The Necessity of Theater

THE NECESSITY
OF THEATER

The Art of Watching and Being Watched

Paul Woodruff

OXFORD
UNIVERSITY PRESS
2008

OXFORD

UNIVERSITY PRESS

Oxford University Press, Inc., publishes works that further
Oxford University's objective of excellence
in research, scholarship, and education.

Oxford   New York
Auckland   Cape Town   Dar es Salaam   Hong Kong   Karachi
Kuala Lumpur   Madrid   Melbourne   Mexico City   Nairobi
New Delhi   Shanghai   Taipei   Toronto

With offices in
Argentina   Austria   Brazil   Chile   Czech Republic   France   Greece
Guatemala   Hungary   Italy   Japan   Poland   Portugal   Singapore
South Korea   Switzerland   Thailand   Turkey   Ukraine   Vietnam

Published by Oxford University Press, Inc.
198 Madison Avenue, New York, New York 10016

www.oup.com

Oxford is a registered trademark of Oxford University Press

Library of Congress Cataloging-in-Publication Data
Woodruff, Paul, 1943–
The necessity of theater : the art of watching and being watched /
Paul Woodruff.
p.   cm.
Includes bibliographical references and index.
ISBN 978-0-19-533200-1
1. Theater—Philosophy.   2. Gaze.   3. Theater—
Psychological aspects.   I. Title.
PN2039.W66 2008
792.01—dc22   2007030683

2 4 6 8 9 7 5 3 1

Printed in the United States of America
on acid-free paper

In Memoriam
Barbara Jane Bestor Woodruff
1914–2003
who knew the art
of watching well

Acknowledgments

M y thoughts on this subject have been enriched over the years by more people than I can remember. I have specific thanks, however, for a lifetime of conversations on theater with my friends Michael and Theresa Holden. My mods tutor at Merton, R. G. C. Levens, first helped me see what was theatrical in the art of ancient playwrights. My late colleague Robert Solomon has deepened my thinking about the emotions and encouraged me to write about theater during many years of conversation. Stephen Halliwell's work on Plato and Aristotle has been invaluable.

My debts for this manuscript are more easily paid. I am especially grateful to my former student Matthew Johnson, who gave me the title, along with welcome encouragement, and read several versions of the early chapters, making useful suggestions. Jerrold Levinson got my engines started again by asking me to write on philosophy of theater and telling me how to do it (Woodruff [2003]). C. D. C. Reeve made comments throughout and even went over subsequent drafts of bits on difficult topics. Edward Garris has also been helpful with suggestions. My colleague T. K. Seung has been my ally in many projects and has continued to rally me through this one. David Sosa, another colleague, helped me through thorny issues relating to free will. James Collins has helped me on many topics, especially on performance wisdom. Greg Scott has repaired several flaws in my understanding of Aristotle.

Charles Griswold has improved my grasp of empathy. Christopher Raymond and Feiting Chen helped me with mimesis. Chris Morley and Ian Oliver helped prepare the manuscript, especially the notes.

All of the students in my seminars on philosophy of theater have been helpful. Bob Jones and Curtis Luciani have taught me much about theater. Kate Woodruff Lange, who is very thoughtful about theater, was first to read the complete draft; she is responsible for a number of improvements.

Preface

Thirty years ago, I had the idea to write this book, or something rather like it, but I was advised at the time that this would not help my case for tenure. The advice was sound. Philosophers in the twentieth century have not been much interested in theater as such, although film, fiction, and performance studies each has its small share in philosophy. I knew this book would do little to persuade my seniors that I was a competent scholar or philosopher, so I set it aside. But I went on thinking about the subject, with the result that this book distills thirty years' thought and work about the theater. In it I try for an account that is systematic and inclusive. I seek new definitions to use as first principles. I exclude some things that have often been discussed as theater, and I include a great deal that has usually been excluded. Although I am acquainted with established theories of theater from several traditions, I make little use of them in writing this book. I have, instead, aimed to do original work.

Philosophy of theater begins with Plato, for me as for all who write on this topic in the European tradition. But philosophy of theater has a second source, harder to locate, in the experience of theater itself. For my part, I was stagestruck before I was struck by Plato. I wrote short plays as a small child, and, as I grew up, sold scripts as a playwright and librettist before I became a scholar of Plato.

All who write about theater work in the shadow of Aristotle. I say almost nothing about Aristotle in these pages, although I have studied his *Poetics* steadily for forty years. Instead of writing about Aristotle, I have written a kind of poetics of my own. Like him I develop a theory by working out the details of a definition, and like him I am openly prescriptive. Like any art, the art of theater can be practiced well or badly. The theory I develop here helps me make and support judgments of good and bad. I feel the need to make judgments about theater especially acutely because of the connection between theater and ethics. Half the art of theater is paying attention to other people, and that is the entire basis of ethics.

In recent years I have returned to an early passion—my love for ancient Athenian tragedy, which drew me into the classics over forty years ago. I have worked on stage-worthy translations and attempted to elucidate the ethical concept that is central to ancient tragedy— reverence, which is the opposite of the tragic vice of hubris. This pair of virtue and vice has a use in political thinking, because hubris was considered the vice of tyrants and reverence the virtue of democratic people. I went on to investigate the place of theater in the democracy of Athens. From time to time I have written short pieces about emotion in theater, projects inspired by my reading in Brecht, Rousseau, Aristotle, and Bergson. A quiet undercurrent in all my work on this subject flows from Artaud.

A boundary has been declared emphatically in recent centuries by European thinkers who wish to separate art from the ordinary stuff of life. If we could locate this boundary, we would find that theater straddles it. Theater is a large part of our experience in real life. I don't mean that real life apes theater, although that can happen, or that theater apes real life, although that always happens in make-believe theater. What I mean is that human beings apply the art of theater in every corner of their lives. They have to. Like the art of language, the art of theater is one of the things we have to have in order to be human. Don't be surprised, then, to see *Hamlet* mentioned in the same paragraph as the Yale-Princeton game, or a family wedding on the same page as *Waiting for Godot*. We are all in this together.

A note on the notes. For those who wish to probe the subject more deeply, notes are provided at the end of the volume, keyed to the text by page number and short quotation.

Contents

The Necessity of Theater

Prologue

Lighting a Dark Stage

We move in a world of theater; it is all around us. And yet the art of theater is poorly understood and practiced fitfully at best. The art of theater lights a dark stage.

The Unwatched Child

In the warm dusk of a spring evening, in southeast Missouri, under the young trees behind the farmhouse, the child looks out over the flat alluvial soil and listens to the buzz of older people talking over her head. The conversation lags among the grown-ups, who are tired of asking each other how long the war will last in France. It is 1917, and they are grateful in their own silences to be listening to the birds. The mother says, "How beautiful the bird song is tonight. I believe they are on their way north. We do not hear this music every day." And the three-year-old on the hard brown ground is tired of being ignored. She lifts her face to the trees and addresses the birds. "Be quiet," she says. "Let Barbie sing." The grown-ups laugh at this, and remind her of it often afterward, always with the suggestion that she had been too forward as a small child, and how nice she is now that she has acquired humility.

Looking back through her many retellings of this tale, I believe she did learn a lesson that evening, and she never forgot it—that she was not worth watching or listening to. And even eighty-five years later, on her last bed, she would be surprised, pleasantly, if people paid attention to her. But if the tired grown-ups in 1917 had found the time and place to set aside for watching Barbie, who was worth watching (she was uncommonly bright, but even a dull three-year-old is fascinating),

3

that would have been theater. And it would have changed her life. Or suppose she had remembered what she must have known by nature as an infant—how to attract attention. That too would have changed her story for the better. Her parents took her for a budding exhibitionist—for someone who repeatedly demands attention for a scene that is not worth watching or does not know how to set boundaries of time around her demands. They could have taught her how to be worth watching for a measured time, after which they could have resumed their adult conversation.

> *The art of theater makes any part of the world a stage for a time, if only the people around the new stage know how to give it their attention, and the people on stage know how to receive attention. Then the two sides help each other bring off a successful time of watching and being watched. We are speaking of a double art that lights the dark stage.*

The Unwatched Play

Vladimir and Estragon are waiting for Godot. Their waiting fascinates me once again; it commands this stage in a London theater. The actors are superb. (One of them is famous for work in film.) They are sad and funny at the same time; they try to pass the time with brilliant riffs of words, and one of them has occasional small triumphs over an impeding prostate. Their waiting is our waiting, and the silence of their Godot is the silence of ours. It is intense, riveting.

But not for this audience—young teenagers bussed in for an afternoon of theater, their teachers out of earshot for a blessed hour of peace. The students plunge into the delights of theater, now that they are released from the boredom of school. Here, in this balcony, they have made many stages of their own, while serving as a kaleidoscope of an audience. In ones and twos, they are performing for each other. These watchers are an ideal audience for young teenagers, and these performers' acting out is perfectly calibrated to seize the attention of their young audience.

The grown-up actors on the official stage are not put off their stride. They are professionals, and the few adults in the audience (who had not been warned) are able to enjoy the performance, as long as they can close their ears to the rowdiness around them. But the art of theater has failed Beckett's play.

> There is an art of making yourself interesting, and an art of finding other people interesting. These two arts must be practiced together and brought into line with each other. The audience should use their art to find Estragon worth watching, at the same time as the performers use theirs to make him worth watching. But we have two different groups in this hall. The youngsters do not know how to be an audience for Vladimir and Estragon. No doubt the actors know how to reach young teenagers, but they are not doing so now.

The Lost Storyteller

The lecture today is an introduction to genetic theory. It is the first lecture of the course, and the students are eager to find out how it will be. They will learn almost immediately what to expect from this class. Some fall asleep in the dimly lit auditorium, others read the newspaper or start homework for other classes. Many of them are dreaming about sex. As they file out at the end, one says to another, "Death by Power-Point! I am not coming back." "No need," says her friend. "He said the lectures would all be on the website."

Indeed, there is no need. The instructor half turned his back to the students and read from his slides, one after the other. At first his tone and pacing were monotonous, but as the hour waned, he picked up speed so as to complete the lecture on time. Two or three students have actually been paying attention so far, but they cannot keep up with the accelerated pace, and soon they too are adrift.

The instructor's eye never met the eye of a student, and he had no way of knowing whether they were keeping up with him. No matter, he would put it all on the web and they could learn it at their own pace. No one has told him that he should have any purpose in the classroom beyond making information available to the students. But the information is already available in any number of books and canned lectures. No one has told him that he might actually engage the students on his subject through a mutual encounter that would awaken their minds to the wonders of the new science. No one has told him that when he enters that space and the students gather around him in a semicircle, he could be a storyteller, and they could be captivated. He is in fact telling a story, but he does not know the art.

> *Storytelling is part of the art of theater. Our lecturer should see himself as descended from a long line of storytellers, from an old man who sits by a fire in the center of a rapt circle of his people. But no one thought to tell our lecturer that he had any art to learn beyond the science he already knows.*

In the village, people my age can remember gathering after supper around a fire to hear the elders tell the stories of their people. But electricity has come to the village. Now every home has an antenna, and the story circles have come apart, each child in his own home watching the flickering screen. Now the children do not know the stories; they do not know why they are a people.

> *We can lose the art of listening to stories as easily as we lose the art of telling them. What new art will give life to the old stories, now that the old one has been eclipsed?*

The Overwatched Child

Terce has been hiding in his bedroom, but the parents have guests and they expect him to perform again. They are always watching him, expecting him to perform, applauding brightly at whatever he does for them. He dreams of running away to a lonely mountain cave where there is no audience. A few years ago he was grateful for his parents' attention, which meant life itself for him. But now he is six, and their ceaseless pressure on him to perform is irksome. They watch him and bring their friends to watch him, even when they think he is asleep. Terce finds himself living the nightmare of an actor on a stage from which there is no exit, on which the light never dims. And he lives with an audience who will never be simply his parents.

> *Thank goodness all the world is not a stage. It couldn't be. You would not want to be on stage all the time—to be so separate from people you love and from the life in which you love them. To have a stage, you have to have an audience who are not inside the circle of the stage. (Where there is "stage" seating, the real stage is smaller than the physical one.)*
>
> *The art of theater knows its boundaries in time and space.*

The Play That Never Ends

Sometimes, after the last line of the *Tempest*, we in the audience are silent for a while, before the applause begins. Prospero has overthrown his own charms, but we do not want to give up being charmed by him. We want more of this magic, more music and dance, more tenderness of young lovers, more anguish of Caliban, and we want to see Prospero again driving the action with his staff, through his hold over Ariel.

Suppose the charm never broke, and the applause never began. For just this moment at the end of the play, it is not so hard to imagine. When we applaud, we set the actors free and, at the same time, free ourselves from the spell the actors have cast over us. But suppose we don't. Suppose we stay locked in our seats with our hands still. Like the figures on Keats's imaginary Grecian urn, the actors would be frozen as actors and we as audience. Life would stop, if the play never does.

> *The art of theater cues the audience that the performance is over. Shakespeare uses an epilogue to tell them when to applaud, modern theater gives the cue with lights or curtain, and each tradition has its own way. But we must have permission to engage again with our lives.*

Watching Alone

Olivia lives for opera. Every performance within a five-hour journey, every open rehearsal, every broadcast—she will be there, watching and listening, if she can, come what may, whatever work or projects or friendships she must leave behind to be there. Her husband—perhaps he is jealous of this passion—has come to loathe opera. In any case, his love is sports, and he spends what free time he has in a soft chair by the TV, watching any game in any sport that is on display. He and Olivia will not be married much longer. He is sharing less and less of his experience with her, and she with him. They are growing apart. If they found a theater to watch together, that theater would give them a shared life.

> *The art of theater brings people together—or apart.*

Love without Witness

The wedding was legal, let there be no doubt about that. The civic official in Ho Chi Minh City was empowered to declare them husband and wife. The couple spoke their oaths with all sincerity; they were in love and they wanted to make a lifetime commitment. Why then are they planning to do it all over again in Fort Worth? Because Thao's family is in Fort Worth, and her family must witness this wedding. In Fort Worth there will be a mansion full of friends and relatives, music, poetry, a banquet, and champagne. Now they are to be married for sure; the friends and relatives who will cherish this couple in future will see that this is so. Thao and Toan will speak their vows while the audience watches, and the watching will make it real. They will not be playing at marriage.

> *Love needs a witness. And where there is a witness, there is theater. Sometimes theater makes a thing real, as it does for a wedding. Theater is not always make-believe; it can make possible the most important real things that we do. Like a wedding.*

Justice Disappearing

Jawad has been missing for six months now. He has done nothing wrong, as far as we know. But because he is suspected of a crime against the state we are not permitted to know very much. He was taken away in the night, and we have heard there will be no public trial. "Don't worry," we are told. "Justice will be done. You must trust us to do the right thing. A nation at war cannot afford to give its enemies the luxury of a public trial by jury." And so we wait for news, uncertain, dismayed, frightened. How can we know, without a fair and open trial, that he has indeed been our enemy? He did not seem so to us. We are more careful, now, about what we say, not knowing what makes them call us enemies. And they, who claim to be our defenders, are beginning to look more like enemies to us. They say that justice in wartime must sometimes be secret. And they are half right. Sometimes war must be waged in silence and in the dark. But justice is different. The aim of justice is to reweave the fabric of society where crime has torn it, and this cannot be done in the dark. Justice has not been done unless we can see that it has been done.

When war darkens the stage of justice, it eclipses justice as well. Justice, like truth, is often a casualty of war.

> *Justice needs a witness. Wherever justice is done in the public eye, there is theater, and the theater helps make the justice real.*

Upstaged by Life

Tonight the theater is given over for one-act plays, mostly by students. I am here to watch a play by an earnest young playwright who is my friend and former student. The writer is performing with another actor, his friend. They are chewing over unsatisfactory relationships in a subtle, delicate scene, touching—but perhaps too subtle. Suddenly, during a quiet moment in the script, a woman in the front row begins to have a heart attack. The theater is almost round, so that the entire audience is well positioned to take in the scene. The woman is lurching in her seat, her friends have risen and are anxiously asking her questions. The play goes on, but no one is watching. The scene on stage was written to be disturbing, but what we are seeing in the front row is far more disturbing. Riveting. In her torment, the sick woman in the front row has shifted attention from the stage to herself. Later, in the interval, we learn that she is fine and has refused the assistance of the ambulance from the emergency medical service. It is all too bad, for her and the young writer, but what a moment! Reality breaking through the artifice of theater like a shot of sunlight through a rift in dark clouds. Truly, she lit a dark stage.

So Claudius, watching *The Murder of Gonzago*, has an attack of conscience in the front row and calls for lights, lights for him. The rush of lanterns douses the play, and the king, with all eyes on his tottering figure, takes himself off to pray.

> *Real life always trumps the theater of make believe, when it interrupts. But the theater of presence calls out for reality. What I call "theater of presence" aims at the immediacy of the heart attack, at a sense of reality in an epiphany no matter how disturbing it may be. So, in the dance theater of a village that uses stone tools, the god may suddenly show up in the body of the dancer, taking him over, appearing through him to his worshippers. And to watchers in the theater of presence, an epiphany is real.*

There is an art to watching and being watched, and that is one of the few arts on which all human living depends. If we are unwatched we diminish, and we cannot be entirely as we wish to be. If we never stop to watch, we will know only how it feels to be us, never how it might feel to be another. Watched too much, or in the wrong way, we become frightened. Watching too much, we lose the capacity for action in our own lives. Watching well, together, and being watched well, with limits on both sides, we grow, and grow together.

Introduction

Why We Need Theater

People need theater. They need it the way they need each other—the way they need to gather, to talk things over, to have stories in common, to share friends and enemies. They need to watch, together, something human. Without this...well, without this we would be a different sort of species. Theater is as distinctive of human beings, in my view, as language itself. Theater is everywhere in human culture, as widely practiced as religion. This should be no surprise: most expressions of religion belong to theater. Like religion, theater seems sometimes to be on the way out, but it keeps coming back in unexpected disguises—some horrible, some wonderful.

We need many things from the culture in which we swim; language, religion, and theater are three of our basic cultural needs. This does not mean that we all need the same sort of language, or the same religion, or the same kind of theater. Because these are cultural needs, they may be satisfied in a number of ways. We need language in order to live a fully human life, but we do not have to have the English language. Other languages work fine, though some may work better for certain purposes than others. So I may say that something meets a cultural need without implying that it is good of its kind. We may have something to learn from cultures different from our own.

Here are two good examples of theater that go beyond serving basic needs and furnish unique benefits to their communities: the ancient

Greek tragic festival, and modern American college football. They are so different that you may balk at seeing them in the same sentence, and yet they have more in common than the simple structure of watchers and watched. They are both powerful centers for community.

Athens once suffered a particularly brutal civil war between advocates of democracy and of oligarchy. At first the oligarchs had the upper hand and plunged into a reign of terror. Afterward the democrats came back hungry for blood and revenge. And then something rare happened: under pressure from Sparta, the two sides swore an oath of amnesty and reconciliation. After punishing those responsible for the reign of terror, the people settled down to a fair degree of harmony. Many factors made this possible, but one stands out for our purposes: the Athenian men on both sides had shared a tradition of taking part in festival drama. Almost all of them went to see the plays, and almost all of them had danced together in the dramatic choruses when they were young. A few days before the reconciliation, a democratic speaker spoke to the army of aristocrats:

> Citizens, why are you keeping us out of Athens? Why do you want to kill us? We never did anything bad to you. Not at all. We have joined with you in the holiest rituals, in the most beautiful sacrifices and festivals. We have been fellow dancers with you, fellow students, and fellow soldiers.

"We have been fellow dancers." Lucky Athenians to have had a theatrical tradition that bound them together as performers, not merely as members of an audience. A dramatic chorus would live and practice together for a long time before their performance, and they would have to learn to move and sing as one. So the theater in Athens was a powerful source of unity.

American college football is not like that at all. Ordinary members of the university community have no part in the team, nor are they likely to know any team members. The players live and eat apart, they are registered for a handful of courses taught mainly by professors who are friendly to the sport, and they were admitted to the university by a special process. But the big game will draw an audience of eighty thousand, including legions of students, alumni, and supporters of the university.

Faculty often complain about the huge emphasis on football at American campuses. But their complaints fall on deaf ears; no sane president of a university would run down the football program. Why does football flourish at a university? Not because it makes money for academic purposes; at best, sports programs break even. Certainly not because the sport calls attention to academic programs; quite the contrary. Football flourishes on campus because it builds an ardent sense of belonging to the university community. We can't easily assign a monetary value to this sense of belonging, but it plainly has a glorious effect on the morale of students and graduates, an effect that is absent from universities outside the United States, which do not have this tradition. Students outside the United States are more likely to live with their families at home, so that their need is met in other ways, especially through experiences shared by a family rather than those manufactured for a student body. Football theater, as we have it on American campuses, meets a need; other forms of theater could meet the same need differently.

At this point, you might complain: "How can you say that theater is necessary when it seems barely alive? Theater is dying out, while genuine cultural necessities, such as language and religion, show no signs of fading away. You seem to want to say that theater survives in modern life just because we go to football games. But if sports events count as theater, anything does. Your definition is so loose that your claim is bogus; if you are allowed to call anything you want by the word 'theater,' then you won't have trouble finding something to call 'theater' wherever you look."

The complaint has a point. My definition of theater is no good if it does not exclude a lot of things. Wait a bit, and you will see that it does. My thesis that theater is necessary implies that it is culturally universal—that it can be found in every culture. If the "it" I am seeking is a cultural universal, then it should be hard to pin down in terms that are specific to one culture or another. Theater has to be larger than our traditions about it. But I am writing in English, and the terms I use are infected by my culture. In the next chapter I do my best to indicate the essential nature of theater, which turns up, wearing different disguises, all around us. At that point I am able to show why I think ancient Greek tragedy and football belong in the same book on theater.

0.1 Being Necessary

Things change. What was necessary in one era may be disposable in the next. Perhaps it *was* true that the fifth-century Athenians could not have been the people they were without theater, but the case for that would be specific to Athens in the golden age. Unless I can make the case for theater more generally—not just for old Athens—I cannot expect my defense to help with understanding New York or Austin in the twenty-first century. So I will need to ask a big question: What is necessary in human cultures as such?

Any practice that a society must keep alive in order to have a human culture would be necessary in the way I mean. The argument will require strong assumptions about what counts as a human culture, but I don't expect these to be very controversial. For example, a minimal human culture must have language, and it must have a memory. The memory must be robust enough at least to pass techniques from generation to generation (by "techniques," I mean, for example, how to make a knife or how to harvest nuts), and, in a full-blown culture, memory should preserve the stories of that culture.

Let's try some examples to illustrate cultural necessity, starting with the arts.

Poetry

Before literacy, poetry was the principal art of memory everywhere, and so poetry seemed necessary to culture; but after literacy, it appears that poetry is dispensable, and indeed poetry survives now mainly in the precious sphere of art poetry—poets writing for poets—and in the wider arena of self-expression—people writing for themselves as therapy. But neither kind of poetry serves as the vehicle for cultural memory; we could do without poets writing for poets, and we could turn to other forms of self-expression for therapy. So we might conclude that poetry is not necessary in our time. Something else must carry our memories down through the ages. After literacy the vehicle for memory was writing, but now perhaps it is digital media. Time will tell.

But poetry is not so easily surrendered; poetry matters more to us than might appear from the scant space allowed to it in bookstores. There is much more to poetry than what I said at the outset—"poets writing for poets," and "therapy." Moreover, poetry serves us in more ways than as a vehicle for cultural memory. What I have called "art poetry" may no longer be necessary to us; perhaps it has become a province for isolated and peculiar minds. But poetry is still essential to our lives, whether we recognize it as poetry or not. We need poetry to support music, and we need music the way we need language: for the broad sharing of feelings.

Music is certainly universal across cultures, and music calls for words. (Wordless music is rare in most cultures and has limited appeal.) "Words written to go with music" is a good definition for lyric poetry. So we do need poetry, because we need it for music, and evidently we need music. And of course we hear lots of poetry, everywhere in the modern world, if we don't close our ears to rap lyrics or folk ballads. The moral of the story is to keep an open mind about what counts as poetry or theater. Only by narrowing my focus too far was I able to make poetry seem obsolete and therefore dispensable.

Painting and drawing

The need for the graphic arts—painting and drawing—also seems to have faded. In old days (and in times as far past as evidence permits), we know that the graphic arts served the need for a visual cultural memory until photography was invented. After photography we can easily imagine a home without graphic arts, but not a home without photos of children and grandparents. So perhaps what is necessary is visual representation in one form or another. Again, we must keep open minds to see what is necessary.

Poetry and the graphic arts illustrate how technology changes our ideas about what is necessary. Another kind of change involves social practices such as slavery and war and religion.

Slavery and war

There was a time when its defenders argued that the practice of slavery was necessary for human culture. The argument ran like this: culture depends on some people's having the leisure to be cultivated, and such leisure can only be maintained by slave labor; therefore, slavery must be tolerated. This was always nonsense, I think. True, most Mediterranean cultures regarded slavery as indispensable, but their vision was narrowed by their experience. Other cultures (such as the Chinese) flourished without slavery. In fact, culture requires leisure, not idleness, and leisure is compatible with hard work. (My great-grandfather, a poor farmer, read *Pilgrim's Progress* as he plowed his fields. No matter that his furrows were crooked. They worked well enough.) So slavery is not necessary.

As for war, I dream of a time when we will be able to say the same about it that we do about slavery. War has been endemic to humankind in historical times. Without war, we might not need to organize into culture-sharing communities; in particular, we might not need to develop that part of a culture which is expressed in government. Therefore we might reasonably say that without war we humans would not be who we are, because we would be without the chief cause for developing cultures beyond the minimum. Again, I do not believe that this is so. Perhaps we will come to think of war as a criminal activity (as we now do slavery), an activity which it is the duty of world government not to levy but to put down. And then we would say that it is not war but police action that is necessary. The moral here, as in the case of slavery, is not to draw large conclusions from narrow experiences. We don't know many cultures that are not organized for war, but we can't infer from this that war is indispensable. The sooner we try seriously to dispense with it the better, although peace may be too, well, peaceful, for human nature to tolerate.

Religion

Again, we might suppose that religion has become obsolete in modern culture, and, like war, we might expect to be better off without the violent conflicts, the rejection of science, and the sheer human evil that are often carried by religion. But here too we may be up against the cussedness of the human.

Science explains the origins of all things, as much as they can be explained, and the mingling of religions within cultures has shown that a culture is not necessarily constituted by a religion. Members of very different sects, with different practices, can share a culture. So it appears that religion is not necessary for human culture. But religion shows every sign of remaining widespread, almost universal, probably because it helps meet certain social and psychological needs. Plainly, scientific explanation does not compete with religion in satisfying the desires people actually have, which they seek to satisfy through religion, for an account of the universe that gives them the comfort of a prominent place in creation. Some religions do not offer that comfort, but their members nevertheless cling to the companionship that comes from sharing religious practices and beliefs.

Theater

Now theater, like the graphic arts, seems to have been replaced by photography—in the form of film—as an engine of popular culture; in the intellectual arena, theater seems to have been replaced by attention to literature (as opposed to performance). If poetry and painting seem to survive only in eccentric byways, what can I say of theater? Theater appears to be in such dark eclipse that it has no popular audience, except for the tourists who flock to musical productions that ape film in their use of sound, montage, and illusion. And if theater may be eclipsed, surely it is not necessary.

But theater is not eclipsed. The art forms that are vulnerable to eclipse are the fine ones. That is because what counts as fine art keeps changing. We are easily tricked into thinking that the arts are eclipsed in modern society because we confuse the arts with the fine arts. "Fine" in the arts picks out traditions that have special appeal for highly educated consumers, and which may also serve as markers of class status. Such traditions may or may not deserve the importance they are given; either way, they are subject to fashion.

Although art theater has small audiences, we see theater all around us if we open our eyes to what lies beyond the boundaries of fine art. Weddings, funerals, football games, street dancing, church services—all of these use the art of theater. If your main interest is art theater, however, don't lay this book aside. Art theater is important to me, too. I launched this book with the idea that it would concern only art theater, but I found that this was too narrow. Art theater has a lot to learn from theater in general. We would be lucky to achieve on the formal stage the power and immediacy of the ordinary theater that we encounter in our daily lives.

The challenge of film remains. Film resembles theater in several ways, but it does not serve the same need as theater. Why do we prefer to attend our children's weddings in person, when we could stay at home and watch a videotape or a DVD of the event? Why pay a high price for tickets to the big game, drive for hours, and then burn in the hot sun on a hard stadium seat, when you could see the game closer up on TV? Theater is immediate, its actions are present to participants and audience. And in the theater you are part of a community of watchers, while in a cinema you are alone, or alone with your partner, whose hand you squeeze from time to time.

Sometimes film and television emulate theater. A sports bar builds a community of watchers for a game, and they are having an experience very like that of theater. Rowdy college showings of cult flicks may have a similar effect. But these are anomalies. The patrons of the sports bar would jump at tickets to see the real thing. When we prefer theater to film, we have good reasons. Film and theater are not the same.

0.2 The Art of Theater

Theater is the art by which human beings make or find human action worth watching, in a measured time and place. That is the bare beginning of a definition. It does not suffice as it stands, but it is enough to get started.

Any work of theater is the product of other arts as well. I call these the "supporting arts" for theater, although in other contexts these are arts in their own right. The art of dance supports the art of theater, for example, but there is also an art of dance quite apart from theater. Dance does not require an audience. Theater has many supporting arts; every human art, I think, can be used to support theater, because theater can make any human action worth watching. So there is no point trying to list the supporting arts.

Almost everything about my definition cries out for further discussion: "Theater is the art by which human beings make or find human action worth watching." By "watching" I mean paying a certain kind of attention to sights and sounds, and perhaps to other sensations as well. Watching need not be visual. By "making it worth watching" I mean two things: capturing people's attention, so that they think it is worth watching, and (in the best cases) making it actually good for them to watch, so that they receive value for the time they spend. By "human action" I mean to cover all the things human beings do that can be watched— talking, singing, dancing, playing musical instruments, engaging in contests, eating, drinking, fighting, killing, loving, and so on. Forming a thought or conceiving a hope—these are actions too, but are not the stuff of theater because they are not watched.

By "art" I do not mean to imply that theater must belong to the fine arts, and I do not mean to imply that the art of theater belongs only to those who are being watched. What makes a given episode in a football game worth watching may have more to do with the current nature of the contest than with anything this or that player chooses to do. The linemen may be innocent of the art of theater, but many people around them are nonetheless practicing it. Promoters, lighting designers, stadium designers, and so on all have work to do in the art of theater. And so does the audience; they have to pay attention in a way that fits this performance.

Under "human action" I include everything people do, whether or not they act in make-believe. The actor who delivers Hamlet's soliloquy is actually talking, but he does so in the context of make-believe; later he will not actually die on stage (unless something goes badly wrong), but he will actually perform Hamlet's death, and that is doing something. I shall say that theater is mimetic when it depends on make-believe. Traditional European-style art theater is often mimetic, but not all theater is mimetic. A football game depends only to a small extent on make-believe.

My definition begins as a highly inclusive one. The point is to bring together the various kinds of theater to see what they have in common and what divides them from one another. We can then ask questions like: What is the distinctive effect of mimesis in theater? Or: How does introducing a contest into theater change the effect of the action on an audience? Examples illustrate both questions: watching the fencing at the end of *Hamlet*, watching a collegiate fencing match, watching a staged sword duel to the death in a trial at arms. The three experiences have a great deal in common; they are all theater, although they differ in important ways as well.

A good definition does more than include. It also excludes. The word "human" does some real work: bird-watching is not theater. And the word "action" cuts out passive human events: watching a comatose Christian being devoured by a lion in ancient Rome is not theater. Watching a frisky Christian, on the other hand, as he tries to fight off the lion, would count as theater.

0.3 The Art of Watching

For an audience, the art of theater is the art of finding human action worth watching for a measured time in a measured space. We need to find justice worth watching, if we are to have it at all, and there are many other things—such as marriage—that are essential to human society, that cannot happen if we are not watching.

And there is an ethical reason to practice the art of watching. Part of our need to watch theater grows from our need to care about other people. You say you care about Antigone as she is led, protesting her innocence, to her death. If I can see that you are hanging onto every word of the scene, I will believe that you care about her. But I would be suspicious if you were not paying attention to this, her final scene. But because I believe you to be a good and caring person, I expect you to pay attention to Antigone. You pay attention because you care, and paying attention allows you to care. Caring about people in the make-believe world of mimetic theater may strengthen your ability to care about people offstage. Healthy people in healthy communities do develop the capacity for caring into a virtue—a virtue that I call "humaneness," following the ancient Chinese.

A stream of travelers passes by a wounded man on the road, until one of them, on business from Samaria, stops to give aid. You may think that the difference between the good Samaritan and the passersby is that he is good and they are selfish; but it is much more likely that he has been paying attention and they have not. Moral philosophers have puzzled too much over why we should be unselfish. That is a silly question: being human, we all know the value of unselfishness as soon as we know a mother's kindness, and we are all inclined (with a few unhealthy exceptions) to be unselfish from time to time. The really hard question is not *whether* but *when* to be unselfish. And often this question is about paying attention. None of us has the time or perceptual agility to pay attention to everyone. But I cannot be unselfish without paying attention to some others at some times.

Across the road, through the window of the restaurant where I am lunching with a friend, I see an unfamiliar figure struck by a car, who picks himself up and rails at the driver, blocking traffic. A crowd gathers, an ambulance is called, police are summoned. But it is not my affair. After a brief remark about the danger of the crossing at this location, I return to my lunch and conversation.

In a famous poem, W. H. Auden sees what Brueghel painted—a boy falling out of the sky while no one pays attention, and the work of the world goes on. How to notice, whom to notice, when to notice, why to notice other people—these are the really hard questions about unselfishness. It is easy for me to notice my own children (nature is at work in this), and fairly easy for me to act on what I notice in their case.

Almost any passersby would stop and render aid if the injured included their own children. Virtues come easy to those who pay attention, and attention comes easy from parents to their children, or generally among people who feel connected to each other. Toward outsiders, attention comes harder.

We will be better people if we become accustomed to paying attention to other people—to be good and caring watchers. But we cannot watch everything that goes on in the world, and we should not watch everything that goes on in the life of someone we love. So we need to set boundaries, and this is something the art of theater does very well. Theater frames people and their actions in order to make them more watchable. Practice in framing human action as watchable helps us cultivate humaneness.

Through the window of the restaurant I see an unfamiliar figure struck, and this time I am engaged, and I am framing what I see now as a scene, and I am calling on my imagination to give it context. I am the first to call 911. I am impressed by the refusal of the pedestrian to take the accident lying down. He is trying to get somewhere and do something that is important to him. His children are waiting for him at their school, wondering why he has not arrived. I hurt for him, and I carry the pain through the day and into the next, when I call the city about installing a light or painting a crosswalk. This scenario is unusual because it is unusual to care about a stranger who is merely part of the observable goings-on. To frame an incident as drama—even when it is an incident from real life—requires an effort of imagination. We need imagination in theater also, but in theater we have a lot of help from professionals who know how to stimulate the imagination.

Hard as it is for me to see the unfamiliar figure as framed in a drama, it is harder for me to see myself (except perhaps as I would like to be seen). But we ought to pay attention to ourselves. This is harder than it may seem. The college sophomore, cut off from family and childhood friends, becomes angry with himself over disappointing grades or social failures. He slides into a depression in which he imagines he disappoints everyone. He is not worth watching, not worth caring about. He may slip into a spiral of despair if he does not find a way to watch himself in a caring way, to see himself as a character in an interesting drama, worth watching. How can he come to see himself as having a future that could excite an audience, even though his troubles are, at the moment, disabling? How can he come to see himself as worth caring about? He must find the answer. His life depends on it.

Theater is the art of finding human action worth watching, and it mostly does this by finding human characters worth caring about. We need to practice that art, on both sides—to find people worth watching and, for ourselves, to make ourselves worth watching when we need to be watched (when we are getting married, for example). The grounds of this need are psychological (we dry up if we feel no one is noticing us), social (a community comes apart if it attempts to secure justice in a forum that is not watched), and ethical (I cannot exercise human virtues unless I practice the art of watching). Willing or not, at one time or another, each of us will be among the watchers and the watched.

0.4 Needing Theater

Now I can ask why we need the art for which I have just proposed a definition.

Needing to be watched

The two-year-old child dances for her father when he comes home, before he takes her in his arms. The smallest child who is capable of any action is capable of making it worth watching, of capturing adult attention for a time. As we grow up we learn (some of us all too soon) that we cannot expect the attention of others as often as we would like to have it; still we are watchers of ourselves and of each other, and if we believe in God or gods we believe we are being watched from above. Even if we don't, we can't always escape the thought that our parents are watching us. In deciding what to do or how to do it, we often ask ourselves what these watchers would think of us. And then we pretend. We tell ourselves stories about what we are doing as individuals, framing our actions all the while as deserving an audience. To imagine yourself totally without an audience would be painful and difficult.

We are under a kind of psychological necessity, then, to engage in the art of theater. Part of being human is to practice the art, to aim at being worth watching. So theater is as necessary as anything else that comes to us naturally. In this way we may begin an explanation for why we perform—for why we do what it takes to capture the attention of other people as watchers.

Theater carries more than a psychological necessity. Communities depend on public events for binding and for healing. Certain kinds of human events must have the community to witness them (or at least they must be such that the community could witness them). Weddings are an obvious example. The plighting of troth is a public event; that is what distinguishes it from a seduction. A lover may be willing to say anything to induce a partner to go to bed, but what will the lover say in public, with the families standing around, and before a representative of communal authority as well? Love needs a witness, then, and finds one in most human cultures; from this need comes the elaboration of wedding and betrothal ceremonies, and this need is also (by a long route) one of the ancestors of the art form known as comedy.

Justice too needs a witness. A body of witnesses makes possible a communal healing of wounds as opposed to the sort of private revenge that leads only to a cycle of violence. From this seminal idea come the traditions of public judgment (older than any system of statute law), public executions, public contests or sporting events, even public examinations. This need, I think, is one of the ancestors of tragic theater. If you were worried about classifying *Macbeth* with a football game, think of the two as having a common ancestor in the idea that certain tensions need to be resolved in public. Even if you are so sure your team will win that you feel no tension, you still need the win to be *public*. Secret victories do not count.

Politics needs all of us to be witnesses, if we are to be a democracy and if we are to believe that our politics embody justice. In democracy, the people hold their leaders accountable, but the people cannot do this if they are kept in the dark. Leaders who work in closed meetings are darkening the stage of public life and they are threatening justice. Worse, they are strangling democracy.

Needing to watch

We must also ask why we watch a performance. All the world may wish to be on stage, but does all the world wish to be an audience? Sadly and painfully, we learn that it does not.

The delighted mother, if she is not distracted by her other burdens, watches her small son prance for her. Lucky child! There is no theater without audience, and he has an audience wrapped around his finger. She watches because the performer is her son. But most people will pay no attention to the prancing child, unless he is in their way. He is prancing between tables at a restaurant. Customers, wishing to be intent on each other, are annoyed, and when a waiter with a heavy tray almost trips over the little boy, a manager asks the mother to keep him in his seat.

Theater is an art—and not simply something we all do by nature, like breathing—because it can be done well or poorly. And since no one *needs* to watch anything in particular, theater must be done well, so as to make people want to watch. Because we feel the need to be watched, we must learn the art of capturing an audience. But this is not all: the audience themselves truly have needs that are satisfied by theater, and though there is no performance they need to watch, they are nevertheless better off for being watchers from time to time.

One part of being human is the desire to be watched; another is the desire to share experiences with members of a community. We become close to each other when we watch the same things. If you and I went everywhere together, like young twins, we would have as close a connection as two people could have. Because we would have had identical experiences, you would know what I meant when I spoke, better than anyone, and I would trust you more than anyone to understand me.

In communities, people approach this sort of closeness by sharing what they watch on special occasions. In traditional societies, entire communities share religious performances of various kinds, and these generally fall under my broad definition of theater. Modern communities, because they tend to blend different religions, are increasingly unable to share traditional religious events. Something must take their place, and in many modern societies it is professional sports that bring people together by means of shared experiences. You who have bought this book because you love theater may be disturbed by the thought that the prevailing theater of our day is football or soccer. Very well. Perhaps we would be a better society if we were bound together by *Antigone* instead of the Super Bowl. But it's not obvious that this is so. Besides, *Antigone* now belongs to an elite, although it was made for a popular theater; but the art of an elite is not the glue of a society. Art theater has a place in our culture, and it will have a very large place in this book. But it cannot be the whole story.

0.5 The Place of Art Theater

Yes, you might say, that's all very well about watching and being watched. But this is not what we mean by "theater." What we call "theater" in English happens on a stage, where there are costumes and actors, and the actors are working from a script. They have an educated audience, who have been looking forward to seeing *Antigone* or *Macbeth* or *The Seagull*, and they have paid in advance for the experience. What does that have to do with the need to watch and be watched?

Let us agree to call what you have in mind "art theater in the European tradition," or just "art theater" for short. This, I submit, is a formal, cultivated expression of the art I have been discussing, the one that makes human action in general worth watching. Art theater is a good thing. Bare, naked survival is not enough for us; we want to be comfortable in all weathers, and so we need clothing for physical comfort, although we might find ways of surviving without it. Art theater is part of our cultural clothing—sometimes warm, sometimes gaudy, and not absolutely necessary to survival in an equable climate. But highly desirable, because necessary for our comfort.

After all, we do not really need art theater for survival. Art theater is part of European civilization, and we don't need that either. Countless people have done without European civilization, and many more will do so in the future. Civilizations decline, and the art forms they contain often perish sooner. We need something along these lines, however, just as we need clothing, but what keeps us from freezing does not have to be in the style we have evolved in Europe and America. Fashions may change. The theater of our comfort need not be *Antigone* or *The Laramie Project*. But it has to be some sort of theater.

A culture may be judged by the sort of theater that binds its members together. If you are disturbed by the thought that football has this role in the United States, you should ask what it is that art theater provides that is not provided by football. Why would you rather belong to a community that is bound by watching Sophocles' *Antigone* than one that is bound by watching the Super Bowl? Do you long for the past as you imagine it? Are you a snob about the fine arts? Or can you show that there is value in an experience of the *Antigone* that is missing in an experience of the Super Bowl, and that this suffices to outweigh the value of watching the big game? Could it be that you are drawn to the greater truth of the *Antigone?* Or to the greater intensity of emotional experience?

Intensity of emotion cannot tell in favor of *Antigone*. Yes, in watching the play, you care deeply for a doomed tragic figure, but you never try to change the outcome. Real emotions make you want to take action, but in the art theater there is no action for you to take. Contrast the stadium, where you actually try to change the outcome by cheering or booing.

Perhaps *Antigone* tells a kind of truth that football cannot: about timeless human issues of daring, reverence, obedience, and social order. But the play is fiction, after all. (It is not even traditional myth; Sophocles has altered the myth he received into a quite new shape.) To prefer *Antigone* on grounds of truth we would have to explain how it is that a work of invention can convey truth. The football game is really happening, and by watching it we are learning facts about what has happened in the world. What could be better than that?

So, if you wish to make a special case for *Antigone* on grounds of truth or emotion, you will need to answer hard questions about truth and emotion in theater. I do believe that these questions are answerable. They are at the center of this book. But they will turn out to be red herrings for the issue about art theater. Of course I have other factors to consider—chiefly plot and character—and these also are central to this book. The one area in which art theater usually excels is in plot. An invented plot works itself out during the time allotted for performance, while games are rarely so neat.

0.6 Needing the Art

The whole art of theater is the one we must be able to practice in order to secure our bare, naked cultural survival.

The word "necessary" does not mean much by itself. We should always ask "for what goal?" "Bombing was necessary," says the general, appealing to military necessity—something on which he would like us to let him have the last word, since he is a military expert. But surely it was never absolutely necessary. Perhaps it was necessary to achieve this goal (say, unconditional surrender by the enemy) at this cost (few American casualties). If so, we may still ask whether we should seek that goal, and whether it is reasonable to try to do so at that cost to our side. Perhaps the general has the wrong goal and he should not do what is necessary to achieve it. That is an illustration of the relativity of necessity. I cannot simply say that *The Laramie Project* serves a need; I must go on to say what that need is.

I have two lines of argument—one general, and one particular to this or that play. The general argument is very simple: through art theater we practice for the larger art which I have claimed is necessary merely to being human—the art of making or finding human action worth watching. Folks in the audience are practicing the generosity of imagination that they will need in order to be good watchers of anything human; folks in the cast and production crew are practicing the various skills that catch the attention of an audience and help them bring imagination into play on a given subject—skills the performers will need in order to bring great communal events before the attentive eyes of the public. That seems clear enough, but I have a great deal more to say about this later in the book in chapters on character, empathy, understanding, and so forth.

The second line of argument deals with particular plays, and this too I pursue in the various chapters to come. One play now: *The Laramie Project*. I have said that justice needs a witness, and you understood me to mean that trials should be open to the public, so that when a decision is made the public will know that healing can begin, that what was done in the courtroom was justice, and not personal—not just another stroke in an ongoing quarrel. Yes, but I meant much more than that, and *The Laramie Project* illustrates my meaning very well.

It is a documentary play, bringing to life on the stage a series of interviews with people of Laramie, Wyoming. The subject is a murder—and not just any murder, but a murder that may express views held by many members of the community who would have been accomplices if they could. The young men who actually had blood on their hands have now been tried and sentenced. The public knows what they did, as well as what has been done to them in consequence. But what of the larger community—friends, enemies, neighbors, parents, acquaintances, preachers, police? What did they do? What has happened to them? And what have they learned?

The larger community is not only the people of Laramie; those real people whose voices sound in the play stand for all of us, except that they are closer to this crime. The play gives them a voice—gives all of us a voice—and calls all of us to witness. It is not a trial, but it is like a trial, full of testimonies and depositions. And although no one but the audience reaches a verdict, and their verdict is only to join in grieving for Matthew Shepard and us all, that is a kind of resolution. And that is a kind of justice, but not without theater. For this you need to be present, sharing the moment. *The Laramie Project* serves the need for justice for the entire community—not the formal justice of a trial, but the informal justice that helps restore the torn fabric of a community. Everyone's thoughts are given a voice. Justice for the killers and for the victim, for those who love and for those who hate, and for the divided hearts of us all.

PART ONE

The Art of Being Watched

ONE

Defining the Art

When you say this you set yourself against me.

—*Antigone*, line 93

Two young women steal out into the twilight before dawn. They come to share the news and a secret, two devoted sisters who were damaged at birth by having a half-brother for a father, and are now wounded by a second family disaster—their two full brothers have killed one another in battle. Antigone tells her sister the news: their uncle, the king, has declared one brother good and one brother bad. One has been buried with honor; the other lies condemned for bringing war against his own people, and his penalty is to rot unburied on the plain, food for wild dogs and carrion birds. Anyone who buries the dead boy will be stoned to death.

The secret is that Antigone will bury her brother at all costs. Her sister, Ismene, is horrified. She is bitterly unhappy about events, but she says they are out of her control. She knows her place as a women in a city ruled by men. Antigone listens but her purpose is unchanged, except that now she is angry at her sister, and the close ties between them are cut forever.

In five minutes or less, ninety-nine lines of Greek verse, a scene technically known as a prologue, two people and their lives have changed forever. Of these two close sisters, one has become a lone rebel, committed to a course that leads to death; the other has been left terrified with no one to cling to. And all because of a few words. "When you say this, you set yourself against me," Antigone observes at scene's end.

And what she has said herself sets her against everything on earth—her family, her king, her people, the living boy who loves her—leaving her in alliance only with the dead and the gods below earth.

This is theater. We are here to watch, in rows of seats, the performance of these two sisters. We see them at their most human, reaching out to each other and failing to connect, as their passions of love and fear force them apart from each other, and we ourselves take sides, many of us thrilled by Antigone's firmness of purpose, some of us shocked by what we see as rebelliousness or a longing for death, some of us won over by Ismene's calm acceptance of what no one can change. We watch, we care, and perhaps we too are changed by the scene. This is what we mean by "theater," isn't it?

Many things that are quite unlike this, however, seem also to be the stuff of theater. Among theater performers are trapeze artists in a circus, football players in a stadium, a stand-up comic in a club, a cowboy-singer entertaining customers in an espresso bar, and the young woman who makes espresso, with great panache, to the admiring gaze of her customers. Among theater audiences we should consider restaurant patrons enthralled by the preparation of their salad, passersby watching workmen through the fence at a construction site, a congregation serving as witnesses at a wedding, even townspeople gathered by a tall oak tree for a lynching. My account will have to find places for all of these insofar as they are practicing the art of watching. Not all watchers are doing so.

Why does the scene from *Antigone* seem more like theater than any of these? Partly that is because the trapeze artists and the others I mentioned really are what we see them to be, and they are really doing what we see them do. The couple at the altar are truly about to pledge their lives to one another. But the breakup between Antigone and Ismene—this is not really happening in front of us, and the women we are watching are not the Greek sisters of mythology but actresses playing roles. Another part of the difference is that Ismene and Antigone are creating a set of conflicts, which we expect to generate an orderly plot that ends in a resolution.

1.1 Kinds of Theater

I am setting out to define an art that is used in different ways in different kinds of theater. But I believe that the art is roughly the same in all of them, so that we can practice the art in one kind of theater and apply it in another. Here is a list of the kinds of theater I have in mind. I give it for two reasons—so that you'll see the scope of the art I plan to discuss, and also so that you'll know what I mean by these terms, most of which I have invented to serve my purpose. These kinds are not exclusive; they may overlap each other.

Mimetic theater consists mainly of make-believe. The actors are not the same as the characters they are playing, and their actions do not have real consequences for the audience or for the actors. Elements of make-believe occur in almost any human action; that is why I restrict the term "mimetic theater" for theater that stages mainly make-believe. This includes both fictional and historical or documentary theater. You can as easily make believe you are history's George Washington as Shakespeare's Puck. Shakespeare's *Richard II* and *As You Like It* both belong to this category, although one is history and the other comedy. Sophocles' *Antigone* and Aeschylus's *Persians* are also mimetic, although one poet invented his plot on the basis of myth, and the other imagined his plot on the foundation of history.

Everyday theater is the theater of ordinary life, in which we are watching people do the things they regularly do—the waiter assembling your salad by the table with a flourish or lighting the Bananas Foster. Ordinary action often involves make-believe (as when a new waiter plays the part of a waiter or imitates the headwaiter). So this kind of theater can be mimetic (though not mainly mimetic).

Extreme theater summons an audience to contribute to events as they actually unfold by watching them. I have in mind events such as weddings and trials and lynchings, which require witnesses. The audience is then partly responsible for the events. The relatives at a wedding, by witnessing the wedding, take on the responsibility to support it in future. The mob at a lynching shares in the guilt, because it would not have happened without them. Extreme theater is often partly mimetic. The bride is truly a bride, but she is also making believe she is the bride in a recent photographic essay in a fashion magazine. In the lynching, the hanging is real, but the justice is a very serious and deadly kind of make-believe. It is not justice, but the mob reacts as if it were. And the ringleaders are trying to put on a good show.

The most vigorous form that extreme theater takes in our time is the sports contest, and this I would classify as a kind of trial requiring witnesses. It means nothing for Texas to claim that its football team defeated Oklahoma's in a secret game open only to those who played in it. It's not a victory in a contest unless it is widely observed to be so.

Theater of presence is the theater of sacrament. An episode starts out like mimesis but ends real. The dancer puts on the god's mask and at first pretends to be the god. But she aims to invite the god into a real presence in the dance, and she will believe, when she comes to her senses after the dance, that the god answered her invitation.

Any theater that transforms people, or aims to do so, is theater of presence. Sometimes you go to the theater to be transformed, as when you enter into the Bacchic dance in hopes that the god will become present in you. At other times you are moved, suddenly, to become part of the ritual, as when you respond to an altar call. At still other times, you do not even know that you are being transformed, as when, while watching Socrates debating a sophist, you begin to answer the questions for yourself, and so you become (even for a short time) a philosopher.

Art theater is any form of theater staged in the context of the fine arts. This is usually mimetic, as in the case of a performance of *Antigone* or *Endgame*. But everyday theater has been staged in the context of art (as when a performance artist lives and carries our ordinary functions on stage for arts patrons). This is not so much a kind of theater as a context for theater of any of the other kinds.

All these kinds of theater use the art of theater; the performers know how to attract attention and the watchers know how to give it. One goal is the same for both sides in all cases—theater binds together a community around actions that people have witnessed together, actions that have a special importance for them. Of course, different kinds of theater have different goals as well as this common one. Theater may aim to educate an audience, to entertain them, to exercise their emotions, to relieve them of tension, to frighten them into submission. And theater may aim at religious experience.

The line between these kinds of theater is quite fragile, easily broken. A really corking version of the *Antigone* would cross into extreme theater if it suddenly made a jury of the audience and insisted that they pass judgment between the interests of the family and those of larger society. In any event, it will feel real enough, if the acting is strong, when the young girl sings her bridal lament as she is led off to her death; then the audience could feel emotions as gripping as they would if they were watching through a chink in the wall the capture of Anne Frank. Because the kinds of theater share a purpose, the differences between them are less important than what is the same in all—at least to an inquiry like this one, which begins from the common purpose and works back to a classification of ways to achieve that purpose.

1.2 Why Ask?

What is theater? What are the essential features that distinguish it from other art forms? If theater is a species of art, what is art? And what is definitely not theater, either because it is some other kind of art or because it is not art at all?

Perhaps we should not even begin to ask such questions. Philosophers expect to define their subject at the outset of discussion, and this seems an honorable thing to do, but in the realm of art, definition carries the stench of exclusion, of drawing lines between the good stuff, which is appreciated by cultivated folks like me, and the bad stuff, which is amusing to barbarians like you. Why not forego the nasty pleasure of exclusion and simply enjoy to the full whatever comes before us, without asking what it is, without asking whether it is really theater, or whether it is really art at all?

I wish to know what theater is in order to show that it is not, as it seems, a dying art form. True, so-called legitimate theater has been pushed almost to the point of extinction by the landing of an enormous meteor on the cultural landscape. Film has shaken audiences out of theaters and into the multiplexes. Filmmaking uses many of the same talents as theater, but it is a different art form (for reasons we shall see shortly), different both in the making and in the experiencing. Still, film takes up space in our lives that would otherwise be occupied by art theater. What survives is mainly in the everyday or the extreme category.

Long before film came on the scene, theater was in danger of being eclipsed by its own scripts. Aristotle wrote of tragedy as *poiesis*, as the making of poetry. By the late nineteenth century, when universities took on the study of literature, scholars began to study the scripts of plays as texts, leaving live, ephemeral performances as elusive as butterflies on the wing. But a bright-colored corpse pinned inside a glass case is not a butterfly, and a script is not a theatrical event. Unlike a script, an event in theater is ephemeral. Even a production is always in motion, so that scholars who write about it take a risk. Before their work is published, they may find that the caterpillar they described in such painstaking detail has grown a new color and taken wing.

So my questions are two: What is theater, apart from a script or something that can be done on film? And why has it been important to us? If we knew the answers, we would know whether to plead for its survival. We would also understand better how to recognize theater in different cultures and be able to consider whether there is a universal theater, as there appears to be a universal music, an art form that can draw on the streams from many different springs of culture.

1.3 What Philosophy Asks

Philosophy asks what things are. Since the beginning of this sort of philosophy in Europe, with Socrates and Plato, it has tried to free itself as much as possible from particular cultures. Philosophy seeks universals. So for theater it should ask not what is theater merely in New York or off-off-Broadway or in East Austin or Borneo or in ancient Rome, but what is the common enterprise to which theater belongs in all these places. Then, of course, philosophy should make distinctions, in order to give each sort of theater a place in relation to the others and to show family differences and resemblances. This is one of philosophy's projects—taxonomy of ideas.

Taxonomy for its own sake is an arbitrary task and not much use even in biology. We find different ways of dividing categories, different ways of forming families, each way useful for different purposes. The great pioneers of taxonomy, Socrates, Plato, and Aristotle, did not pursue it for its own sake but as part of a larger project to understand what is good and how different things aim at the good. Their definitions and distinctions belong to a broad study of the purposes of things. My scope is less ambitious than theirs (here, only theater), but, like theirs, my quest is guided by the intuition that things are best defined by their purposes.

The purpose of theater, stated simply, is watching. Like my classical predecessors, I take it that any truly explanatory purpose is a good one. Philosophy is not neutral with respect to good and bad, and for most of its history it has not tried to be. I have already said why I think it is good to be watched, good to watch, and good to create the conditions in which watching takes place. There are various strategies for causing human action to be watched. Some strategies are better adjusted to the purpose than others, so some kinds of theater are better than others. My study of theater aims to provide a systematic background theory for judgments of value.

In the world of theater, value judgments cannot be merely matters of personal taste. A work of theater is not like a painting made for the taste of a single patron. To bring a play to the stage, a large number of people must find the play worth performing, and then (usually) a larger number must find it worth watching. Such a union of personal tastes would be unlikely if there were no merit in the work itself. Sophocles' *Antigone* won acclaim for its writer-producer when it first saw the light, and it has been considered a model play for thousands of years. This is no accident of cultural history (though its survival has been contingent on many factors). *Antigone* is one of the best plays ever written, and readers of this book who admire the play will, I hope, discover new ways of explaining why it deserves their admiration.

There are other things that philosophers might do about theater besides defining it in terms of its specific purpose. They might construct large theories about art or meaning and then bring them to bear on special subjects such as theater. Semiotics has been a powerful example of this approach, but I will not emulate it. This book is just about theater.

Then there are things to do about theater which philosophers do not do, and which I will not do in this book. After all, theater has a history, so historians may write about it. So may anthropologists, social psychologists, gender studies experts, economists, and so on. People who actually do theater also write about it, and they often do so very well. They frequently take on philosophical issues, and so I will make use of their work when it is most helpful, paying special attention to two giants of twentieth-century theatrical theory—Brecht and Artaud—and to those who follow their influence. Philosophers, generally, have not written about the questions I am asking here. Although I respect what Plato and Aristotle and their successors have said about theater, I do not find that it touches the subject as I understand it.

1.4 What Theater Is

Theater is something we human beings do, when all of us who are involved are alive and present, and at least some are paying attention to others, for a measured time and in a measured place. Some of us do things, while others watch. From this angle, theater looks like the most basic of all the arts, because its medium is simply us. But from another angle, theater is among the most derived of the arts, because it brings together some combination of choices from a long menu of the arts. I cannot think of an art that is not used in theater from time to time. A contemporary list would have to include acting, dancing, singing, playing musical instruments, writing, painting, designing clothes, photographing, lighting, and sound mixing, as well as applying video or digital effects in a live setting.

We could say that theater is the art that uses all of these other arts in a certain way. But such a derivative account is not satisfying, because the list of arts it gives contains no essential elements of theater. None of the arts I listed in the preceding paragraph is necessary for theater, not even the elements we most closely associate with theater—writing and acting. We can improvise without a text, and we can be watched without acting. We do not need sets or costumes or lighting. We need only ourselves in theater. Theater is human action being watched.

If we need only ourselves for theater, then this is the most basic truth about theater: theater is the art that takes *us* for its medium. But to make us a medium for art, theater has to make a frame for those of us who are to be watched, and another for those of us who are to be watchers, for the measured time of the performance. Typically, theater measures out a place for itself and draws a line between the watchers and those who are to be watched; at the same time, it measures out the time, a beginning and an end, for the watching to take place, because we will not be watchers indefinitely. We must know when to start watching, and, before we start, we must know that there will be an end—so that we will know that the price of paying attention will be reasonable, and that soon we will be free to get on with attending to our own lives.

Measuring the time of watching is not enough. Why should a potential audience take any time at all to watch the players? This question points to an element that is nearly universal in theater—engagement. The players seek to engage the audience in what they—the players—are doing, or, if not in what they are doing, then in what they are make-believe doing, during the measured time and within the measured space that is a stage. The players seek to hold the attention of their audience by exciting them, catching their intellectual interest, or making them care about something. There are heaps of ways of doing this, and they have just this in common: the players try never to let the audience become bored by what they, the players, are doing for the whole of the measured time.

Supporting the definition

I said that theater is the art by which human beings make human action worth watching, in a measured time and space. (I hope my readers will not mind my repeating this like a mantra.) I simply announced this definition as a hypothesis in the introduction, where I briefly explained some of its terms. I have no way to prove such a hypothesis, but I still have ways of supporting it—partly by showing weaknesses in its competitors, partly by showing its strengths, and partly by bringing out the elegance of its form.

I need the whole book to display the strength of the hypothesis, as I track the many questions and answers that arise from it. Formally, however, I can point out already that the definition has an elegance that should delight philosophers trained in the classics. I define theater in terms of four elements: those who make theater ("human beings"), what they make it from ("human action"), the basic form they use in making it ("in a measured time and space"), and their purpose ("to make it worth watching"). These neatly correspond to Aristotle's four "becauses"—four factors in explanation: the maker, the material, the form, and the purpose. But is this classical elegance any use for the study of theater? The only way to judge the case is to read on.

As for competing definitions, a brief review should suffice here.

1. *A kind of mimesis.* Aristotle defines tragedy and comedy as kinds of mimetic poetry. But to think of theater as limited to mimesis is to sell it short. We cannot omit to study real rituals, real contests, and real events, and to ask why they are so gripping, if we want to know how to captivate an audience for *Antigone.* In some traditional cultures, performers do not aim at make-believe or representation. When they act as gods or heroes, their goal is to become gods, to be taken over, so as to be not themselves. Among Europeans, the distinction is more readily understood in traditional sects that believe in sacraments and accept transubstantiation, than in reformed ones that deal only in reminders and representations.

Mimesis is precisely what Plato despised about theater. Plato complained (1) that theater is essentially mimetic and (2) that it always aims to galvanize emotion in the audience at the expense of reason. But on the definition of theater I have just given, neither of these is essential. Football in a stadium is theater, and most of it is not mimetic; the stand-up comic in a bar is theater, and she uses mimesis. But she neither whips up emotion nor undermines reasoning. Mimesis does not always cause the trouble Plato says it does; still, we will be looking at a more powerful kind of event if we cast our eyes beyond the mimetic.

2. *A collection of examples.* We might consider an empirical strategy, gathering together things we think are theater and asking what are the most important elements they have in common. I can't help using examples, but I do not believe that they can take us very far by themselves. We have no way to settle disagreements about what we should count as theater. We depend on judgment to select good examples, and then we depend on judgment again to pick out what is most important in those examples. Besides, our concept of theater has soft edges; many things seem on the boundary between theater and other art forms. You may want to put movies into the category of theater and exclude football; I have reasons for wanting to do the reverse. You may make Shakespeare's plays your main paradigm of theater, whereas I would admit his work only as one paradigm among others, some of which are non-European. Besides, part of my aim in defining theater is to support judgments of value, and the pure study of examples will not do that. I hope to explain why a

good performance of *Antigone* is better as theater than a typical football game. The explanation, which arises from my definition, has to do with plot and character—but that is to anticipate.

3. *The sum of the arts used in theater.* We might build an account of theater from definitions of the arts that are used in theater. That would be all very well if we had a convincing way of selecting the arts that are most important in theater—aside from falling back on the empirical method that I have already set aside. Also, I think that we lose sight of an important point if we treat theater as derivative of other arts. Theater is universal in ways that many of the arts it uses are not, it appeals to fundamental human needs, and it is found in cultures that have no concepts of writing or acting.

4. *A species of the fine arts.* We might set down an account of the fine arts as fundamental, and mark off theater within that. My reason for resisting this should be clear enough by now. "Fine arts" is a concept that was born in European cultures fairly recently; it has its uses, but it can blind us to the real scope of the arts. For example, if we look only at art poetry, we see a dying art that has lost its importance in modern cultures. But if we simply look at poetry, we find an art that is very much alive. Poetry lives with music, which has always depended on its companionship. And if we want to know where to look for the secret of vitality in poetry, we would be foolish to look at its fineness when it belongs to the fine arts. So it is with theater. It is all very well to produce Chekhov for a cultivated audience who can discuss the fine points of staging and interpretation. But Chekhov himself would not be satisfied with an arts audience. He did not write in order to give fuel to an elite culture industry.

Scope of the definition

The competing approaches to defining theater are all too narrow, in my view. So I will have to defend the very wide scope of mine. My main defense is the book itself. If in the end I have said something useful about theater here, then the broad approach is useful. We should expect the broad approach to be useful because it will allow us to draw on a variety of cultural traditions. The broader the scope of the definition, the lighter the load of cultural baggage that it makes us carry; and the less cultural baggage we carry, the more we will learn from theater in traditions other than our own.

Broadness helps within our tradition as well. I have defined a class of events that meet certain needs, including the whole range from classical mimetic theater and dance to the extreme theater of public events. Extreme theater continues to be robust in modern cultures, while art theater appeals mainly to an elite. If we can find the source of the robustness in the theater that is robust, we may be able to give the performance of *Antigone* a shot in the arm.

Broad as it is, my definition may seem too narrow. Why insist on measured time and space, for example? Why couldn't theater go on everywhere, forever? Because an event would lose its audience if it went on forever, and no one would be free to be in the audience if everyone was on stage. But take away the audience, and the watching ends. If no one is watching, it's not theater, though it may truly be a performance.

Another way that my definition may seem too narrow: Why insist that the medium is human action? Why not watch animals or gods? And why actions, as distinct from events in general? The answer is that my subject is the art of theater, and an art, by definition, is a kind of learning that guides human actions. The dance of the cranes may strike us as highly artful, but they cannot teach us their dance in the way we pass an art along from one generation to another. We can imitate the dance of the cranes, but that is another thing, our art, not theirs. A secondary answer is that actions are more interesting for us to watch than events. That is why disaster films show people taking action during the disaster. Action has a story line. The rising of a river has a story line only by anthropomorphism—only if we imagine the river as having human qualities, like Homer's river in the *Iliad* that surges over its banks in a rage against Achilles.

1.5 What Theater Is Not

As broad as it is, however, my definition is narrow enough to exclude two art forms that are frequently confused with theater: literature and film. Neither of these takes human action as its medium; the medium of literature is the text, written or memorized, and the medium of film is, of course, film. Besides these interlopers, there is a third sort of art that theater is supposed to belong to but doesn't—fiction. Theater may or may not involve fiction. Last, theater has been identified with hypocrisy. That charge also is false.

Literature

Literature has no necessary part in the definition of theater, which does not require a text. Literary critics have for generations pleased themselves by taking theater to be little more than the enactment of literary texts, but this treats theater as an ancilla to something else, rather than as an art form. True, texts are often well taught through performance, but teaching literature is not a specifically theatrical goal. Further, performing an act of reverence to a written text, like any other ceremony of reverence, can be a sort of theater. But this is not what theater is.

Film

Theater is different from film in being a live performance (though a presentation of film may be *used*, properly framed, in a live theatrical performance). The art of making films does not make human action as such worth watching, and the art of watching them makes fewer demands on its audience than does the art of watching human action.

In theater, the arts of watching and of being watched are intertwined, and each affects the other. Those who wish to be watched must adapt to the present audience; no two audiences are the same, so no two performances can be precisely the same. Even if the audience members are the same, their moods will vary from one evening to the next. The interaction between actors and audience builds a tension that energizes a live performance in theater. Theater calls on its double art to build this tension, but the art of film does nothing like this.

The art of filmmaking seeks to make the film worth watching, not the action it is supposed to represent. In film there is only the art of making film. There is no art of film watching. Because film cannot adapt itself to different audiences—to different ways of practicing the art of watching—it must impose itself on its audience, leaving us no room to practice anything like the art of watching we employ in theater. Film requires us to watch in a certain way; its artists often choose where we should focus our attention.

Film has at its disposal powerful effects for controlling emotions, effects that are not available in theater—enormous close-ups of a human face, or music coordinated with the realistic depiction of action. The weaker effects common to theater allow for a wider range of audience response than in film, and members of the audience, seeing the action from different angles, will have different experiences of the same play. But there is one angle for everyone in a film showing. If you see the actor's right profile in a given scene, so will I, no matter where I am sitting.

Because it controls the way it is watched, a film may be shown in the same way for any number of consumers over the years. Although it may deteriorate or be recolored, and its soundtrack may be redubbed, it cannot be adapted as a whole to a new time or place without being remade. Good films die, while good plays adapt. A film, like a book, is completed and published in a set form. "Cinema is a time machine," as Susan Sontag observes, while theater brings classics up to date.

The actor's work in film is different, moreover, because a film actor does not need to have a sense of the whole beyond the scene being shot. Indeed, no one knows exactly what the whole film will be until the final cut is made. But there is no cutting and splicing an actor's performance on stage. In short, actors take over from the director in a performance on stage, developing their own relationship with their audience, but, in producing a film, the director and production staff take over from the actors.

The line between film and theater is obscured by the practice of recording performances on film or video and transmitting them to large audiences, as now often occurs with opera and with sports events (which are a kind of improvisational theater). The showing of a film is a kind of performance; audiences can respond and thereby affect each other's experience of the film, and the cult showing of certain films (such as *The Rocky Horror Picture Show*) works like theater to build a sense of community through a ritual of engaged watching.

If I am right, a performance of *Antigone* has more in common with a football game than it does with a film of *Antigone*. In the same way, a man has more in common with a woman than either one has with a photograph of the other. One could make love with a man or a woman, but not with a picture.

Fiction

Theater is not essentially fictional, in the traditional sense of fiction as invention. Purely documentary historical material may be presented in theater, and although the representation of history is certainly mimetic, it need not use invention, though it will use the tools of selection and arrangement that are available to all historians.

I have already argued that theater need not be mimetic. I can maintain this even for a broad definition of mimesis, such as Kendall Walton's. Walton treats all representation as make-believe, and all make-believe as fictional; so on his account all representational performance is fictional. But not all theater involves representation, and even in representational theater, directors often wish to leave open the question whether events transpiring on stage are representational or actual. The actor playing a jealous husband may actually be a jealous husband, and the audience may witness a real murder on stage. They may even find that their seats are not safely removed from the action, when an actor bursts through the fourth wall and confronts a spectator directly, or when spectators are asked to decide what happens next. Such events are rare, but the possibility of reality breaking through is always present in even the most mimetic theater and brings a unique excitement to the genre.

Hypocrisy

Hypocrisy is pretending to be something you are not, as when a lying philanderer poses as a paradigm of moral probity or an atheist takes a lucrative job as a televangelist. The word is formed from the Greek word for actor, literally, "one who speaks for another." The word "theatrical" is often taken to imply "hypocritical," and the art of theater has been identified with the art of pretense. That is one of the reasons that theater has been banned by puritans. That is also why it seems to be sharp criticism even now to call a politician theatrical. But all democratic politics is theatrical, since democracy can only happen in a public forum, and candidates who are incapable of theater will never make it past their first campaigns. There is nothing intrinsically hypocritical about knowing how to get people's attention and keep it for a certain time. But that is theater. Even mimesis does not imply hypocrisy. There is nothing hypocritical about children's games of make-believe or let's pretend, and yet these are mimetic through and through.

1.6 Art

I defined theater as an art form with a range that may have surprised you, including weddings, football games, and public executions. These, you may well say, do not belong to the fine arts. Very true: theater is not a fine art. It may be fine or vulgar, and it may cater to elevated or quite ordinary tastes. But because it is generally considered to belong somehow to the world of art, I should consider what it is to be a work of art.

You might hear, "That's not art, it's pornography!" Or, "Not art, only kitsch!" Or, "Not art, only a decoration." Or "Only entertainment, not art." Or "Yes, that is art, so you cannot call it pornography, and you must place no restrictions upon it." But the greatest excitement in the art world is usually at the boundaries or frontiers of art, where artists try to invest new kinds of work with the dignity of the fine arts.

Art has never been defined to the satisfaction of those who need definitions. That is partly because there is no one context for art; art is sometimes a political concept, sometimes a legal one, sometimes a normative term, and sometimes a barrier that revolutionary artists delight in breaking down (while still being artists). The modern notion of the fine arts as systematically related to and distinct from other human endeavors is fairly new, a new sandbar built up by shifting currents of thought in Europe during the early modern period. "Sandbar" is the image I want, because I regard the concept of fine art as a navigational hazard.

There are heaps of artworks that are accused of not being art; perhaps an artwork that does not provoke the "That's-not-art" objection is just not very interesting. So it would be foolish to try to fix the boundaries of art; the aim of the art game (which I do not wish to play) is to make those boundaries move. But I do need to examine the ideas that come into play when the art game is played—especially the properties of things that deter critics from accepting those things as art. I will call these properties "defeaters," because they are used to defeat a claim for the status of art.

The main defeaters for claims to art are as follows.

1. *Pedantry.* For example, being pedantic or being instructive is supposed to be a defeater. Few critics would accept an instruction manual as fine art, and, for the same reason, many have objected to Brecht's play, *The Caucasian Chalk Circle*, because, they say, it is built to convey political instruction. "That is too pedantic a play to be a work of art," you might hear. Generally, when a performance exhibits one of these defeaters, critics might say, "That's not theater," meaning "That's not the kind of theater we want to consider."

You should be suspicious of this sort of thought. Brecht's play is written as "theater for instruction"—his own term—but it is, for all that, a good play, and squarely in the European theatrical tradition. Christianity has used theater for instruction since very early days, and there was a time when there was virtually no other kind of theater. We have evidence that the ancient theater of Greece served an educational purpose in a democracy that called for its citizens to think through tough questions about the use of power. Theater is actually a very good medium for instruction, as many successful teachers know. When a performance fails to be worth watching, that is not merely because it is instructive. The aim to instruct may lead to bad theater, but what is bad about it is something else. Good instruction is always good theater.

A troop of young advisers stages a skit for incoming university students, designed solely to make them aware that rape by close acquaintances may occur, while giving them tips on how to avoid the danger ("stay sober," "always take 'no' for an answer"). A critic might say that the skit has no artistic values ("no production values"), and indeed it was never intended to be fine art. But it is a kind of theater.

2. *Utility.* The problem about pedantry is a special case of a broader problem about utility, or usefulness. Utility is a well-known defeater in the art world. Art is not supposed to be useful or even to look useful. Marcel Duchamp hung the urinal upside down and labeled it "Fountain" so that it could be perceived as art, and not as an object of use. It would be a strain to pay attention to the art qualities of the urinal while using it for its original purpose, and it might distract other museumgoers as well. Pornography is used for sexual stimulation, and that is one reason that it is not considered art. But art can be stimulating in many ways.

3. *Competition.* If you catch your audience's attention by showing them a competition with winners and losers, you have stepped off the high ground of fine art as it is usually defined. That is one way in which a football game differs from art theater: people watch it partly to see who wins. And yet many admired ancient plays are built on competitive speaking in both long speeches and line-by-line exchanges. And the plays themselves

were entered in competition. Ancient Greek audiences were loath to watch anything that was not competitive; they watched to see who won. Most kinds of competition are inherently theatrical; without an audience as witness we cannot be sure the game was fairly won.

4. *Lack of originality.* Reproductions, imitations—anything derivative is said to be out of bounds in the modern world of fine art. That is because we are heirs to the idea (new in the eighteenth century) that an artist is a creative genius. This conception of the artist has no place in traditional cultures, however, and theater in particular has a history of deriving itself from earlier models without shame or loss of merit.

5. *Frequency and novelty.* The art world resists accepting as art either objects that are too common (such as tablespoons and games of catch) or those that are too rare. The first time an artist wrapped a building in fabric, many people found it hard to accept the event as art, but with greater frequency comes greater acceptance. There is a comfortable zone in which art usually takes place, outside the common sphere of life, but not so far out that we are unprepared to see it as art. Artists of the previous century made many attempts to break out of this zone, but the verdict of history will probably be that they succeeded only in expanding the art zone. By contrast to the other arts, theater has seen few boundary disputes. It has never been limited to a zone. It can be mundane or utterly astonishing, as long as it brings watchers to its measured time and space.

Theater has many ways of making human action worth watching. Some of them create value of the kind that is recognized in the fine arts. Some do not. Try to think of all the things that might draw you to watch a performance, and all the goods you might hope to gain from doing so. You will probably never get to the end of the list: beauty, wisdom, epiphany of the divine, ritual, resolution of conflict, a sense of belonging, a chance to hold hands with your friend, a rush of feelings, sexual excitement, relief from boredom, a change of pace. There are many reasons to watch, and a definition of theater should try to make room for all of them, somewhere. But they are not equal; some are more worthy than others to be watched. What *is* worth watching?

TWO

What Theater Makes

The child playing Hamlet remembers most of her lines without prompting, although Gertrude has forgotten everything, and all Claudius wants to do is play with his sword. Somehow the play winds to its bloody end, bodies strewn around the stage. The parents in the audience—entirely delighted by their children's brave and clever performances—applaud wildly, after turning off their video cameras. This was Shakespeare's *Hamlet*, abridged, simplified, and altered both by the director's tact and by errors in performance. But still, this was *Hamlet*.

Or was it? When can we honestly say that the play is being performed? In this case none of the audience demanded money back; all knew what to expect. After all, they had been hearing about the production for months from the excited actors. But if someone had demanded a return on the cost of a ticket, an answer is ready: almost all performances of *Hamlet* cut scenes or speeches; some, like the children's version, cut characters as well. Ophelia's part was eliminated from last night's production after her mother expressed concerns about asking children to play at madness and suicide. But is it still *Hamlet*?

More hangs on this issue than the price of a few tickets. Questions like "What makes *Hamlet Hamlet*?" look like philosophers' parlor games, but in fact they call for serious answers. Such questions make us decide what we think is truly important about what theater produces.

For *Hamlet* the question is what makes this piece of theater *Hamlet* and not any other thing. Philosophers have used the word "essence" for this kind of importance, and they have held that the aim of definition was to state an essence.

Since we have a definition of theater in front of us, we should ask whether it helps with the problem about *Hamlet*. If it does not, then it cannot be a good definition. But don't expect too much; theater, like all human art and culture, does not allow a high degree of precision in definition. So don't look for clear boundaries around the play *Hamlet;* look for the center. That should be good enough. (I say later what I mean by "center.")

Now according to my proposed definition, the art of theater makes human action worth watching for a measured time. What is most important about *Hamlet*, therefore, *as a piece of theater*, ought to be what makes it worth watching for the time it takes.

What makes *Hamlet* most worth watching is Hamlet himself—this fascinating young man: disturbed, brilliant, passionate, reflective, book-loving yet capable of violence, Hamlet, the lover who drives his love insane, the dutiful son who insults his mother. He is captivating, but we are not prepared to watch a lifetime of someone's being Hamlet. We will watch him for the time it takes for him to get into a difficult situation and out of it. This kind of play gets its hero clear of complications through death, so we will watch Hamlet till he dies (and that had better not take too long). What makes us keep watching to the end is the plot, which promises us a cue to stop watching and go home before our patience runs out.

So here we have the two essential elements in a play like *Hamlet*: character and plot. They are the elements that make this play worth watching. But they do not turn up in every theater piece; they are the elements of mimetic theater only. A more general theory says that the essentials of theater are structured action and role. In a football game, the structure lies in competition by the rules of the game, and the roles are the positions of the players. In a wedding, the structure is that of a certain sacrament, and the roles belong mainly to those whose lives will be changed by the ceremony, while the roles themselves are defined by the ways in which the lives will be changed. In all cases, what is essential to the structure is that it promise an end to the action we are asked to watch, and what is essential about roles is that we must be able to care about at least one of them.

2.1 The Product of Theater

Theater is the art by which human beings make human action worth watching in a measured time and space. That helps as a starting definition, but it leaves many questions open. This art seems to produce various kinds of theatrical events, such as the Yale-Princeton game of 1965 or the middle school performance of *Hamlet* that I just described. It also generates kinds of events that can be carried out on many different occasions, such as football games and the play *Hamlet*.

What does the art of theater make? It makes events, in which some people watch other people in action for a measured time. We speak of events in two ways. We produce *kinds of event*—generic events such as football games or weddings—and we produce *particular events*, which are *instances* of those kinds of event, such as the Texas-Oklahoma game of 2005 or last night's performance of *Hamlet*. Kinds of event may be more or less specific; football contains college football, and college football contains the Ivy League sport. On the fine arts side, we speak of Shakespeare productions, productions of specific Shakespearean plays, and so on, and these are all kinds of events. So now I can define my terms. By "a theater piece" I mean a *kind* of theatrical event that may be repeated. By "a theatrical performance" I mean a *particular* event in theater that may not be repeated.

A particular performance is easy to pick out but not so easy to explain. The art of theater produced last night's performance of *Hamlet*, which we watched in the school auditorium between 7:30 and 9:00 PM. But what was it we saw? It was one in a series of performances—the sort of series that is called a "production." It purported to be a performance of Shakespeare's play, *Hamlet*. In this, it was an instance of this year's St. Sebastians School's production of that play. But what does it mean to say this? What is it to produce a particular play?

Don't expect clean or final answers to questions like this. Any classification scheme will leave some cases to dither about, and there are bound to be some *Hamlet*-like events that are not quite *Hamlet* and not quite anything else either. We should not be put off by these hard cases, and we must be especially careful not to allow the hard cases to make us think the whole business is arbitrary. It is not. As long as there are clear cases of *Hamlet* in performance, we can ask what features of those performances make them clear cases, and then we may reasonably debate how well those features show up in the questionable cases. That is what I meant by looking to the center rather than to the boundaries.

We should not throw in the towel and say that we will arbitrarily call events in theater whatever we want, as long as other people let us get away with doing so in our time and place. "If St. Sebastians calls it *Hamlet*, it's *Hamlet*," we would then say, forestalling further discussion. But that would be relativism, and it would sell the art of theater short. When Shakespeare created *Hamlet*, there was some *thing* he created as an artist in theater, and I would like to be able to say what that creation amounts to.

We must not let just anything be called *Hamlet*. Suppose Portia seduces Hamlet in the first scene, and the love-besotted boy does not even hear the ghost of his father calling to him. Later, Claudius outfits Hamlet with an army and sends him off to do battle with Fortinbras, and, although distracted by the antics of Falstaff, the young prince is successful in battle and returns in glory, only to find that Portia has been sleeping in his absence with his beardless young cousin, Troilus. The ensuing duel is interrupted by Mercutio, with fatal results for all concerned, and Portia dies by her own hand, clutched to the breast of her best friend, Rosalind. This is not *Hamlet*, and no change in language or culture would license us to call it so.

An easy solution would be to declare that to perform *Hamlet* you must perform Shakespeare's text. But this fails, because Shakespeare himself did not take that view. He did not leave us a definitive text for any of his plays, and in the case of *Hamlet* he evidently left us two different versions (of which more anon). Even plays that have come down to us in a definitive text may be translated or edited for production. Besides, even if there were a definitive text, you could perform that text without using the art of theater—if you made none of it worth watching, for example. Theater is a performance art, and nothing written down perfectly represents a performance.

The play we saw last night was not a performance of a text written by Shakespeare. The language had been modernized, scenes and characters omitted, and speeches shortened. But the performance did have something to do with Shakespeare's text. Was it an instance of what Shakespeare created? Faithfulness to text alone will not decide.

Besides text, there is a growing and changing performance tradition, which explains, for example, why Hamlet wears black, and why the Yale game is interrupted by an amusing contest of marching bands.

In both kinds of cases we face hard questions about what counts as what. Is Trobriand cricket a kind of cricket? Or should we say that it is a kind of dance derived from cricket? If we answer that Trobriand cricket is cricket because it follows in a historical tradition from the English game, we are adopting too loose a criterion. Trobriand cricket is a kind of sport, and a kind of theater, but its aim is the opposite of cricket's. By that, we would rightly say that anything performed in the *Hamlet* tradition is *Hamlet*. But my crazy scenario with Hamlet and Portia belongs to the *Hamlet* tradition, and that is surely not *Hamlet*. So this does not work either. Faithfulness to text is too strict a rule, and faithfulness to tradition is too loose.

Let us be clear about one thing: the art that produced Shakespeare's *text* was the art of composing with words, specifically, the art of writing poetry. But the art that produced last night's *performance* was *theater*. Where does the art of words meet the art of theater? The same question goes for football. Football is also linked to words, to a book of rules or to oral traditions about the rules for football. But a football game is not constituted by those rules.

2.2 What Is *Hamlet* (the Play)?

Hamlet is a theater piece. A theater piece is a product of the art of theater which may be repeated on many occasions, in many places, and in many different ways. It is to be distinguished from a production of *Hamlet*, such as the famous one with Richard Burton, which may be repeated fairly often, but usually with a fixed cast, a fixed design, and so forth. Both theater piece and production must also be distinguished from a performance, which happens only once, and which may be an instance of both. The theater piece, *Hamlet*, may be repeated both in many productions and in many performances of each production. By contrast, football (the game) is a theater piece that may be performed in many ways, but there is nothing quite like a production of a game. The Yale game of 1965 happened only once, and a reenactment of it would not be a game.

The questions "What is *Hamlet*?" and "What is football?" belong to ontology. We have a good idea what the *Mona Lisa* is, and clear criteria that would enable experts to pick it out from a collection of fakes. But we do not have clear ideas about how to decide whether the school play I described is, or is not, *Hamlet*, and we do not have clear intuitions about what sort of thing the play is. It is not at all like a carved rock or a painted canvas. Certainly it seems to be something apart from its many performances and productions. But what? On what basis may we say that this or that belongs to the essence of a theater piece?

In keeping with my proposed definition, I propose a way to deal with these questions: we must assume that certain noncontested performances are performances of *Hamlet*. Consider what makes the action of these performances most worth watching; then take that to be the essence of the thing.

We must start by setting aside features of the performance of *Hamlet* that are shared with performances of other theater pieces. Yes, the play is beautiful and exciting, and, yes, it seems to reflect, albeit vaguely, some basic truths of the human condition. But so do lots of theater pieces. *King Lear*, for one, hits the same standard, roughly, on all points. So *Hamlet* is not the play that it is because of its beauty or its truth or by any other general quality it has, any more than the one I love is the person she is because of her beauty or virtue.

We must also set aside special factors such as the fame of an actor, or our family ties to the costume mistress. These are special because they may affect only part of an audience and because they do not discriminate among theater pieces. I don't care what play she is in, I will watch avidly if my daughter has any role, however small. But no one else in the theater is there because of this tie. And such special factors attract me only to certain scenes—the ones with my daughter—and not to the play from its beginning through its middle to the end.

What makes *Hamlet* worth watching to the end in every successful performance, and for every audience, is Hamlet himself, and the play is worth watching to the end because only then is the conflict between him and his elders worked out in a climax of revenge. (By a successful performance I merely mean one worth watching.)

So I would say for a start that the barest essence of the theater piece known as *Hamlet* is (1) that its main character is Hamlet and (2) that it is about resolving certain conflicts generated by Hamlet's felt need to seek revenge for the killing of his father. Some elements of the play are essential to it, as almost everyone will agree, while other elements have varying levels of importance, about which reasonable people will disagree. Whether the Ophelia subplot is essential is hard to judge; I would say it is merely important. Most of us, I suspect, would accept an Ophelia-free production as an abridged *Hamlet*, but some would not. Rosencrantz, by contrast, could be painlessly cast away (though few directors would do so after Stoppard). In any event, *Hamlet* is rarely performed without some abridgement.

Hamlet, then, is a performance in which the lead role belongs to the character Hamlet, and the plot consists in resolving a nest of conflicts arising from his father's death. We can make the point general: to find the essence of a piece of mimetic theater, identify the main character (or characters) and the principal conflict (or conflicts) that are resolved in the plot. By "plot" I mean structured action that keeps our attention and measures the time for a theatrical performance. By "character" I mean someone who attracts our close attention.

Setting up a conflict and resolving it is the most common way to make a theater piece command our attention, and this is the most common way of building a plot. Most games set up competitions that lead to a decision, but not all have winners and losers. A game of toss on the lawn may draw an audience for a moment. Each throw and each catch has its tiny moment of suspense, but they do not sustain our watching for any measure of time. Conflict would have helped. A scoreboard might rivet us to the scene.

Plot generally (but not always) consists in the development and resolution of conflict. Conflict attracts our attention to action because we want to see it settled, as it is in a game when one side defeats the other, or in a revenge-tragedy when one side wreaks revenge on the other. Because we want to see a conflict resolved, the actions that are most important to a play are those that set up or resolve its conflicts.

In dances, concerts, ceremonies, and public executions, the structure of the action rarely depends on conflict. Some dance performances are types of mimetic theater—some even take their action from plays—and represent a plot, with all the traditional elements of conflict and resolution, but some do not. Other dance performances take their structure from the structure of the music which they follow; others may have their own kind of dance structure. Music and dance, when separated from words and mimetic theater, depend on structures that are clearly apparent only to seasoned audiences. How many concertgoers understand sonata form or know a development section from the introduction of the second theme? No matter, if they can hear the music at all, they hear it building and resolving complexities, and they recognize the cadence that signals the coming of the end of the piece. Even in music there is something like conflict and resolution.

Weddings are good examples of ceremonies. In many cultures they end with a kiss between bride and groom, who in this way allow the audience to witness the token of their love. In some cultures, however, a wedding is represented as resolving a conflict of families. And so even this may fit the usual pattern. But many ceremonies build to moments like the wedding kiss, moments in which the lives of those involved are supposed to be forever changed. So it is with confirmation, with induction into high office, even with Holy Communion. Execution is the ultimate life-changing ceremony. In all such cases, the ceremony ends as soon as possible after the lives are changed.

Roles are essential to theater because action requires choice, and if there are to be choices, there must be people to make those choices. In games, the roles are filled by players in defined positions. In mimetic theater, roles are filled by what I call characters. (I am using this word in a technical sense to be explained later.) To be a character, a person must affect the audience in two ways: characters must be such that (a) the audience can take the characters to be capable of choice, and (b) the audience can care about what happens to the characters.

Of the two essentials, character and action, action is provided by the performers. Character, however, is the product of a collaboration between the stage and the auditorium. Writers and actors, for their part, must present characters in such a way that the audience can respond to the characters as characters. When an audience practices the art of theater, they do so on the basis of their culture and their personal ethical dispositions. All present in a theater are practicing the art of theater, because the performers cannot bring a theatrical performance into being by themselves. When Rosencrantz and Guildenstern abandon the players in midscene, in Stoppard's play, the players are right to feel betrayed. They cease to practice the art of theater, and they cease to play characters, when the audience turns away and there is no watching to be had.

How many roles for characters must there be in a theater piece? Enough for conflict, in most cases; enough for ceremony in others. A play needs at least one character for a conflict, and most conflicts call for at least two. *Prometheus Bound* has only one character (in my sense); the hero's conflict in that play is with Zeus, who is offstage throughout. Not all conflicts are resolved in the plays they animate; *Prometheus Bound* is an example of a play that leaves its conflict hanging, while resolving the issue of how its one character will face that conflict.

In competitive games such as football, there must be two teams, and each team must have at least one player. That gives us the essential cast of characters. In many cases, props are also essential: balls, nets, and so on. The players may tag or tackle, they may adopt various different rules about field position or passing the ball, but it is still football if it turns on a certain kind of conflict—in this case a competition governed by certain basic rules—which offers the characters—the players—a choice of actions which we find interesting to watch, and which belong to the game of football.

So, in general, you may define a product of theater by pointing to the structure of actions and the definition of roles. This works equally well for kinds of theater (such as football) and for specific events (such as this year's Yale game). And it answers the question with which I began: of course the St. Sebastians play was *Hamlet*. There was a girl on stage playing Hamlet for over an hour, during which her conflict with Claudius ripened and burst and ended in bodies strewn about the stage. That's *Hamlet*.

2.3 What *Hamlet* (the Play) Is Not

First of all, it is not a performance or a production, because it is something that is repeated each time *Hamlet* is performed or produced. Second, it is not a particular string of words, because the play is often performed in translation. Third, it is not a text, even when "text" is broadly understood to allow translations. This is especially clear in the case of *Hamlet*, which, as I have pointed out, is almost always abridged in performance. To my dismay, none of the film versions, apart from Kenneth Branagh's, contains the marvelous soliloquy about Hecuba, yet all are marketed, and accepted, as film versions of *Hamlet*. To make matters worse, we have two very different versions of Hamlet, both of which may come from Shakespeare's hand. The "bad quarto" edition—short, violent, shorn of meditative passages and much else—still has a claim to be *Hamlet*. For most written plays there are textual variants, and in many cases no particular reading has more authority than another. Even if we had the final manuscript copy in the author's own hand, we would be wrong to identify the play with the text, because the play belongs to the art of performance, not the art of writing.

A fourth alternative is that what is essential to the play is fictional truth—what is true within the frame of the play. For example, it is fictionally true that Gertrude is Hamlet's mother. In the St. Sebastians production, it is fictionally true that Gertrude is hysterical, but this does not hold for all productions. Different things are true in different productions. Directors and designers and actors must decide many points for themselves: Is the ghost real or a sham? Is Claudius really guilty as charged? Is Hamlet mad or shamming madness? Has he slept with Ophelia? Is it true or false that he wears black? Does he need corrective lenses in order to read? We can't simply identify the play with what is fictionally true in a given production of it. So if the play is to be identified with some set of its fictional truths, we need to specify the set of truths that makes the play what it is. And if we pursue this question, we are soon led back to my suggestion that we fall back on truths about character and conflict. They are what matter the most, because they are why we watch the play.

2.4 The Case of Music

A musical performance may be theatrical. Will my criteria for a theater piece work for a piece of music? Not smoothly. Because Beethoven's Opus 131 is a performance piece, it is not identical to a text. We may think of it as a kind of musical idea that may be instantiated on any number of occasions. But that is intolerably vague. What sort of musical idea? What are its essential features—features that must be reproduced in anything that can honestly be called a performance of Opus 131? At least, the notes must be played, most of them, more or less accurately. Must they be played by a string quartet? Apparently not; the tradition in classical music allows us to use "Opus 131" for transcriptions, keyboard versions, synthesized performances, and so on. So it is the notes (not the inscription of them, or the assignment of parts to instruments) that seem to make this piece the piece of music that it is. (By "notes" I mean relative, not absolute, pitches. Opus 131 may be transposed into a new key.) To bring Opus 131 before us, we must play all the notes shown in a certain text, which represents the musical idea that is Opus 131. You may not, for example, omit the development section of the opening movement or rewrite the ending to bring it to a climax in a key change unauthorized by Beethoven. That would be another piece of music. Opus 131 is more strictly lined up with its text than *Hamlet* is with any of its texts.

Still, I think that structured action and role serve as the essentials in a piece of music. Opus 131 in every instance has a certain structure, even if it is transposed as a whole for a set of different instruments. The structure is musical, and only by a very loose metaphor could we compare it to a conflict, but it is no metaphor to say that it leads to a musical resolution and that the structure promises from the very first note that there will be a last note, that the piece will have an ending. As for roles, there are four of them, and they are clearly defined, the inner voices giving substance to the piece, the lowest voice providing its foundation, and the first voice usually taking the melodic lead.

2.5 The Game Analogy

We can give a rounder account of what it is to be a theater piece by unpacking the analogy between plays and games. I have taken *Hamlet* and football together in this chapter because they have important features in common, so that one sort of theater helps to illuminate the other. Think of an enduring work of performance art on the analogy of a certain game, such as football. Usually we agree when football is being played, as we agree when *Hamlet* is being performed, but standards for both will be subject to change. Performing *Hamlet*, on this analogy, would be like playing football. In both cases there are roles to fill and rules to follow, and these may be done more or less appropriately to the game at hand. To do them well requires more than a script or a playbook, since it requires also a certain evolving tradition of performance. Suppose, then, that an enduring work of art theater such as *Hamlet* is an artistic game that may be played in various ways. How far will this take us?

Start with football. Football is being played whenever a player is performing as quarterback (sufficient and necessary condition). If this seems too slim an account of football, look how much is packed into it: performing is more than practicing; the player is not performing as quarterback in drills or in life off the field. In drills, he is merely practicing to be a quarterback. In order to perform as quarterback, the player must be engaged in a game. A game takes place in a measured space—the field—and during a measured time, and it draws the attention of onlookers if any are present. So whenever a quarterback is at work, theater is happening too. Besides the measured space and time, certain other conditions must be met. The quarterback must have a team, and they must face an opposing team. Both teams must be trying to win, more or less following the rules of this version of football. The rules are football rules if they belong to the tradition that became collegiate with the Princeton-Rutgers game in 1869.

2.6 Performing Hamlet

So let us play a game of *Hamlet*. You be Hamlet, I'll be Claudius, and your sister can be Gertrude if she wants. This is a game we could play, and if we played it for an audience, we would be performing *Hamlet*. *Hamlet* is being played whenever a player is performing as Hamlet, just as football is being played when anyone is playing at quarterback. For this to occur, four conditions must be met, analogous to those necessary for football to be played.

1. *Space and time.* The player performs in a measured time and place. The prince of Elsinore in the tenth century who was perhaps named Hamlet or Hamnet was never playing Hamlet. He simply was Hamlet, day and night, wherever he went, and at all times, so he did not meet this condition. The St. Sebastians *Hamlet* satisfies this condition; that makes it a theater piece, although it does not make it *Hamlet*.

2. *Tradition.* The tradition of *Hamlet* has been broken, repaired, invented, but it has been causally linked to Shakespeare's production of the play. The tradition is largely carried by printed versions of the text, but since the restoration of theater in the later seventeenth century it has been transmitted in other ways, as one generation of actors and directors pass on performance tips to the next. The St. Sebastians *Hamlet* belongs to the *Hamlet* tradition; but that does not make it *Hamlet*.

3. *Structured action (plot).* In order to play Hamlet, you must play someone who is in a certain situation that calls for choice. Earlier I pointed to conflict as an essential feature of the play, and, indeed, we can understand Hamlet's situation most simply as conflict with his uncle. Many other conflicts come into the play, related in one way or another to this one, and we will have to ask, for each one, how important it is to the play: Must Hamlet be in conflict with himself? with Laertes? with Ophelia?

    In any case, Hamlet has a tough decision to make. He feels he should seek revenge for his father's death, but he can't be sure that he has a good reason for thinking, as he does, that it was his uncle who killed his father. He has seen a ghost. His father is dead. His uncle is king. His mother is now married to his uncle. He is in love with a young woman. He knows how to play the recorder. Wait! Is that necessary? The boundaries of Hamlet's situation are fuzzy, but we know what is at the center: Hamlet is caught in events that seem to call for revenge. The situation calls for other characters and at least one other actor. You cannot play Hamlet all by yourself, because Hamlet is in conflict with, in love with, disturbed by, and friendly with, other people.

The player must take action, on the basis of choices shown on stage, and in some coherent way, in order to perform *Hamlet*. He must act coherently and on the basis of choice; otherwise he will not be taking action in the full sense, as we shall see. But there is no fixed rule about which choices must be shown on stage, or how actions follow from choices, or how choices are made to appear coherent in a given abridgement or production. The play, *Hamlet*, provides a broad umbrella for variations in what is loosely known as plot, and these are loosely held together by the common tradition from which they derive. Yes, you might play Hamlet leading to a happy ending, if you stick closely enough in other ways to the structure of the play. That's an odd way to play the Hamlet game, but keep in mind that you can play football games in odd ways also. We may decide to trade a few players after each play, for example. But it's still football we are playing.

The action on St. Sebastians' stage is structured by a plot that includes the main elements of Shakespeare's. So it is a candidate to be classified as *Hamlet*.

4. *Character.* To perform Hamlet, you must perform him as a character, and not as a piece of human scenery. As I said earlier, that requires a certain kind of attention from the audience, a willingness to see you (when you play Hamlet) in a certain way—as a character in the full sense.

The girl from St. Sebastians is playing Hamlet. She is melodramatic, occasionally forgetful, and not always audible. But she is certainly playing Hamlet, from ghostly visitation through indecision to a surprising revenge on a stage littered with bodies. This play is *Hamlet*.

2.7 A Test Case: *Antigone*

Sophocles and Jean Anouilh both wrote plays called *Antigone*, the one in Greek, the other in French almost 2,400 years later. Are they two versions of the same theater piece, or are they different pieces of theater on related themes? We can agree that they are both theater pieces, designed to be performed in measured time and space. And we can agree that they belong to the same tradition of material about Antigone.

To be the same play, however, they must meet a more stringent condition. What makes them both worth watching must be pretty much the same, and this, according to the theory I have proposed, consists in plot (structured action) and character (focus of audience engagement).

Reasonable lovers of these plays may disagree. I disagree with my former self: once upon a time, for a very long time, I spoke of Anouilh's play as a version of Sophocles'. I have recently changed my mind. Plot and character are quite different in the two plays.

Sophocles' central character is Creon; he has half the lines in the play, and he engages our attention more and more as the play crashes to its end. The plot is his—his struggle to contain rebellion, his vacillation over whether or not to listen to others, and, ultimately, his grief-stricken recognition of what he has done, which we see when he takes responsibility for the deaths in his family.

Anouilh's central character is Antigone, as advertised by his title. She is the one whose choices and actions guide the play. Creon is a fixed quantity, a piece of immovable political scenery—or that, at least, is how he tries to see himself. For him there will be no recognition, no acceptance of responsibility, and no grief. For Antigone, however, there is an enormous choice—one not given her by Sophocles. She can, if she wishes, keep the whole thing secret and live a false life as a productive wife for Creon's son and as the mother of his grandchildren. She must make this choice in full knowledge that the brother she buried may not have been the one she thought, and that even if he was, he had not been as good a man as she had thought he was.

The action here is structured by a different plot, and, as a result, the focus of audience engagement is on a different character. So this is a new piece of theater.

We must now turn in more detail to action and character.

THREE

Action Worth Watching: Plot

*The stream and the broken pottery: what was any art but
an effort to make a sheath, a mould in which to imprison
for a moment the shining, elusive element which is life
itself—life hurrying past us and running away, too strong
to stop, too sweet to lose?*

—Willa Cather, *The Song of the Lark*

You would expect to see steam rising in the theater if it were not
so dark where the audience is seated. Excited by what they are
watching, couples are beginning to grope at each other. Lone viewers
are starting to grope for themselves. It is time for the management to
turn on the auditorium lights or to send an usher down the aisles with
a flashlight, playing it along the seating. This may be pornography, but
the house wants to maintain a sense of decency.

The management may also believe that what they have staged is
worth attention in its own right, and, if so, they will want us to pay
attention to the stage rather than to each other or to ourselves. If the
play excites me to the point at which I start to lose myself in my partner, it has not been worth watching to the end. Paying attention to my
partner is a good thing, in itself, but it is not the same as paying attention
to the action on stage. If the action on stage were really worth watching
for its measured time, then I would wait and turn to my partner later, at
a better place and time.

Change the scene now to the parking lot outside a football stadium.
In a light drizzling rain, the audience is streaming out to their cars, but
we hear subdued cheering still from inside the stadium. The game is far
from over. But it has been a lopsided contest, and the outcome is not
in doubt. The audience has lost interest, whether rooting for winner or
loser. Wearing one color or another, dragging their dripping banners,

they slouch homeward. It has not been a good afternoon, and they have no reason to wait for the final whistle.

Management tries to avoid scenes like this. Colleges play in leagues that offer good competition; professionals try to even the odds as much as possible within and across the leagues through the draft system. The problem is that many people come to see who wins. In a well-plotted performance, the denouement does not come until close before the final curtain, so the audience wants to stay until the end. But in a game, there is no guarantee that the denouement will wait till the end, though each running of the ball or each inning in baseball, like every scene in a play, has its own plot structure that may hold an audience for a brief time.

Both the sex show and the football game suffer from the same flaw: they don't have good plots, and people come to them not for watching the action (in most cases) but for something else—to the sex shows for stimulation, to the game for seeing who wins. That is why the management must make a special effort to keep audience attention for the measured time, since there is constant danger of a mismatch between the aim of the audience and the measured time. Perhaps a few watchers are so interested in observing technique that they are not stimulated by the sex or don't care who wins the game. But they are the exception. Action worth watching *for a measured time* has a good plot, and a good plot is a large part of what makes it worth watching for that time.

Of course a plot that keeps us in suspense to the very end is not good enough, if the very end does not come until we have lost patience. A baseball game that remains tied for eleven innings has an exciting plot, for a while. But it is too long to sustain excitement in all but the most avid fans. A good plot sustains our interest from beginning to end.

Sex shows and football games are not ideal specimens of theater, though they are theater. They rub against the definition in two ways at once—and this shows the power of the definition, that it gives them some edges to rub against.

First, what makes the sex show and the football game worth watching does not necessarily make them worth watching for the measured time. The value of any activity needs to be adjusted to the time the activity takes. For example, if you think that what makes your life worth living is your plan to make $5 million, think again. Your length of life is not measured to fit your goal. You may meet your end before making all that money; or you may make the money at thirty and live to be ninety. Either way, what makes your life worth living *for the time that you have* cannot be making $5 million. The goal and your life span are out of synch.

A theatrical performance, unlike a life, has a time span measured out in advance. It is easier to make a play worth watching than it is to make a life worth living, because (in a well-plotted play) we know that we'll have exactly the right amount of time to resolve the conflict in the play—and we can end it right there. That's because the author used the art of theater to design a plot that unfolds in the time allotted.

Second, the sex show and the football contest do not seem to be making the action worth watching. If they were, the audience would not wander off before the end of the show or the game. In a good specimen of theatrical performance, it is the action itself that we find worth watching. In the football game, the people fleeing the stands are not interested in the action as much as they are in seeing who wins, and they have seen that before the action is over. In the sex show, the couples that are turning to each other are here to become excited about each other, not to watch the action for its own sake. In the same way, if I am watching a cooking demonstration by an expert at making apple pie, and I came here only to learn how to make crust (being confident of my fillings), I will leave as soon as I have learned what I came for. I did not come for the action. So once more we have an example of bad theater. The pie demonstration is more pedantic than theatrical. But it could have been both. If it had a better plot than the mere steps in a recipe, it might have held my attention for the full time.

And how long is the full time? The action of ordinary human life is rarely worth watching for very long. After a while, even the nosiest neighbor loses interest in your doings and peeps only occasionally through your windows or over the fence to see what you are up to. The reality shows on TV are carefully edited to be worth watching for the measured time of those shows. Theater frames human action in a measured time and space, in order to mark off what is supposed to be worth watching, and then uses various other techniques to make it so within its frame.

3.1 Value

The sex show, the lopsided football game, the interminable baseball game, the dull demonstration of pie making—all of these are specimens of theater, but they are bad specimens. They show what theater ought not to be. They may be good specimens of something else—an effective cooking lesson, a stimulating sex show. But they are bad theater, and they may be just plain bad as well.

A good specimen is one from which you can learn about the nature of the species. A definition states the nature of a kind of thing, according to the classical system I am using. It follows that a good specimen is a good illustration for the definition. A bear that has lost its teeth is not a good specimen of bear, nor is a baby bear that has not yet grown its teeth. You would be sadly mistaken if you learned from these examples that bears are toothless. When I define bears as having the potential for teeth, I imply that toothless ones are either not fully developed bears or not very good bears. And that's right, even though they may be good bears in other respects. If I defined human beings as having the potential to be over six feet tall, I would imply that many of our companions were either born defective or have not fully developed. Too many, really; so I do not want to posit that definition. There are plenty of good specimens of humanity under six feet tall who can teach us a lot about what it is to be human. Declaring them to be poor specimens does nothing to advance our knowledge of our species.

Defining things is not innocent. It implies judgments of value. Do not be lulled into thinking that when you argue about definitions you are safely confining yourself to facts. If you are queasy about values, set aside this book. But first please consider this: the value judgments I make here are all part of a tentative undertaking. My definition of theater is merely a hypothesis to explain what we generally do and what we generally value in theater. The value judgments that stem from the definition are simply parts of an expanded hypothesis. How well the hypothesis works depends on how well the whole book works, when all is done. If my definition condemns a great many kinds of theater, then it is undermining my project. Perhaps we should give those kinds of theater a chance to teach us something positive about what theater can be. But we won't give them a chance if we let my definition put them in a class with toothless bears—as examples we should not learn from.

My method is this. Propose a definition. Then see what values it implies. If you don't like the result, and you have a reason for not liking it, go back to the definition and change it till it gives you the results you want. This method would be circular if I thought the definition provided grounds for the value judgments. But I don't. The definition and the values it implies are all part of the same hypothesis, which I believe I can defend as a whole, by writing this book.

Definitions are not innocent. If a definition of theater does its job it excludes some things that might look like theater, and if it does the job really well it gives some things the privilege of being better specimens of theater than others. Classical philosophers defined a human being as a rational animal (meaning, "having rational potential"). That classical definition leaves out all the apes and monkeys that do not have a rational potential, if "rational" means "able to use language more or less the way human beings do." Quite right! Apes are not human, and nothing follows about who's better or worse. But within the human species, some specimens will have more potential for rationality than others.

Does it follow that smart folks are more human than the stupid ones? No, because both groups would be human in virtue of their potential for rationality under the definition. But the smart ones would be better specimens, because they would better exemplify the defining features of the species. If, that is, the classical definition were right. But it can't be right. If it were, Star Trek's Lt. Data would be a better specimen of humanity than Romeo or Juliet. And that's absurd. Rational we may sometimes be, but we are also capable of laughter and love and lulling each other to sleep with words that have no meaning. And these capacities also mark us as human. A definition implies values. If you cannot accept the values that a definition implies, go back and revise the definition. This is one to go back and change.

With this example in mind, consider my proposed definition of theater: theater is the art of making human action worth watching. Few words anywhere are innocent of value, and these are as guilty as words can be: "art," "worth," "watching," "human," and "action." The first two I will set to one side for the time being. "Art" has its own section in chapter 1, and I will not add to it here, except to remind you that I do not mean fine art here—just art, which is a learned way of doing things.

"Worth" can be read in two ways—subjectively for things certain people like, and objectively for things that are truly rewarding. I mean to define theater as an art that aims to be truly rewarding and not merely to be liked by some people. This is bold.

By "truly rewarding" I mean "should be rewarding for anyone"—anyone, that is, who belongs to the target audience for a given theater piece. The puppet theater of Java may not be the least bit rewarding to me until I have learned enough about Javanese culture to follow it. But once I have learned this, and I join the target audience, I take on a responsibility to try to find this performance worth watching. The art of theater is not entirely up to the performers. Part of my job in the audience is to be the kind of person who can be rewarded by watching such a performance.

Health is worth having both ways; people like being healthy, and being healthy should be rewarding for anyone. I say "should" because health would be a false benefit for villains like Adolf Hitler. If he had totally lost his health before taking power, he would have had to curtail his life of crime, and then he would have died a better man. So in a case like Hitler's, health is not a benefit. But that is his fault. You have to be living a terrible life for health not to be good for you. What is truly rewarding is what benefits you if everything else about your life is as it should be. Another way to make the point: you should try to live your life in such a way that good health—and all other truly rewarding things—are rewarding for you. When I say that health is truly rewarding, I am spelling out what it means to say that health is worth having; it means that you should live your life in such a way that health is good for you.

My proposed definition of theater is loaded. It implies that theater aims at something that is truly rewarding. And I mean what I say: if theater is not beneficial to you, you should change your life—or else change the theater to which you are exposed.

3.2 Action

Theater is the art of making human action worth watching, in a measured time and space. The adjective will be redundant if (as I expect) all action turns out to be human, but the point is worth making explicit.

I chose the word "action" with some care. By "action" I mean an event under a certain kind of description—described as a person's doing something. The form of the description would be "A's Q-ing," where A is a person, and Q is an active verb that is not stative. "Paul's taking up the cello" names an action. So does "Paul's falling in love." But "Paul's being in love" does not, because that refers to a state of being in love, not an event. In the same way, "Oedipus's understanding" does not name an action, because the verb refers to a state Oedipus is in—a condition, stretched out over time, in which he understands something. But "Oedipus's trying to understand" or "coming to understand" both name actions.

"Oedipus's being trapped by the gods" is not an action, because the verb is passive. Actions include speaking, hoping, lamenting, fighting, flying into a passion, learning, forgetting, taking a seat. At the end of his life, in Sophocles' last play, when Oedipus takes his seat on sacred ground and will not move, he is taking a decisive action, one that he recapitulates with each refusal to move, with the result that his simply sitting there is not merely a state; it is an action extended over time, like that of a modern protester sitting in all day and all night against a war or a judicial crime.

Strictly speaking, the definition of action excludes whatever events we may wish to watch that are not human. But why be strict? Why not see drama in the burglary of squirrels framed in the window as they raid your bird feeder and the jay screams? Why not see action when a wind bursts out of the northern sky to toss treetops against darkening clouds? There is a good reason why not: in neither case is the event due to a person's choice. The north wind is not a person, though it may be delightful to think so. Neither is the larcenous squirrel. Both have been given parts in a natural sequence of events that leaves them no scope for choice. That is why we try to deter the squirrel and to protect ourselves from the wind, but we do not think of punishing either one for the harm they do. We expect Creon to see what he has done and accept responsibility for it, and that recognition scene will be the climax of *Antigone*. But we can't expect a hurricane to show up shedding tears of regret for striking the coast by a great city and killing many innocent people. Tragic heroes sometimes act like hurricanes (as Ajax does in his madness, or Macbeth in the dream of his ambition), but at some point they wake up and remember their humanity. Hurricanes never wake up.

Imagination is often part of our watching; it may allow you to see action in natural events. You may learn to see drama in the building of the storm as the clouds gather toward climax and spill into thunder and rain, releasing tension and transforming a baleful threat into a blessing for the crops. In such a case you are thinking of the elements of the storm as if they were capable of action, and that effort of imagination may help you appreciate and come to terms with the storm. You could actually stage a play in which actors take the parts of clouds and lightning and rain. Watching this play would be watching action; merely watching the storm build and break is not. But watching the play would teach you a way of watching the storm. And, I think, watching a good brief storm would help you understand the structure of a good plot. Such an exercise of imagination is anthropomorphic, in that it sees natural processes in terms we usually reserve for human beings or other persons—terms that imply that choices have been made.

Even in the case of human beings, I think, we need to exercise imagination in order to see events as actions. Watching workers at a distance, swarming over the steel frame of a rising building, I could see them as I would see ants crawling on the trunk of a tree, with no thought for the choices that may have led them to that steel frame or the decisions that they will make later today on their way home. Human action at a distance looks a lot like a natural event; we need to make an effort to see it as human. The effort has an effect analogous to that of a zoom lens. Good filmmakers understand this; when showing a great army in motion they zoom in on an individual at some point, in order to show that this is an army of people.

We need to humanize events if we are to see them as the stuff of theater, and that requires us to imagine that they are the results of choices on the part of the agents. Humanizing a storm is not so very different from humanizing your enemy in war or humanizing unknown homeless people camped out across the street. It is all too easy to see human beings as forces of nature, but it is wrong, and it develops bad habits to do so. Human beings do make choices. On the other hand, to see forces of nature as capable of human agency is usually harmless, and it develops a good habit of watching—the mindful sort of watching that is on the lookout for human agency.

"Human" names a species, and so "human action" appears to be a descriptive word. But speaking about a species is not merely descriptive, because some members of a species may be better specimens than others. As with theater, the definition of human both sets boundaries and picks out a center. Some of the things we do are more human than others. We humans can both fart and talk, whereas horses can fart but not talk. Talking, therefore, is a more human activity than farting, and we should not be surprised to find that good theater pays more attention to talking than to farting. Abstract philosophizing attracts a few people, and it might be the principal activity of those superhuman beings—like Aristotle's gods, if they existed—whose lives are fully rational. Although it involves choice and can be described in terms of action, abstract arguing is not as human an action as debating a particular case of law. Debating guilt and innocence is a lot closer to the center of what we do than is abstract contemplation of being quâ being—Aristotle's favorite subject.

We should not be surprised, then, to find that a good play shows us a debate, such as about whether Helen is guilty of starting the Trojan War, but no good play shows us an abstract debate about the general link between guilt and free will. The debate about Helen leads to even better theater when the play shows us Menelaus shrugging off arguments entirely as he feels the resurgence of his love for Helen. Love is more human than any kind of argument—closer to the center of what we are.

What are the most human actions? They are the ones that exhibit the abilities that are most distinctive of our species—communicating and forming communities. That is why theater often draws us to watch people working up to a wedding; a wedding play is about people forming commitments and expressing those commitments to each other; on this basis they are forming the atoms of community. They do most of this by talking. But talking is not the only action that grounds community; besides making talk we make music, dance, sports, and many other things that are worth watching.

We can see an event as a better or worse specimen of an action, depending on how much choice we allow to the agent. "The canoe's bow sinks as it drops over the waterfall, filling and spilling its hapless driver into the waves, where he is pinned under the surface and drowned by a down current and an overhanging rock." So described, the drowning is an event, not an action. But try this: "The canoeist realizes too late that he has steered his boat into the gap that leads to the steepest part of the falls; he tries to slow the boat with backstrokes, but he picks up speed nonetheless, takes the falls leaning back but is unable to keep the bow from going under; alone in the water, he tries to keep his head above the surface, but he is not strong enough to resist the current; he slides, flailing desperately, under an overhanging rock, from which he does not emerge, and where, we must suppose, he drowns." This describes the same event as action, at least up to the last moment. The more your play lets us see events as actions, the closer it is to the center of theater.

Action is the stuff of theater. A capacity for action is one of the distinctive marks of humanity; so is the imagination needed to watch people in action. The art of theater makes a pair of demands on us—for the performers to present action to their audience, and for the audience to understand the behavior that they see as arising from choice.

3.3 Plot Design

From these elements we can sketch a general treatment of plot. What makes a good plot?

First, a plot should be sized to fit the measured time it is to fill. By "sized" I mean that the actions should have a structure which spreads what is worth watching throughout the measured time, so that the audience does not lose interest before the end. Sex shows and football games, remember, did not reliably meet this criterion. Mimetic plots have the advantage that they can be designed to hold the audience precisely until the end. That is partly because the end in mimetic theater is not given by the clock but by the plot itself. A good plot does not merely fit into the measured time; it is itself the measure of the time.

Second, a good plot makes *action* worth watching. Action is a human phenomenon; the more human are the actions on stage, the better the plot. Talking is more distinctively human than eating and farting. Because we share those two functions with many animal species, it appears that eating and farting can occur without the kind of choice that humans make. Talking, however, shows a mind at work, trying to execute its choices through words. We should therefore expect a good plot to show us more talking than eating or farting. Ancient Greek theater is full of talk. But singing, dancing, and many other behaviors are also the stuff of theater. Farting has a very small place in it.

Third, since a good plot presents actions to us, and actions flow from choice, we should expect a good plot to show us the kind of situations in which choices are made. Choices are made by characters acting under these conditions: when the characters are (a) more or less sane, (b) acting freely without duress, and (c) behaving coherently. A coherent pattern of action makes it clear that the agent is the one taking the action. Suppose there is no pattern in Macbeth's actions; sometimes he kills, sometimes he pardons, sometimes he seems interested in power, at other times he cares only for music and dance. How would we explain this? Perhaps the witches have driven him around the bend, and he is no longer in control of himself. Perhaps he acts differently when Lady Macbeth is around, because she is manipulating him. Either way, Macbeth himself drops out of the picture and the women take over the play. We see them as taking action, rather than him, because of the greater coherence of what they are doing.

From these considerations come limitations on plot: characters must not be completely mad in a good plot, and they must not be totally under the control of others. To show that they are sane and independent, each character must have enough to do in the plot that he or she can establish a coherent pattern, and this limits the number of characters that may be used in a given time. So a good plot has only a few characters in the full sense, though it may have a lot of human scenery.

Fourth, since a well-measured plot is often mimetic, its makers (when it is mimetic) must know what effect they wish to produce. There are many things an audience might take away from watching an original action: they might be educated by it, excited by it, shaken emotionally, moved to hilarious laughter, or put to sleep. The makers of mimesis, if they are masters of their art, are able to control the effects fairly closely. Consider this example. Not long ago I let a heavy woodworking tool fall on my head, causing a nasty injury. Now you want to present this on stage, by way of mimesis. How will you arrange the scene? So the audience will laugh? Cry out in horror? Intervene in order to save me (or the actor playing me) from danger? You will probably achieve only one of these effects, and you may use the conventions of stagecraft that are alive in your culture to determine which effect you will have, through the complicity of the audience. Modern audiences sometimes laugh when Agave carries in the bloody head of Pentheus, her son whom she has killed under the illusion that he is a lion. But directors aim to wring a cry of horror from the audience. How can this be corrected? Only by theatrical techniques that are in tune with modern audiences. Directors must know whether the plot aims for a laugh or a shriek at this point, and then they should supply mimetic techniques that can achieve the desired result.

Good plots may fall into many different categories, not all of them mimetic. Ceremonies and rituals may be well measured without being mimetic, and sports events may have more shape than is given by the clock. All of these may lend their structures to mimetic plots as well.

3.4 Pleasing the Emperor

Today Philostratus has been appointed to be the master of circuses for the emperor. His predecessor was declared an honorary Christian and fed to the lions, after presenting a series of shows that the emperor found boring. The emperor is easily bored. Philostratus has only a week to prepare for the next circus, and his planning is severely focused by the thought that he too is in danger of being declared an honorary Christian. He quickly gathers groups of citizens and asks them why his predecessor's shows were boring, and what they think would be more worth watching. The consensus is that the shows have been monotonous. Christians with arms bound and feet tethered have been herded into the arena of the Colosseum, the door of the lion cage has been raised, and the hungry lions have quickly dispatched a few people and then commenced to feed on them. No conflict, no drama, no human interest.

Philostratus does not have much latitude, as the supply of Christians is growing, and the emperor is determined to use the circuses for two purposes at once—entertainment and religious hygiene. So Philostratus decides to introduce action, conflict, suspense, human interest. He frees the Christians from their bonds and gives them weapons; he even gives them a little training, so that they can put up a fight. If he can make it appear that the Christians could actually defeat the lions, the audience will be spellbound, watching in suspense, hardly daring to breathe, while the action takes place. And that last clause is the key: there will be action in this show, and a contest, and people will find that worth watching.

Indeed, the emperor did find this worth watching, on the only day the circus was presented in this format, but the Christians successfully defended themselves, even bringing down the best in the pride of lions. Although well entertained, the emperor was not pleased with the outcome, and Philostratus's conversion to the new religion was announced the next day. It is not enough to observe the rules of good plot design. Each audience has its own expectations. When the emperor asks for Christians and lions, the lions have to win.

Staging Choices

The old man on the hill is fulfilling his destiny. He has come to Athens to die on this sacred spot. We do not know what brought him here, because he is blind, and the young girl leading him does not know her way. Soon, in this place, the god will speak to the old man, but we will not hear what is said, and up to now the god has apparently been silent during the journey. Now, however, because the odd pair has arrived on stage, we are to see what keeps them on this hill.

He could easily be dislodged. The natives do not want anyone here, and when they hear who he is—the cursed man who slept with his mother and killed his father—they are even more eager to have him out of their domain. But their king will decide to give him sanctuary.

Then Oedipus himself is tempted three times to go back to Thebes, and as far as we can tell, he could go there if he wanted. First his daughter tempts him to return and heal a family rift; then his brother-in-law tries to force him home to save Thebes from a civil war; and, finally, his son begs him—as only a child can beg a parent—to come home and save his life and his crown. But Oedipus decides against them, all three. And we see why in each case. The family has abandoned him, the city wishes merely to make use of him, and his son is already launched on the infamous crime of fratricide. Oedipus has three good reasons for making the three decisions. We watch and listen while each decision is made and the result comes roaring out of the old man's mouth.

He is choosing his fate. The death which the gods foresaw and foretold and perhaps even foreordained—for this he is choosing to take these steps along the way, all the ones we are shown on stage: wandering far from Thebes, rejecting his family, offering a gift to Theseus. Or so we feel, with a chill in the spine, as we see the unregenerate old man in his rage come, through his own agency, to be in closer and closer harmony with the gods. This is thrilling, a stunning series of scenes. Imagine how dull it would have been if he had been led, meekly consenting, to his last moment. But this is a tragic hero. He takes action and refuses to be acted upon.

And so, in the *Oedipus at Colonus*, the play of Sophocles that brings us closest to the actions of the gods, we are shown one human choice after another: Oedipus's determination to sit in the sacred place, his refusal to return to Thebes, his curse against his sons, his plan for his own death, Theseus's decision to assist him. And whatever the gods may be doing to consummate Oedipus's marvelous death, no action of theirs is shown or even described on stage. The messenger from offstage is not allowed to see the death which he reports, and the one man who does observe it is forbidden to speak of it.

Sophocles has made Oedipus's last day worth watching by filling it with action arising from choice. And yet if any event is beyond human choice, it should be this one, in which Oedipus is claimed by his destiny. Sophocles seems to have done the impossible, to have conjured choice out of a close web of fate. How has Sophocles pulled this off? Even plots that leave nothing to fate seem to raise problems for the staging of choice. How is it possible for any playwright to put choice on stage?

4.1 The Possibility of Theater

An old axiom states that what is necessary must at least be possible. So far I have been sailing along as if only the necessity of theater were at issue, but now I am in danger of striking a reef that would sink the entire project. Theater, as I define it, must at least be possible, but the problem of choice puts this in jeopardy. Theater, as I define it, is the art of making human action worth watching. So theater must put actions on view, and they must be recognizable as actions. But actions imply choice, and how could the art of theater put choice on view? Three problems.

The first problem concerns the structure that theater gives to events. In order to make events worth watching, theater gives them the structure of a plot, which unfolds in accordance with probability or necessity. Good plots seem immune to the disturbances we would expect from characters who enjoyed freedom of choice. The stage generally shows actions that are planned or fated. Mimetic theater knits a plot tightly together, so that the actions presented to the audience all fit into a plan, which the audience recognize with delight. But action implies choice on the part of the agent, and in a well-made plot the agents' choices are all planned by the art of theater. Apparently, audience members are asked to believe both that choice is taking place and that it is planned. But that would appear to be impossible.

Tragic theater especially tends to show events that fulfill a fate that was foretold long ago. Events governed by fate cannot issue from human choice. So once again an audience is asked to do the impossible—to accept the events on stage as actions, and therefore as arising from choice, and to believe that those same actions are due to fate. But fate, we think, defeats choice.

Second is a gap between what choice is and what theater does. Theater shows externals, but choice appears to be internal. Choices, if they take place at all, seem to take place in the mind, and the mind is not directly accessible to theater. So how will audience members be able to recognize actions when they see them, as opposed to events that do not spring from choice? In short, "staging choices" looks like an oxymoron, odd in the same way that "thinking in public" seems odd. Don't we think and choose privately, in our heads? (We'll see that theater proves that we do think and choose in public.)

Third is our grand, longstanding worry about freedom—the fear that choice is not possible for human beings at all, in view of the ease with which science can explain and predict human behavior. The debate on this is as old as philosophy and as new as today's brain science; I have only a little to add to it here.

So it would appear on these counts that theater is impossible. Theater is supposed to put action on view, but (says the third objection) there is no human action because there is no human choice. And, say the first and second objections, even if human choice does occur, we cannot show it on stage because choice is internal, and even if we could show choice when it occurs, we could not show it at all in tragic theater (because its plots are driven by fate), and only with great difficulty in other genres. So theater, as I have defined it, is either impossible or dreadfully difficult.

The easiest way to show that something is possible is to point to an example of it. There it is! They are doing theater! So it must be possible. But the objection runs too deep for this response; it cuts at the heart of our definition of theater. The question is whether we can really cause action—events proceeding from choice—to be watched on stage. Somehow the audience must be able to tell that choice is taking place or being represented. So each problem presents me with two challenges, one theoretical and one practical. The theoretical challenge is to show how theater is possible. The practical challenge is to show how the art of theater does stage choices.

The first problem, the one about fate, will get a short answer here in the example of Oedipus, who chooses each step that leads him to his assigned death in the *Oedipus at Colonus*. The playwright shows this by offering him temptations, which, one by one, he refuses for reasons that are plainly his. Although the result was foretold as a matter of fate, his refusal in each case meets the conditions for choice, as we shall see. Whatever the tragic poet meant by fate, he did not mean that it defeats choice. If he did, he would have built no suspense in these scenes of temptation; they would be dull, flat, and lifeless. But as it is, they breathe with passionate life.

The second problem was that choice is often defined as a mental event, of which only the chooser is conscious, and which, in the best case, is the culmination of a process of deliberation known only to the chooser. If choice is a mental event that is present only in the mind, then it defies presentation on stage. Some philosophers define choice as a purely mental event; they would take the subject of this chapter to be agency rather than choice. I believe, however, that my subject is not the same as agency; choice is a public phenomenon which explains agency and which I attempt to explicate in this chapter.

The third objection claims that science proves that human beings lack the freedom needed to make choices. This objection arises from confusions about freedom, which I attempt to dispel mainly by showing how freedom is shown in theater.

Now for an example. Let's leave mimesis out of the discussion for a while—since that adds an unnecessary complication—and consider a case from extreme theater, the kind of theater that actually changes lives. Weddings put choice on display—the choice of two people to form a new family unit, faithfully, and for life. In private, the man might declare such a choice and not mean it, in order to have his will with the woman, but saying it in front of witnesses makes it an oath. An oath must be both chosen and public. No one can take a binding oath in the privacy of his own mind. Witnesses must take note, be they family, friends, enemies or, as in many traditions, a divine observer. God is supposed to be an ideal witness, who is aware of choice in ways that are denied to humans. But the requirement of human witnesses seems to be universal, and that is what makes oath taking a kind of theater. A wedding must be staged in such a way that the human audience are good witnesses to an oath proceeding from choice on both sides. To be a good witness is to have good grounds for believing that what you think you saw actually took place. The staging of a wedding has at least this goal: to give its audience good grounds for thinking that a wedding took place:

GEORGE   I wish I could get married without all that marching up and down.

MR. WEBB   Every man that's ever lived has felt that way about it, George; but it hasn't been any use. . . . All those women standing shoulder to shoulder making sure that the knot's tied in a mighty public way. (Thornton Wilder, *Our Town*, Act II)

In an actual wedding, an honest and successful one, the principals, at least, believe they are making choices. Though they may have decided in private long ago to be married, the action of their marriage takes place now, in public. And because it is an action, it implies choice. The importance of the choice as choice is emphasized in conventional ways of staging a wedding. For example, the two oath takers may be separated physically from anyone who might coerce them and presented in such a way that it is clear they are not raving drunk or mad. Witnesses may be asked to speak up if they know of conditions that might defeat the possibility of choice in this case. In some traditions, the choice is made, and the action taken, by the families, not by the bride and groom, and that is reflected in different conventions for staging their weddings.

Stagecraft is in play whenever oaths are taken. The occasion is solemn, witnesses are present, and everything possible is done to convey to the witnesses that a choice is being made. Far from making us doubt what we see, the stagecraft of oath taking helps us recognize what is going on. A marriage really took place today. The happy couple are sworn to each other, now, for life. We saw what we need to see, now, in order for us to hold the couple to their vows.

The public taking of vows is a paradigm for what we really mean by choice. So there is nothing odd about my title after all. Staging choices is as familiar as a wedding, as common as a promise, as public as an oath of office. Plainly, then, theater is possible. We do know how to give an audience grounds for believing that choice occurs. But I have not really answered the objections; all I have done is show how deeply our culture is committed to the staging of choice. But how good, really, are the grounds for believing that choice occurs? And what are the devices for staging choice in theater?

4.2 Freedom

Choice implies freedom, it seems, but we are not certain that we have the freedom it takes to make a choice. The art of theater must presuppose that we do. A metaphysical abyss drops at my feet. One step forward, and I will bring us tumbling into the debate over free will and determinism. The arguments, which I will not cover here, seem endless. If the defenders of free will are right, our freedom is such that no finding of science could put it in doubt that we are free. Free choice is possible, and so is theater as I have been accounting for it. But what if they are wrong about free will?

Hard determinism would deny free will and, therefore, choice as well. We do not need to take this position seriously: anyone who asks us to choose hard determinism as the correct position cannot deny that we are free to choose. Still, one variant of hard determinism is worth mention. Fictionalism says that we make believe that we have choices, by means of the stories we tell about ourselves, even though we do not in fact make choices. On this view, theater would be possible, for it would represent fictions of choice. But, since any story about choice would be fictional, even extreme theater would be fiction. We must have been playing at make-believe, in watching the wedding, when we believed that choice and action occurred. But this seems to fly in the face of experience. We know what it is to make believe, and we were not doing it at the wedding.

Compatibilism argues that people may make genuine choices that are subject, like anything else, to causal explanation. If compatibilism is right, then choice is possible, and theater too, as far as this issue is concerned. Many thinkers since Hume have been compatibilists, but the position has been under fire from free-will theorists in recent years. Much hinges on what the two sides mean by "causal explanation." Some compatibilists, the soft ones, consider that explanation in human affairs is weak, riding on causal rules that do not always hold. Other compatibilists, the hard ones, have a robust theory of causation, appealing to causal factors that determine a result.

Defenders of free will would say that whatever can be explained can be predicted, and whatever can be predicted cannot be subject to choice. If we could know in advance that Oedipus would curse his sons, then he was not free to choose whether or not to curse them. That apparently was determined at the time there was advance knowledge that he would do so.

Soft compatibilists would reply that the only thing we know in this case is the history of Oedipus's choices—the pattern of choices he characteristically makes—from which we derive the expectation that he will curse his sons. This, they say, is not advance knowledge at all; predictions in human affairs are soft. Such predictions tell us at most what we may reasonably expect.

The defenders of free will are not satisfied by this answer. The fear that drives them is not of soft predictions but of prediction by determining factors. In theater, especially, determining factors appear to be in play. There is nothing soft about Oedipus's fate, as Sophocles presents the story. The gods know he will die in Attica on the sacred hill at Colonus, bringing a blessing to Athens and leaving a curse for Thebes. This they know precisely in every detail. That is an extreme case, of course. The gods have made no plans for Willy Loman (in Arthur Miller's *Death of a Salesman*), yet the audience knows he is doomed, and none of the blows that strike him down falls unexpected. But the extreme case of Oedipus is the one we need to study, for even he seems to be making choices. How could any credible theory make space for choice in a world as tightly governed as that of Oedipus?

Sophocles, like most ancient thinkers, is almost certainly a hard compatibilist; that is, he holds that the course of human events is determined in advance and that this course of events consists mainly of freely chosen actions. If challenged, he would probably defend his view by appeal to what modern scholars call "dual causation": his characters, like characters in Homer, share causation with the gods—like the poet who says in the *Odyssey*, "I am entirely self-taught, and I learned all I know from the gods." One outcome, two causes—human and divine. Homer often tells both stories concurrently, with human and divine action intersecting to produce a single result. Sophocles, however, stages only the human story in his plays. For every action he shows on stage there is a human explanation, consisting in believable human choices, made by believable characters, and influenced in believable ways by events.

Some readers, however, claim that Sophocles shows events governed by fate, leaving no room for human choice. I say "readers" because I do not believe that anyone watching the action on stage could believe that it is represented as devoid of choice. We need to keep clear the distinction between what Sophocles shows on stage and what he lets us believe happened off stage. On his stage, we never see the gods taking control of human events. Sophocles stages no miracles, brings in no gods on a machine (as Aristotle rightly points out). It was offstage that Oedipus broke one taboo, by marrying his mother, and desecrated another by killing his father; and perhaps he was compelled by fate to do these things. But Sophocles does not stage those events for us. What he does stage is plainly designed to show us Oedipus in action—choosing to investigate the king's death in *Oedipus Tyrannus*, choosing to abandon his city and family in *Oedipus at Colonus*. And the explanations Sophocles suggests belong to the softer theory. Oedipus curses his sons because they insulted him, and he has shown in many actions that he is the kind of person who responds to an insult with murderous rage.

Mimetic theater often shows us people working toward fates that have been determined for them, but working toward those fates by a series of choices they make themselves. The tension in mimetic theater between fate and choice is one source of the pleasure that theater gives us. But we should ask whether such theater is coherent—whether, on reflection, we can reasonably believe both that Oedipus chose to curse his sons and that he was fated to do so. If we must decide which story to believe, then we should decide on the basis of what we see on stage, and what we see on stage is a sequence of actions that strongly appear to be driven by choice. Sophocles leaves fate in the shadows of legend and dim report. He is a poet of choice.

Poets like Sophocles do not try to explain the compatibilism which they appear to hold, so they offer us no theory on this topic that we can evaluate as philosophers. We should be clear on one point, however.

What drives the staged actions of Sophocles is choice, not fate. If we are to judge only by his work as a playwright, we cannot conclude that he is a determinist.

4.3 Choice Defeated

Theater, as theater, is committed to the way of choice. Theater makes people worth watching by treating them as capable of action and choice. Theater proceeds with this advantage: we usually believe that the people we watch have chosen to do what we see them do. By default, we believe in choice, but this belief is defeasible. By that I mean we are prepared to abandon belief in choice if any of a number of factors is present.

We do not think a wedding has occurred if the groom holds his bride at gunpoint when she is supposed to take the oath, or if she is staggering drunk, or if she is so unlike herself that we feel she has been brainwashed or hypnotized (that is, if she does not act like the woman we knew). These are among the conditions that defeat choice—or, more precisely, defeat the hypothesis that choice occurs in a given case. So, first of all, the art of theater must steer clear of conditions that would defeat choice. But good steering does not simply avoid the shoals; it has a mark for which it steers, which I consider in the next section.

To illustrate the defeat of choice, consider one simple scene: in *Oedipus Tyrannus*, Oedipus condemns Creon for plotting against him, in spite of Creon's clever defense oration. We see this as an action he takes, arising from a choice he makes. We might have seen it otherwise, had Sophocles written the scene differently. He could have defeated choice. Here are four scenarios, between Oedipus and Creon, in which Oedipus would neither choose nor act. Each represents a condition that defeats choice: insanity, incoherence, external force, and what I call "mechanism," or internal force.

Insanity

Suppose Oedipus is demented, totally out of his mind, when he meets Creon, and he does not know what he is doing. He perceives Creon as a serpent and tries to drive him out of Thebes to save the city from peril. Then we would not suppose that he chose to drive Creon out of the city. His target was a serpent. In the scene as Sophocles wrote it, however, we do not doubt the sanity of Oedipus. He has shown similar bad judgment before, only moments ago, when he flashed out at Tiresias. He is the sort of person who does things like that.

Scenes of insanity are familiar in ancient myth, but Sophocles does not show them on stage. The *Ajax* shows a man who has recovered from an episode of dementia and who is now actively working out what action to take, now that his dementia is behind him. Under the spell of the goddess, he attacked cattle in place of his enemies, but now he is bitterly ashamed.

Not everything that smacks of madness defeats choice. In the context of mystery religion, for example, what looks like madness can be a higher kind of sanity. In the *Bacchae*, the madness that leads Pentheus to dress like his mother is not imposed on him but brought out of him by Dionysus, and with it comes the ability to perceive divine power more clearly. Pentheus in a dress is more Pentheus than ever, but Ajax lashing a bull is not the hero we admired and Odysseus cheated. Pentheus, we feel, somehow chose to sashay up the mountain in drag, because the desire to do so came from him. But Ajax never chose to flog the bull; he wanted to flog Agamemnon.

Incoherence

Suppose Oedipus is stopped in his tracks by Creon's fine rhetoric. "My dear fellow," he answers, putting his arm around Creon's shoulders, "How could I have been so obtuse? I should have tried harder to see the matter from your point of view. Of course you have no reason to plot against me. Now let's put our heads together and see if we can solve the mystery of the old king's death." In this scene, Oedipus would not be demented in the usual sense—not raving mad—but he is not himself, and we have seen nothing to explain the sudden change of heart. Even Creon would not believe it—perhaps Oedipus is trying to fool Creon into betraying himself. But how unlike Oedipus this would be! Up to now he has been direct and straightforward, quick to anger, suspicious, unwilling to listen. A modern audience, trained in the devices of science fiction, would suppose that some alien creature had taken over Oedipus's body if he behaved so strangely now. An ancient audience would suspect that his mind had been seized by a god. Either way, the Oedipus we came to know in earlier scenes isn't here, and we cannot accept what we are shown as the actions of Oedipus.

As it is, Oedipus's actions hang together; from the start he has been proud, affectionate, prone to flashes of anger, and more than a little blind in his judgments of other people. So when he lashes out at Creon, we believe the anger is his; and when he calms down in the presence of Jocasta, we accept the relaxation also as his.

External force

Suppose Apollo appears in all his epiphanic splendor (represented by an actor kited onstage by a derrick). The god's force is irresistible. Everything stops, and everyone does his bidding. The scene is now his, the actions are his, and the string of human actions is over. Playwrights who introduce such devices use them at the very ends of plays, for just that reason—the god who speaks from a machine leaves no scope for human action. The same effect could be achieved by a magical potion, a spellbinding orator, or the exercise of physical force. Suppose Creon's secret bodyguard burst out of the crowd and, holding a knife to Oedipus's throat, extract from him a promise to lay off Creon. That could have happened, but it did not. This is Oedipus's play, and Sophocles wisely reserves the main action for him, not for Creon.

Internal forces

Suppose the play's prologue tells us that Oedipus has been programmed by the gods to do certain things and that the plot is arranged to make this credible. We would then believe what the prologue had told us, because we would see that Oedipus behaves like an automaton and not like a human being. He is not affected by anything he perceives or is told, he never pauses to think; perhaps he even moves like a machine.

Sophocles' Oedipus may be predictable, but he does not move like a machine. Machines are not affected by the voices of the women they love, but Oedipus is moved by Jocasta. He calls back his condemnation of her brother Creon because she asks him to do so. Perhaps if she had been present from the start he would never have lashed out at the man.

Unpredictable characters and totally predictable characters are alike in that we would not see them as making choices. To attribute choice to someone, we need to have in mind an explanation in which that choice figures, along with a coherent pattern of behavior. An unpredictable character would not meet this condition. On the other hand, a totally predictable character seems to be at the mercy of internal forces. Theseus in the *Oedipus at Colonus* personifies Athenian civic virtue, and we can never imagine *him* doing anything other than what he does. We can always predict that he will do what his perfect virtues call him to do. The play does not make it clear to us that Theseus is making choices, and, as a result, he is not a very interesting character.

Theseus's scenes would not be worth watching if they did not show him interacting with more interesting characters, including Oedipus and Creon. He is in the play mainly as a foil for Oedipus and Creon, to show that a ruler does not have to be as contemptuous of suppliants as they are. But suppose Theseus were an automaton, a victim of internal forces, a slave to his own virtues. Then he could not serve as a foil to Oedipus; his example could not show that a ruler could choose to treat a suppliant with respect. On this hypothesis, the stage showed us only Theseus's bowing to the necessity of his virtue. But that would be absurd; there is no "necessity of virtue." Virtue cannot be an internal force that defeats choice, because it is, by definition, "up to us." If Theseus were an automaton, he would not be virtuous. To say that his behavior arises from his virtue implies that it arises from choice, even though the play does little to make us believe in his choices.

We have discussed four ways a playwright could defeat choice. Any one of these scenarios would have spoiled the Oedipus-Creon scene. It would have made Oedipus less worth watching, because he would not be taking the action we see. And that, in turn, is because he would have been denied the freedom to choose. These scenarios are examples of stagecraft that takes choice off the stage. What sort of artistry would bring choice onto the stage? Choice, we shall see, follows character.

4.4 Choice Presented

In the glade a young shepherd holds an apple, which he is about to present to one of the three women in front of him. We have heard the story; these are goddesses, and the youth is to judge which of them is the most beautiful. The painting represents the judgment of Paris. Judgment is a kind of choice. We believe that it is a choice because we have heard the story, and we have heard that Paris will be rewarded for making it as he does. In the painting itself, as opposed to the story behind it, there is nothing to make us believe that a choice is taking place in this scene, aside from the fact that there is only one apple and there are three women. So the painting does show us that three different outcomes are possible. But it does not show us that a genuine choice made by Paris will cause the prize to go to the love goddess. Perhaps Paris is out of his mind, under the spell of Aphrodite; perhaps he is being moved by an unseen force. We have no way of knowing. This painting illustrates a story, and it is the story, not the painting, that reveals the choice.

Choice is presented within a series of events, on or off stage, in mimesis or in real life. When someone behaves consistently enough that we can reasonably attribute some piece of behavior to him or her, then we rightly call the behavior "action" and see it as proceeding from choice.

Let's tell a different story. Suppose that Paris is not making a choice. This boy has always been devoted to Artemis; no other goddess has ever appealed to him. But now Aphrodite has cast a spell on him, and he has no choice but to give the apple to her. In his beguilement, he thinks he is making a choice. We, on the other hand, who know Paris well, would rightly conclude that his ability to choose has been disabled by love. Whatever he says, we know better. Aphrodite has acted on him and through him; he has not been permitted to act at all. Or to choose. If Paris were able to observe his own behavior from a distance he would see that he has been beguiled into thinking he is choosing when he is not.

The example shows that choice is a public phenomenon and not present in any special way to the mind of the chooser. The feeling of making a choice, which Paris has in this version of the story, does not make him the true agent of his judgment. We could tell another story in which he lacks the feeling but does in fact serve as the agent.

There is no action without choice, no choice without a character who makes the choice, and no character without a history of actions. I use the word "character" as a technical term in this book, which I explain in the next chapter. Not everyone who is visible on stage is presented as a character; some people might as well be scenery. And not everyone who is presented as a character is seen as such by the audience. How well people are presented and seen as characters depends on the art of theater. Characters are people worth watching, and they are worth watching partly because they take action. If they take action, of course, they are capable of choice.

The art of theater, then, knows how to supply the stage with characters who are presented and perceived as capable of choice. Take what follows as instructions to the playwright, director, and performers: in order to present people as characters capable of choice, present them as sane, coherent, and free of external force. It helps also if they appear to be open to reason—capable of acting differently if they see things in a different light, and therefore free of internal forces as well. These points hold equally for mimetic and extreme theater—as well for comedies as for weddings. Both cases, also, require an effort on the part of the audience to perceive the characters as they are presented, that is, as capable of choice. Consider first a harder case than Sophocles' Oedipus—a character who, unlike Oedipus, really is threatened by insanity or incoherence. Hamlet.

Sanity

Hamlet may be feigning madness. He might actually have gone mad from his contact with the ghost. Or he may waver between real and feigned madness, throwing in an occasional fit of sanity. If the text does not provide all the information necessary for a sound diagnosis, actors and directors may choose how to present the prince. Still, Hamlet is almost always played as sane most of the time, with an applied intelligence that suits both the brilliance of his speech and the cunning of his contrivances. An actor who introduced symptoms of real madness into his portrayal of Hamlet would risk losing the confidence of his audience. Hamlet may be quicker to speak than to act, but we find him most compelling when he is in action. Actions come in many forms: sparing the life of the king at prayer is an action, one of the most remarkable of this play.

We believe that characters are sane enough to make choices when they give reasons for those choices—as Hamlet does for sparing Claudius—and when acting on those reasons is consistent with other actions of the characters. I will say that actions are consistent, for our purposes, when they may be attributed to a coherent character.

Coherence

Hamlet is a coherent character because his actions form a pattern that does not defy reasonable expectation; if it were otherwise, we would begin to doubt that they are actions in the strict sense. We could not predict what he will do, but once he has done it, however surprising it may have been, we accept it as *his* action, because it fits into the pattern he is building on stage. Aristotle would have said that his actions are *eikos*—usually translated "probable." A more accurate translation would be "in accordance with reasonable expectation." In rhetoric, anything that meets this test is supposed to be credible, believable. To be a character, Hamlet must deliver a series of actions that we may credibly attribute to the same man. That is, he must act in a way that helps us believe his performance is a series of actions that are linked causally to one another, not symptoms of madness, not a random string of events, and not the product of external forces.

Actions come in patterned sets that conform more or less to our expectations. Such patterns belong to our experience in real life, and they are heightened by the plotting of mimetic theater. The coherence of a character, on stage or in real life, allows for such prediction as we are able to make in human affairs. But this coherence does not defeat choice. Far from it; in the absence of coherence, we will doubt that choice is taking place.

Freedom from external forces

In *Oedipus Tyrannus,* Oedipus apparently chooses first to exile Creon and then to rescind the penalty. That's how it looks on stage. But what if Oedipus is acting under hidden constraints? Suppose these are just two more events in an elaborate scheme planned by the gods and brought about by them in order to fulfill an oracle? Sophocles and his audience believed in oracles. "Why should we dance?' asks his chorus in the *Oedipus Tyrannus*, why pay any attention to sacred shrines and festivals if oracles are not fulfilled? But if oracles about human events must be fulfilled, then those events do not flow from human choices, and they cannot be staged as actions. Is Sophocles confused? It seems he accepts both determinism (in his beliefs about divine influence) and free will (in his manner of telling a story through depicting action). But these views are not compatible, according to many philosophers.

If we humans were controlled by strings like marionettes, or by laser beams emanating from remote-control devices in the clouds, we would not be capable of action. Sophocles the playwright knew this well. His Oedipus is not a plaything of the gods—not, at least, as

Sophocles shows him on stage. The only curse at work in the action of the play *Oedipus Tyrranus* is the one Oedipus calls down on the murderer of Laius, and every scene brings at least one choice to our attention. Oedipus is presented as free from external forces because he stands apart from other men, and because he is subject to no deus ex machina. No one threatens or coerces him to do as he does, and no god (judging from what we see on stage) overrules his ability to choose. Sophocles is a great playwright mainly because he knew the difference between action and other kinds of event, and because he presents action on his stage at every opportunity.

Why, then, do the oracles come true, if Oedipus's actions are governed by choice? And why is their truth so important to Sophocles and his audience? They must believe that choice is one of those things that can be predicted, explained, and even determined in advance—all without the exercise of external force. That belief is reasonable. If determinism poses a threat to action it would do so through forces that are internal.

Freedom from internal forces

The best way to show that Oedipus is free from internal controls is to show that he is open to reason. In *Oedipus Tyrannus*, we see Oedipus as open to reason in the scene with Creon because he is, soon, persuaded by Jocasta to relax his anger. If he acted at random, or if he appeared to be hard-wired (as we would say) to destroy everyone who stands against him, he would not listen to Jocasta, and we would not see him as rational. Wind-up toys and random decision generators are not characters.

Sophocles often provides foils to show that a character's choice of action is not inevitable, even when it seems to flow from ingrained habit. Other people act differently in her exact circumstances, so why couldn't Antigone act differently? Theseus is a foil for Oedipus, Ismene for Antigone, Chrysothemis for Electra. In these cases we see how each hero is tempted to act out of character and why each one does not do so. Oedipus does eventually follow Theseus's example part way and allow his son to speak. Antigone hears Ismene's argument but rejects it entirely, convinced (wrongly, in her passion) that the argument puts Ismene in the enemy camp. Electra would have an easier life if she relaxed her anger; she knows that, but her sense of injustice is too strong to be easily abandoned. In these three cases we see a character brought to a point of decision by a foil, then choosing to proceed in accordance with the pattern she is establishing on stage.

Foils are powerful, but theater has a still stronger technique for showing that a character is open to reason: display him in circumstances in which he chooses to go against his ingrained habit—for a reason. Ajax is the blunt, plain-speaking hero, loyal and truthful, always steering clear of shame. And yet Sophocles shows him telling a whopper of a lie to the woman who loves him and for whom he evidently cares. And why? Because he is in extreme circumstances, because his suicide plan requires it, and because he has chosen suicide in order to escape from shame. Like many suicides, once he has made up his mind what to do, he seems a changed man. His loved ones believe what they hear, because Ajax never lies. We in the audience knew that Ajax was out of his mind early in the play; here also we know he is not himself, but we understand that this new anomaly arises freely from Ajax's choice.

4.5 Living Choices

A well-lived life should be worth attention. At the very least, you should find your own story engaging. In presenting yourself to yourself and to others, then, you should keep in mind the rules that good playwrights follow. Like a good character in a play, you should be making choices that are explicable—choices that appear to come from a mind in working order. Your choices should be reasonably coherent with each other, also, so as to support the thought that there is a real person—you— behind those choices. I formulated these first two rules after studying what playwrights did, but then I was delighted to recognize them as old friends from Plato.

In Plato's dialogues, Socrates presses people to give reasons, and he presses himself to make choices that cohere with choices he has made before. On a famous occasion, he decided to refuse an opportunity to escape from prison, and to accept, instead, the penalty of death that the Athenian people's court had voted for him. Had he decided otherwise, he felt, he would have made a mockery of his lifetime commitments to justice and the rule of law. Of course he had reasons for those commitments, but he knew that they were not grounded in godlike knowledge. At the end of his life, Socrates cared deeply that the whole of it be coherent. It was.

The other two playwright's rules are harder to follow. Playwrights show their main characters making choices that are independent of external force or inner compulsion. Good characters are never simply victims. Plainly it is not entirely up to you to avoid force and compulsion, though you can try to stay out of reach of tyrants and away from choices that lead to addictions. Even in the worst times, however, you can, like Prometheus chained to his rock, focus on the freedoms that remain to you. Your mind is free as long as you believe that your future is not wholly determined by the powers that oppress you; as long as you have the freedom to think and to protest, you are not wholly a victim.

FIVE

People Worth Watching: Characters

I am trying to keep my attention on my companion in the restaurant. I love to be fascinated by her, and that is why I am here, with her, trying to listen while she tells me about her day. But the dining room is crowded, and she is being upstaged. A noisy table of six behind her is debating various dates for a wedding. One possible date excludes a favorite uncle; another would leave out a much-feared cousin, who takes over events like this, but whose anger at being left out would be hideous. The young couple are cheerful participants at first, but they turn morose and simply hold hands while their parents grow louder and louder. This is high drama, but it is not what we came for, my companion and I. Although the main spectacle is behind her, she hears the shouting and tries to follow my eyes, craning her neck.

If I could direct events for my own benefit, I would have insisted that the table for six be merely scenery. They should be *human* scenery of course; they should seem to talk and move and engage in various other actions. But they should be careful to remain scenery nonetheless, so as not to draw attention away from the important business at my table. My partner and I intended to be the principal characters. Why don't these people speak nonsense to each other, like actors in a crowd scene? That would be as meaningful as most dinner conversations.

Am I unfair to the table of six when I wish to write them off as scenery? Not at all. They are principal characters in their own drama, and we are certainly no more than scenery for them. I cannot really pay attention to one person unless I withhold or withdraw it from someone else. Sometimes I like to say that I can attend to two conversations at once, but my companion knows better; when one of my ears is catching someone else's words, she knows it immediately, and she is hurt. In life, as in art, most people are scenery for us most of the time. We do not have the brainpower to track more than two or three conversations at once or to watch more than three rings of a circus, let alone really attend to more than one conversation. Part of the art of living well is knowing where to pay attention and where not, in the different circumstances we face. It is often difficult; now, for the two of us in the restaurant, we'll never get it right until we leave this venue and start the evening again.

The art of theater saves us the trouble of deciding where to direct our attention. It brings out certain characters in whatever action we are watching at the expense of others. Had the restaurant scene taken place on stage, it would have been badly directed, a failure of the art of theater. No stage is big enough for both a romantic couple and a quarreling family, unless one is consigned to be a backdrop for the other.

5.1 Being a Character

By "a character" I mean a person worth watching, as opposed to one who belongs in the scenery. In theater, the people we watch lie on a spectrum between scenery and full-blown characters. The full-blown characters are the ones we pay the most attention to. Hamlet is certainly a character. So is Ophelia. Horatio is more like scenery, while Rosencrantz and Guildenstern barely emerge from the backdrop. In *Antigone*, the watchman is a character (albeit a minor one), but Creon's guards are scenery, and the messenger is something else—a narrator whose identity is submerged in the story he has to tell.

My subject in this chapter is full-blown characters: By what means do they capture and retain our attention? There is an artistic question for the performers and an ethical question for the watchers. What can you do, as a writer or director, to make the characters in your play worth watching? That is a question in art. What can you do, as a watcher, to help you see other people as emerging from the scenery—as deserving attention in their own right? That is the parallel question in ethics. As an ethical question in real life it demands an answer even more urgently than it does in theater watching.

A character is a person worth watching for the measured time of theater. The people who are most worth watching satisfy two conditions: they are active as agents, and they are able to engage our emotions. Victims aren't worth watching for very long; we get the idea immediately. People we can't have feelings about aren't worth watching either.

My definition of character fits all the theatrical arts (film and video too), and an analog should work for literature: a literary character is a person whose story is worth following. My definition is not arbitrary. It is a way of spelling out what is meant by my definition of the art of theater. Theater makes action worth watching, and there is no action without agents. Who are the agents behind actions worth watching? They are the characters. In a moment, I will look into various competing accounts of characters in theater; generally, they are marred by the confusion of "character" with "fictional character." First, notice three features of my definition that may strike you as odd.

1. Being a character is a matter of degree. People may be better or worse characters depending on how well worth watching they are and how well attuned the audience is to the characters' situations. If this bothers you, think of "character" on the analogy of "foreground" in painting. Some objects may be placed or lit better than others, and so some of them will be more clearly in the foreground than others

2. Being a character requires the complicity of the audience: for *you* to be a character in theater *they* must see you as a character. An uninformed audience in football may see only the quarterbacks and receivers as characters in the drama that unfolds, but a truly sophisticated audience may see the entire rank-and-file team as characters. Do not be alarmed by this. Remember that the whole art of theater requires the complicity of an audience; they must understand their job as audience members, if theater is taking place.

3. It does not matter where characters come from, as long as they are worth watching. For the purpose of theater, real life, history, fiction, and myth are all equally good as sources for character. Whether you invent a person or find one in history is irrelevant to the art of theater, which can try to make anyone worth

watching for a while. Showing up at a party is one thing, and being noticed is another. The need to be noticed is the same in real life and in theater. The things we do to get attention are pretty much the same also, although in real life, at a party, we have less control over factors such as lighting and noise level.

5.2 Mimesis and Imagination

Characters come from both sides of the art of theater—from performers and audience. Characters do not need to be made up, and yet imagination and mimesis have roles in their making.

The quarterbacks in a Super Bowl game have no doubt used a great deal of invention—theirs and their press agents'—in becoming the characters they are on game day. But they are flesh and blood people; their source is not fiction. A fictional character is one who has been entirely made up—like Rosalind in *As You Like It*. A historical character is drawn from historical facts—like Shakespeare's *Henry V*. A mythic character is drawn from traditional myth—like Oedipus. Some characters come from the shadowy boundaries—like Falstaff, who has a little history behind him but is mainly fictional, or like Antigone, who has a few small roots in myth but much mightier ones in Sophocles' imagination.

Stage characters may or may not be drawn from life. Being lifelike does not make a stage character worth watching by itself, because in life, sad to say, not everyone is worth watching. And not all characters worth watching are lifelike; many great characters are, as we say, far bigger than life. What makes a stage character lifelike is mimesis—which fools us into reacting to stage characters as if they were real, more or less.

Stage characters may be mimetic whether they are fictional or historical. Mimesis makes a representation have an effect on an audience that the real thing would have. So we would succeed in mimesis if we made an actor's stage performance of Henry V inspiring in the sort of way that Henry V would be if we could bring him back from the abyss of time. In a somewhat similar way, the presenters of a football game would succeed in mimesis of war if their game affected the crowd as war would if they were watching a battle.

Not all theater is mimetic, because not all theater *represents* characters or actions. The bride in the wedding is really a bride. Still, much has been done to make her bridelike, and some effort needs to be taken to make her lifelike as well. If she strikes the audience as a zombie, or if she seems to be mouthing her oaths like a ventriloquist's dummy, the audience will doubt that a wedding has really taken place. Zombies cannot take oaths.

A character serves as the agent of actions worth watching, and agents make choices. To see the bride as an agent we must see her as making the choice to which she takes oath before her family and friends. This then is the minimum for a character: she must at least *seem* to be an agent, and therefore to make choices. This may involve some element of mimesis; by listening to others, the bride may have learned how to sound as sincere as she actually feels.

The audience must join in the imagining that makes our bride a character. They must imagine certain things and hold back from imagining others. On the negative side, the audience may not allow their imaginations to be clouded by thoughts of determinism. They must not see the bride as a statistic in social science, and they must not—not while watching the wedding, anyway—reduce her scientifically to a collection of cells operating on the analogy of a machine. They must not imagine that the bride is a zombie.

On the positive side, the audience must imagine that the bride is an agent in a narrative not fully known to them, but one in which the choice made in the wedding is decisive. We do not know all about their falling in love or about the hopes and dreams that have led them to the altar. We imagine, nevertheless, that there is a story about these things, and it explains the choices they are about to make. In a well-made play, we would have less to imagine; the playwright would have seen to it that we knew what led up to the wedding. But either the writer's imagination or ours is required, because we must be able to suppose that the event we are about to watch has an explanation of a certain sort—that is, a story of the kind that leads to a choice. Actors are often trained to imagine a wider story behind their characters than the writer has supplied.

Imagination helps to provide an audience with a context in which choice is a plausible hypothesis for them to make. The greater part of this context is real or imagined history, but part of it looks to the future, and this is wholly imagined. We imagine, as we watch the wedding, a home in the future, with children and then with grandchildren, as one commitment leads to another. We imagine that the bride and groom see themselves as making choices which, they will recognize themselves, define their lives in the future.

Saying that imagination is necessary to character does not imply that character is imaginary. Many characters are real people, and many of these are really worth watching, but it still takes imagination to see them as characters and as worth watching.

5.3 Being a Particular Character

What is it to be this or that character? What is Hamlet, for example, as a character? What makes him the character he is? What is the essence of Hamlet? I said that half the essence of *Hamlet* (the play) was that someone played the character Hamlet in that play. So my account of the identity of theater pieces leads to this question and requires me to work out the identity of characters. This group of questions belongs to ontology. I consider briefly two bad answers to the question: text-based and quality-based.

The text-based account of character identifies a character in litera-ture with the text that constitutes that character—the lines the character says, and the lines said about him or her. This is an attractive suggestion, because it locates the character in the textual tradition and because it is economical. Like other applications of positivism, it does its work with-out appealing to any strange or spooky entities. It runs into a number of problems for theater, however. If I am right that the play *Hamlet* is not a text, then, by similar arguments, I will be right to insist that the char-acter is not a set of text fragments. To make matters worse, characters seem to cross texts. The positivist account would make it hard to explain our belief that Falstaff shows up in three different plays by Shakespeare, a film by Orson Welles that cuts two of them together, and an opera by Verdi. Is Falstaff the same character in *Henry IV* and in *Merry Wives*? This is not a question about texts. To answer it we need to ask what is most important about this character.

The quality-based account of character depends on an ontology of universals and particulars and is due to a false way of reading Aristotle. On this account, fictional characters are universals, whereas historical ones are particulars. Fiction constructs characters out of fixed qualities—like bravery—that can be shared among many people, real or imagined— while history refers to actual individuals, whatever qualities they may turn out to have had. If fiction constructs a character out of fixed qualities, then it cannot change the qualities of a character in midstream. That is, if what it is to be Rosalind is to have a mixture of courage and loyalty and sensitivity, then she must show that mix of qualities consistently.

Quality-based theories of character are attractive because they account nicely for certain kinds of fiction—most obviously the sort of fiction that uses stock characters slavishly. Such theories are disturbing for the same reason; quality-based consistency of character tends to reinforce stereotypes. Such theories do not account for a character like Falstaff, however, who starts out looking like the stock character *Miles Gloriosus*— the braggart soldier we know from ancient comedy—and grows in *Henry IV Part II* toward the bitterness of failure and self-understanding. We never looked to see Falstaff confess failure: "Master Shallow, I owe you a thousand pounds." But when he does, we have seen him through so many events, so many changes, that we are prepared to accept this moment of weakness. The braggart in Falstaff returns for a few lines, but we see this now as a changed Falstaff's attempt to put a face on failure.

Stock characters in themselves are not very interesting. We are captivated by Falstaff partly because he turns out not to be the stock character—not to be defined simply by the qualities we saw in him during his opening scenes. Another reason we are captivated by Falstaff is that our hero, Prince Hal, genuinely loves him, even though Hal's love is painful to both of them at the end. Generally, plays that use stock characters effectively do so either by breaking the type or by introducing nonstock characters (like Prince Hal) to react with them. Shakespeare does both.

As for historical characters, the particular historical reference has the advantage that it allows change. Prince Hal can grow up to be King Henry V; his growth fascinates us, keeps us on the edge of our chairs. And still he is the same person, because he belongs to the same particular history. But since a good playwright can do this for fictional characters like Falstaff, plainly the historical reference is not necessary. Fiction can affect us as if it were history; to do this, fiction invents a character who is defined in fiction much as a character is defined in history through relationships with events and other people.

The main defect of the quality-based theory is that it gives different accounts of fictional and historical characters. And yet the two kinds of character seem to be treated the same by the art of theater, and many examples of theater seem to blend fiction and history. The art of theater must work equally hard to make them worth watching either way. We should, therefore, try to find one theory of character for all cases.

Both of these philosophical approaches are hopeless when it comes to explaining what makes a character worth watching. In fact, if either approach is right, characters are not worth watching at all over the measured time of theater—stock characters won't hold our interest for the time required, because we have no reason to expect anything about them to be different at the end; historical characters, because their history won't fit into a measured time. Unless—in both cases—the art of theater makes them worth watching.

My hypothesis is that what makes Falstaff a particular character is precisely what makes him worth watching. Obviously his initial qualities would not make him worth watching if they remained fixed. His readiness to change intrigues us, so does the love he shares with Hal, and so is the impossible dream of the future that sustains him. His complex relationship with Hal fixes him so firmly that he could make gargantuan changes and still be the same Falstaff—he could give up lechery and drink and even his penchant for falsehood—and we would still know him for Falstaff.

Now we can see why we feel that the Falstaff of the *Merry Wives of Windsor* seems like a different character from the one we met in the history plays. He is still lecherous, bibulous, mendacious, and ineffectual. But he is not *Hal's* Falstaff, and he has no dreams for their future together. Belonging to Hal is the heart of being Falstaff.

Or so it is for me. You may see him differently. Perhaps what makes him worth watching, for you, is simply his lechery. Your Falstaff would then be the same in the first *Henry IV* and the *Merry Wives*; he would also be the same as countless other lechers we have seen on stage. Your Falstaff doesn't quite match the one we meet in the second *Henry IV*, while mine runs the same through the history plays but does not fit the one in *Merry Wives*. What makes him worth watching in the histories, to me, is the drama of his complex relationship to Hal. He is not worth watching in the *Merry Wives*. That play is justly named: the wives are the characters that engage us; Falstaff here is a stage prop.

You are wrong to think Falstaff's essence is his lechery, I think, because my Falstaff can sustain a story much better than yours can. Mine sustains the two parts of *Henry IV*; yours provides little more than scenery for a drama about middle-class marriage in *Merry Wives*. Mine accounts for Falstaff's particularity; yours makes him a type that could turn up under many names.

Characters are worth watching, I said at the outset, when we see them as agents with whom we become emotionally engaged. Agency and emotional engagement belong to particular people, not to universal qualities. The art of theater, for the most part, seeks to endow characters with particularity, and it accomplishes this by placing them in a web of relationships.

5.4 Agency and Éthos

The word "character" has two meanings: it can mean a person in a story or theater piece; it can also mean a set of traits. These two meanings are not confused in Greek, and Aristotle has them right. The characters in a play he calls "agents" (*hoi prattontes*), and the character of an agent or of an action he calls *êthos*, a word I will not attempt to translate. A good poet aims at consistency of *êthos* in his agents.

What is consistency of *êthos?* The criterion will have to be soft, if it allows characters to develop. Otherwise, if Rosalind's courage fails (as it does when she sees Orlando's blood), she will become a new character. But that would be absurd. Aristotle's solution is to require that changes in a character be within the range of reasonable expectation, what he called *eikos*. The range has to be wide enough that we can be surprised, but not so wide that we cannot believe that this character was responsible for that action. Aristotle wisely points out that we should expect people to do unexpected things.

It must be possible for the same outcome to be *eikos* and completely unpredictable. Aristotle is not requiring that the audience be able to infer action from character. What he *does* require is made clear in the *Poetics*: a writer should prefer what is believable but not possible to what is possible but not believable. In tragedy as in rhetoric, the gold standard for what you can get away with is what the audience will believe. Consistency, then, does not require that an agent's behavior be predictable—only that it not be so surprising that we in the audience would not believe in it without an explanation for it from outside that character's agency, as ancient Greeks did when they inferred divine intervention from a surprising turn of events.

Euripides failed on this score, as Aristotle observed. Euripides' Iphigenia in Aulis changes so abruptly that we cannot readily believe that she really agreed to be sacrificed in order that her father could have fair

winds to waft him to his disastrous war. She seems a counterfeit character, or, at best, a victim of the gods. "He is but the counterfeit of a man
who hath not the life of a man," says Falstaff. In successful living as in
good theater, the life of a human being is largely a matter of agency, and
this depends on consistency. In the end, we cannot believe that Iphigenia has been living the life of a woman.

Harold Bloom asks: "How can you create beings who are 'free
artists of themselves,' as Hegel called Shakespeare's personages? After
Shakespeare, the best answer might be: 'By an imitation of Shakespeare.'"
Perhaps so, but I have argued that the first great artist of character in the
European tradition is Sophocles.

Sophocles' characters do not always run true to type, but when
they do not, he makes their behavior credible. Creon, for example, is
the type of a tyrannical leader in *Oedipus at Colonus*; but in *Antigone* he
veers in and out of the path of tyranny—in it when he refuses to accept
advice; out of it when he listens to the chorus of old men, whom he
has asked to serve as his council of elders. The principles Creon states
in this play are rarely tyrannical. He is a good example of what Aristotle
would have called "consistent inconsistency." When he is moved by fear,
he acts like a tyrant; when he takes time to consider good judgment,
he does not.

We have a parallel in his son, Haemon, who might have been the
type of the passionate young man. About this type, Aristotle wrote:

> The young, as to character, are ready to desire and to carry out
> what they desire. Of the bodily desires they chiefly obey those
> of sensual pleasure. . . . They are passionate, hot-tempered, and
> carried away by impulse, and unable to control their passion.

But Haemon is quite able to control his passion. His opening remarks
are respectful, and his long speech is as well argued as his father's: rational, considerate, and thoughtful. He knows that this is the only way a
young man might impress an older one, and he is doing his best to act
grown up.

Then in the dialogue that follows their debate, however, the two
men enrage each other. They summon up changes in each other in ways
that are *eikos*—in accord with reasonable expectation. Haemon brings
out the tyrant in his father, and Creon calls up irrational passion in his
son. Although the sudden violence of the scene is surprising and unpredictable, it belongs to the range of what can be reasonably expected.

When the father calls the son a woman's toy, what else would we expect but blind rage? And when the son implies that the father's style of government is tyrannical, shouldn't we expect him to reply with insults? Neither character has a fixed *êthos*, but both deviate in ways that do not defy expectation. No need to bring in a god on a machine. The agents here are human. People do things like this.

Shakespeare does not follow the rule of consistency as closely. In *As You Like It*, the bad duke and the bad brother both experience miraculous conversions; the poet does not give us even the comfort of a deus ex machina. But no matter, these people were never much more than scenery anyway. Rosalind is a real character, one of Shakespeare's best. Her *êthos* is clear: she is courageous, resourceful, faithful, and witty. Yet her courage and her resource fail her when she sees Orlando's blood.

But this failure falls neatly in the range of reasonable expectation. For all her pluck, she is a woman and she loves Orlando. We believe this. She really did faint, and she really did try to cover it up. Cracks in *êthos* are a major source of energy in theater and one of the best ways to support the agency of a character.

5.5 A "Center of Love"

What is it to be a full-blown character, one who commands attention? The people we want to watch are generally people we care about—people we are affectively engaged with, positively or negatively. Simply put, the point is this: in the art of theater, a character is someone who can be a certain kind of target for emotion. Effective characters, to coin a technical term, are carable-about, just as effective thoughts are thinkable. Caring about is not the same as caring for; you care about villains if you are eager to see them punished. There are many different ways of caring about someone you watch. Some of them depend on our having emotions *on behalf of* the person we watch; others depend on a closer connection, as occurs when we see the person *as representing us*. Either way, the theater people cannot manage without the help of the audience.

The art of theater is practiced on both sides of the line dividing action from observation. To be a character (as this is to be understood in the art of theater) is to be watched in a certain way. The audience must be prepared to watch in this way, and the writer, director, performer on the other side must make it possible and attractive for the audience to do so. But this is not just a matter of theater; we are better members of the human community if we know how to see other people as carable-about.

In most cases, in life as in theater, we are able to see a person as carable-about if three conditions on our imagination are met. We must be able to imagine, in the normal case:

1. That the person has a past.
2. That the person has hopes for the future; that is, that he or she has a goal, an aim, a passion or a project of some kind.
3. That the person is a center of love, that he or she loves and is loved, cares for and is cared for by, other people.

In his two most famous poems, the World War II poet Keith Douglas packs all three into his way of seeing enemy soldiers, one long dead, with a picture of his girl in his pocket (in the poem "Vergissmeinnicht"); the other turning to dust as he presses the kill button:

> Now in my dial of glass appears
> the soldier who is going to die.
> He smiles, and moves about in ways
> his mother knows, habits of his.
> The wires touch his face: I cry
> NOW. Death, like a familiar, hears
>
> and look, has made a man of dust
> of a man of flesh. This sorcery
> I do. Being damned, I am amused
> to see the centre of love diffused
> and the waves of love travel into vacancy.
> How easy it is to make a ghost. (Keith Douglas, "How to Kill")

He writes of "the centre of love," imagining the man as having had parents and friends. It is a heroic and extraordinary effort for the young soldier; World War I poetry has nothing quite like it, though Wilfred Owens's "Strange Meeting" comes close.

The converse is true. If you wish to have no feelings about a person, you treat him, as we say, "like a number." This may be an easy strategy for combat soldiers in thinking of the enemy. Medical professionals may find themselves less tense if they quiet their imaginations about the lives of their patients. The same goes for teachers. If I do not have time to listen to a student's difficulties, I may feel better if I do not imagine him as having parents who dote on him, a lover who has just jilted him, or grand but inarticulate hopes for the future. But we will live better lives if we can find ways to see people as full-blown characters rather than as numbers.

The most important case is yourself. To avoid the worst effects of depression you need to see yourself as carable-about —to imagine yourself with a future, to remember your past, and to believe that you are a center of love. Sometimes all of this is hard. But in your own case, as in the case of caring for others, the practice we have in theater can be a great help to us. And this point goes for film and video and novels as well as for live theater; all give us practice in finding people like us carable-about.

There is another reward for seeing people as carable-about. In theater, you will not find the play or the game boring if you care about the people involved. And life itself will be more interesting when you practice the art of theater in it. You cannot be bored if you care about what is going on around you.

Notice that the three conditions are conditions on imagination, not on truth. It does not need to be true that the soldier is a center of love. In truth, he may be an utterly unloved and obnoxious orphan, whom no one will mourn. Seeing people as carable-about requires you to treat questions of truth with cheerful abandon. Imagination is rewarding.

We are told that Gorgias made a case against truth in theater during the fifth century BCE. In theater, he thought, justice requires that the poet deceive the audience. In effect, he is saying, an undeceived audience should ask for its money back. At the same time, wisdom requires that audience members allow themselves to be deceived. They will be bored if they don't. A robust imagination will help us in real life, if it helps us see people as carable-about. But outside theater, imagination and caring both have obvious limitations. Truth matters, for one thing, and we lack the power to care about everyone on whom we could bring our imaginations to bear. It is not always wiser to be deceived or more just to deceive.

5.6 Limits on Comic Characters

Let this be our initial answer: a character worth watching is one who has a past, a future, and people to love and be loved by. If you want to see a real person as standing out from the scenery, find out these three things about her. If you want to bring a fictional character out of the scenery, make up as many of these three things as you can. That is what effective writers do, and good actors and directors often try to fill in the gaps left by writers, if they want to lift a given person out of the scenery and make him a character.

This answer does not go far enough, however. Being carable-about about in a particular way is not the only way of being a distinctive person in theater. In comedy, especially, a person may be marked by an excessive display of a single trait—boastfulness, for example, or miserliness—or by a single obsession. Such persons in theater are not carable-about, but they are fun to watch, up to a point. By "stage villain" I mean a figure in theater whose only attribute is villainy. Stage villains are people we simply love to hate. They are very useful in theater; so are the other stage figures who are defined by a few fixed attributes—the jealous husband, the hopeless lovers, the grasping miser, the cruel landlord, the *miles gloriosus*, and all the rest. They are not scenery, plainly, but they are not characters in my full sense, because it is not for their sake that we wait to see how the play comes out. Because they are quality-defined, their behavior strikes us as mechanical, as mere consequences of their qualities, and so they do not strike us as full-dress agents. Also, because they are identified with their qualities, they do not offer us much to care about. Qualities do not engage our emotions. People do.

What holds us through the measured time of comedy is often a character who is carable-about, whose cause we do take more or less seriously. Sometimes this is a slave or a servant involved with the principal persons of the plot. In *Much Ado about Nothing*, Hero and Claudio are no more than stock lovers who are victims of abuse, with the result that they cannot mean much to us. But Beatrice and Benedict, who take the cause of Hero, are characters in the full sense, and they hold us through the play.

In *Comedy of Errors*, the intricacy of the plot is enough to keep us laughing and attentive. When comedy can hold our attention with no recourse to empathy, it has no need for characters in my full sense.

Even when comedy has characters, they cannot satisfy the first of my three conditions. Comic characters do not have a past—not the sort of past that might explain how they came to be who they are. We know where Othello came from, and his quick explosive anger is something we can understand. We know how Oedipus came to Thebes, and so we know why he thinks he can solve puzzles better than anyone. Take away the past, and these characters would become absurd, and the absurdity they would bring to the plays would move them across the line into comedy. The converse is also true: give a past to comic figures and you can make them the stuff of tragedy.

To see this, try a thought experiment. Alceste, in *Le Misanthrope*, is a center of love; he has dear friends and he is himself in love, up to a point. He also has a project: to be an example of honesty to the world. But he does not have a past. It is because of his friends and his project that we do have some concern for him, and we are a little sorry for him (as are his friends) at the end. He is never wholly ridiculous. But suppose we supplied for him a story to explain how he turned out the way he did, that his hypocritical campaign against hypocrisy was due to abuse he received as a child from an uncle who was in holy orders. Then he would not be funny at all; we would be not merely sorry for him but angry on his behalf, and the play would be turned upside down. There would be nothing comic about it, and he would have become a full-blown character.

Sacred Space

At midday, on the green lawn in front of the tower, three students are spinning a plastic disk, winging it across the hedges and walkways. The players are beautiful in themselves, young and shirtless, and they play beautifully as well, performing the most difficult throws with accuracy, sometimes rising gracefully to make a high catch. They are well worth watching. Passing students and faculty pause for a moment and then move on. No one stays to watch for long; no one could plan to stay till the end, because this game promises no end. Perhaps the players will stop before the next class period, perhaps sooner. Or perhaps they will go on until they drop. There's no way of telling.

You and I are on our way to a meeting, but we are early, and we stop to join the audience, appreciating the skill and grace of the players. Just before the clock strikes, we move on without regret. Watching the game has been an unexpected dividend to a day dedicated to other plans; there is nothing to stay for.

This game keeps no score and no official clock, so it has no structure to measure the time it will take. That's why the spectators feel fine about starting to watch in mid-throw and turning away whenever they feel like it. How different it is to watch *Hamlet:* leaving this play before the final curtain feels like a violation; coming in during the first scene with Ophelia is hardly better. The disk throwing is watchable enough, but it has no boundaries in time, and there is nothing for us to violate by coming late or leaving early.

6.1 Marking Time

The art of theater works in a measured time. Measuring time is necessary, because without it we lose interest. We need to know that this
claim on our attention will come to an end, after which we will be
able to talk loudly with our friends and consider our bodily needs. You
may say that I am working from a formal European conception of theater, because some traditions allow lengthy performances that make few
claims on the audience. People come and go during a Chinese opera,
for example; they talk among themselves and order refreshments from
passing waiters. This is fine, as long as the audience is having fun. But it
cannot be what the art of theater aims at. The art aims at being worth
watching, and the more worth watching a performance is, the less freedom it will give its audience for activities unrelated to watching.

The measured time of theater is descended from the sacred times
of ritual. A period of time is sacred if it is set apart for certain activities:
some activities are forbidden during the sacred time, others may be
permitted only during the sacred time. The Jewish Sabbath is the best-
known sacred time among us now; Sunday is sacred to many Christians,
and so is Lent. In theater time, there is something you are supposed
to do if you are in the audience—watch—and something you are not
supposed to do: anything that would distract others from the performance.

We have two ways to measure theater time. The first is by some
combination of clock, calendar, or planetary motion—from sundown
on Friday to sundown on Saturday, for example. Football game time is
measured by a clock. Some traditions of narrative drama tell long tales,
interrupting them late at night and resuming the next evening where
they left off the night before, as a long book might be read in a family
before bedtime.

The best way to measure time in theater, however, is by plot. Clock
time does not guarantee something worth watching from beginning to
end. A good plot does. A well-made plot will catch the audience's attention at the start and sustain it through to the end. Consider the stroke
of a skillful rower: she engages the water with her blade the instant
it drops beneath the surface, and from then on she is propelling the
boat forward steadily, increasing pressure as the boat itself responds and
moves faster, building to a climactic surge at the finish that sends the
boat away while the oar pops cleanly out of the water, in a moment of

peace at the center of the whirlpool it has made for itself. That's how a good plot propels the interest of an audience: catching, building, finding peace, sending away.

6.2 Sacred Space

Why does theater need a measured space? In order to practice the art of theater successfully, some people must be watching the actions of others. Whether your job tonight is to watch or be watched, you need to know which job is yours; the watcher-watched distinction is essential to theater. We shall see that even this can break down at the end of a theater piece, with marvelous consequences. But one of those consequences is that the event is no longer theatrical. When no one is watching, it's not theater; it has grown into something else. Marking off space in theater is a device for meeting the need to distinguish the watcher from the watched. In most traditions there is a circle or a stage or a sanctuary or a playing field.

Plot measures time better than a clock does, but what could measure space? This is a hard question, because theater space seems to be much more elastic than theater time, and nothing serves the function of plot to give space a structure that is comparable to the beginning, middle, and end of time in the theater.

Back to the green lawn in front of the tower, the flying plastic disks, and the leaping, twirling young men. Suppose that, after our meeting concludes, we return past the same green and see the students still playing. Our meeting ended early, and we have time to watch again. The throws are longer now: one student leaps the hedge to catch a long throw; his friend dashes down the steps to retrieve another. In the pause for retrieval, the third player recognizes one of us, and, as a challenge, throws her an extra disk that had been kept in reserve on top of his backpack. Wordlessly, one of us moves onto the green and we commence to play, a separate game, fully clothed and far less skillful. But on the same ground. The student players shift slightly to make room for us.

The student game never had boundaries, although perhaps the green looked as if it gave the players a spatial boundary. But no. They violated nothing when they leaped over the hedge, and we violated nothing when we stepped through a gap in the hedge and began our own game.

But imagine the outcry if the next football game between Texas and Oklahoma went the same way. In this stadium, there is a line drawn on the grass, and it marks the space for the game. If a player crosses the line, he must pay a price for that. The game will stop if he does not stay inside the assigned space. A parallel rule governs intruders. If you and I, sitting in the front row at this game, grow bored with the poor quality of play, we might decide to start our own game of catch on the same field during the game. But to do so would be to risk being dismembered by the crowd. We would be straying into sacred space. Certainly, this space is sacred to this crowd of football fans. (I almost said "worshippers," but football mania is not worship. It merely resembles worship.) And for an audience member who intrudes on that space the price is much higher than for a player to stray outside it.

"Sacred" is a word we have almost lost in modern times, like "reverence," to which it is related in meaning. Sacred things and places call us to reverence, as do sacred times like the Sabbath; perhaps in our century we are too alert to the dangers of idolatry to recognize that we are, still, surrounded by what we wordlessly take to be sacred. And Christians have come more and more to neglect the Sabbath. Like reverence, the sacred is best known in religious contexts, but, if we are to recognize it now, we must look for it also in the secular world, such as the football field. I will say that a place or an object or a person is sacred if it is held to be untouchable except by people who are marked off, usually by ritual, so as to be allowed to touch it.

What makes theater space sacred? Ritual, or a tradition based on ritual, defines the space and calls for penalties against those who violate it. All theater, football games and *Antigone* included, is the heir of a long line of spaces made sacred for religious ritual. Sometimes the space is permanently sacred, like the *adyton*, the un-enterable room in an old Greek temple. Sometimes it is sacred for the time of the event, and the boundaries of time and place work together. So it is with the stage, after a performance of *Hamlet*, if you are invited as a sponsor to a reception with the cast on the set. Nothing wrong now with setting foot on this space (although, if the performance was good, I dare you to step on the stage afterward without a shiver). So it is also with a trial at law; for the time of the trial the courtroom theater is sacred and may be entered only by designated people and used only according to certain rules.

The sacred room in a temple is permanently sacred; there is no time when it is not sacred. But this does not mean that no one ever enters it. One of the most interesting features of sacred space is that it is not altogether forbidden; consecrated people are allowed to enter it. To understand the sacredness of the space is to understand the rules about who may enter it. Only priests may enter the temple's *adyton*; only players and referees may set foot on the field in a football game; only actors (and perhaps subfusc stagehands) may tread upon the stage during performance.

All who enter sacred space are consecrated to the roles that give them access to that space. Priests of course are formally and permanently consecrated to the priesthood; players put on uniforms and often dedicate themselves as a group to a game through a locker room ritual, usually involving prayer. I used to think that such rituals were only about praying to win, but I see now there is a deeper meaning to the shared prayer, one that prepares the players to occupy space set aside, now, for this game. Actors use a variety of rituals, some shared, some individual. At a barn in Winedale, Texas, university students plunge into Shakespeare; when they are about to perform a play, they take hands in a circl and share in vocal and physical exercises. It is the ritual circle they form that changes them from a group of students to the cast dedicated to this play.

Theater has two ways of measuring its space. The most common way is to draw a line before the time begins. In art theater this is called the *stage*, in sports it is called the *field*, and in religious ceremonies it takes a variety of forms and names (the sanctuary, the shrine, the sacred grove). In each case, the boundaries seem to have been laid down in advance, by convention.

The second way is to see where the actors go. In the twentieth century we began to see theater space defined by action, and this often produces a more powerful effect. Wherever the actors go, they carry the stage with them. Being dedicated as actors, they are sacred, for the time of the theater, and even if they seem to be in our space, in the auditorium, we know that each is in his or her own sacred circle. We shift to make room for them, and we do not banter with the person behind the mask. When we are only inches from a performer we are confronted directly with the sacred majesty of theater. This is Hamlet. Yes, I know, an hour ago she was my daughter, and I greeted her with a hug. But I would not dream of hugging her now. She has just killed Polonius, and she is dragging the old man's corpse through the auditorium. Claudius does not know where she is, and no one has invited us to let him in on the secret.

To know the art of theater in any culture, you need to know how the sort of theater you are doing measures its time and space. You must know this whether you are among the watchers or the watched. Usually, the two groups will have the same idea about where the boundaries are. But not always. Sometimes the boundaries change, and sometimes the performers have drawn lines that are unknown to the audience. Surprise, surprise! The person sitting next to you is part of the play; perhaps you too will be designated, and then you will find that your seat has all along been part of the wider stage. The surprise can go the other way, as when an audience member surprises the cast by joining them on stage—a rare event, because it is a rare cast that knows how to accommodate such an intrusion.

The best theater is prepared for anything. Sometimes we discover boundaries only by straying across them; sometimes by straying we change ourselves into something new. The boundaries of theater space are whatever lines cannot be crossed without transformation. Either individual people or the broader event may undergo metamorphosis. Transformations may be good theater, and theater itself may be transformed into something better than theater. Actors may become audience, audience may become actors, and a theater piece may become a ritual that is shared among all present. That happens when the performers invite the audience to become part of the action and the audience accept. At such a moment, everyone is changed; everyone has found the grace to be allowed to enter sacred space. What begins as theater and passes through transgression may end as sacrament.

6.3 Transgression: Oedipus

A very old man shambles onto the stage from a side entrance. He is lame. He favors a cruelly deformed foot, and with each step he leans on a tall wooden staff, which he holds in one hand. With his other hand he clings to a young woman. He follows her, his face canted upward. He is blind, and he does not know where he is.

So opens Sophocles' last play, the play of the poet's old age, *Oedipus at Colonus*. At the end of an extraordinary set of temptations, Oedipus will rise, throw aside his walking stick, stand up, and, still blind, lead the full-sighted king of Athens to the place that has been promised for them both. Before the end of the play, the old man will have discovered in himself the power to bless the land on which he is about to die, along with the power to curse his errant family. Blessing and cursing—these are the powers of people who are sacred, and so is the power to see what others cannot see, the power that he will soon have to see without eyes.

Oedipus is sacred. But how could he be? He has shown more than his share of human failings, and he will go on showing them during this play. Arrogant and quick-tempered, irascible and unrepentant, he seems an unlikely bearer of divine gifts. And yet he is. His death will bless the land on which he dies and make it inviolable by enemies. He brings a blessing, even though his fellow countrymen have driven him out of his own land as a bearer of pollution.

We in the audience know who he is; he used to be the young man who killed the king of Thebes. Such a man would not normally be allowed to set foot on the land of the murdered king. But Oedipus is worse than that, for the king was his father. And his wife, the mother of the young woman who is now leading him—she is his own mother, and his daughter is his half-sister. Truly, if anyone has trodden on forbidden ground, it is Oedipus.

And now here he is, at the beginning of this play, seated in the center of the stage while his daughter tries to learn where they are. She does not know any better than he does what land they have reached, but we do. This is a place called Colonus, belonging to Athens, and Oedipus has taken his seat on the edge of a mound that is sacred. Soon he will learn from a local resident that he has violated sacred space. Just by being where he is, he has committed yet another transgression without knowing it. He is the most transgressive character in Greek mythology.

Before anything else happens in this play, the manner of his entrance has given the audience signs of his past. There he comes, leaning on the murder weapon, the staff with which he killed his father. And now there he sits, on the edge of a mound no human being is supposed to touch, like his mother's genitals, which he entered without knowing where he was. But his transgressions have changed him in ways he and the audience come to appreciate only as this play progresses.

Oedipus has come under a curse, his own curse. He carries a kind of sacred space around with him—a space most people will not enter, for fear of taking on some share of his curse. And now that he is physically in a sacred space, he is where he belongs, the untouchable man on untouchable ground. Classical languages have the same word for "sacred" and "cursed." Oedipus has crossed the line no one should cross: he has lived on the wrong side of the line. Transgression has not made him a good man, not by any means. He is as terrible as ever. But transgression has made him holy.

I tell you this partly because it is an explosive opening to a great play—a strong catch that will propel the play forward to its astonishing conclusion—his strange exit, to be followed by an event so sacred that we cannot even be told about it by the one eyewitness. But mostly I tell you this because it is an early case of a sacred space presented within a sacred space, and it illustrates the main point I want to make in this chapter—that transgression is enormously powerful in theater or out of it, and that although theater depends on marking off a sacred space, when theater violates its own sacred space it moves us most strongly.

6.4 Transgressive Theater

The most powerful theater is as transgressive as Oedipus himself. Theater can explode the genre that gave it birth, it can lead its followers into sacred ground, and it can leave a mysterious blessing behind when its time expires. By "transgressive theater" I mean theater that sets up boundaries and then violates them. Boundaries that are never violated fall off the horizon of our attention, and theater that does not violate its boundaries lulls us into forgetting that it is theater. Transgressive theater calls attention to its own boundaries, and in so doing it calls attention to itself, to the very fact of its being theater.

Watching an audience

In Love's Labor's Lost, the four young lovers (who have sworn not to fall in love) come on stage one by one, each thinking himself alone, to read the dreadful poetry their love has inspired. Each hides and joins the secret audience for the next. In some productions a hidden lover will make a face at the audience after an excruciating line, signaling a kind of collusion with the audience. His face says: "We are all in this together, listening to this wretched stuff." But then he is brought back into the action, out of the audience. But the moment of collusion is delicious. (Seeing this scene so performed hooked me on theater at an early age.)

When playwrights show us a play within a play they show us an audience. They may be showing the kind of audience they are used to, but they are also showing us to ourselves. Even tiny vignettes within a play have this function: when one character recites poetry to another in *Le Misanthrope*, the players give us a moment of theater in which we may see ourselves watching this very scene, this reading of a poem.

Shakespeare's formal theater within theater includes the aborted *Murder of Gonzago* in *Hamlet*, *The Nine Worthies* in *Love's Labor's Lost*, the rude mechanicals' *Pyramus and Thisbe* in *Midsummer Night's Dream*, and the masques in the *Tempest*. Sometimes audience intrusions destroy the play. In *Hamlet* a performance is cut short by an audience member who is touched too closely by the play; in *Love's Labor's Lost* a particularly obnoxious audience reduces actors to silence or tears of anger. "This is not generous, not gentle, not humble," says a discomfited actor, and he is right. In *Dream* the play is completed for a slightly less annoying audience, thanks to Theseus's compassionate defense: "The best in this kind are but shadows; and the worst are no worse, if imagination amend them."

Theater inside theater may advance the plot (as in *Hamlet*), it may show us our worst tendencies as an audience (as in *Love's Labor's Lost*), or it may invite us to think about the meaning of theater (as in *Midsummer Night's Dream*). In the *Tempest* above all, the playwright brings out the magic of the stage by giving its magician hero a mastery of performance.

Theater inside theater often stages transgression, but the result, in itself, is only mildly transgressive. When we watch a staged audience we have a triple vision: we see the play-within-a-play as we would normally see a play, in its own space. But we also see the surrounding play as a play, and we become aware of ourselves as an audience. In our minds, for a moment, we let the line dissolve between the audience we are watching and us as watchers. We are all in this together, we and Theseus and his court, together watching the rude mechanicals perform their play. The watched audience has the freedom to say what they think about the play, which we do not, but we know they are speaking for us.

Audience transgression

Shakespeare illustrates audience transgression of a kind he probably experienced. Wealthy patrons seated on or near the stage of the Globe apparently had no qualms about interrupting a performance with criticism serious or jocular. In *The Knight of the Burning Pestle*, Francis Beaumont, an Elizabethan playwright, shows members of the audience not just crossing the line but hijacking a play entirely, bringing in their own actor, creating a character for him, and micromanaging the plot. The play reverses the usual pattern, however. The interference comes not from rich nobles in privileged seats but from ordinary folk who make up the bulk of the audience—a merchant and his wife. They want their apprentice (a handsome lad on whom the wife has a crush) to play the lead role, and they have their way. But the tension between their taste and that of the players continues to animate this brilliant play, which combines satire of Elizabethan theater with an adaptation of *Don Quixote* to a battle in which the enemy is venereal disease. Hence the obscene pun in the title.

In modern theater, audience transgression is almost unheard of, and with its decline a lot of fun has gone out of the theater. But the transgressions I have mentioned are all staged. They are part of the plot, and that is why they are fun. We would not take so much pleasure in the disruption by an audience member of a formal play for which we had bought expensive tickets. The most famous theater disruption of my lifetime was the killing during the Rolling Stones' concert at Altamont, a live festival also captured on film. It was, at least, memorable for all concerned. But the art of theater cannot produce this result. The art of the audience is to pay attention to the performance, not to interrupt it.

Theater space has a special feature: in many cases, it cannot be violated and remain as theater space. Other sorts of sacred space remain sacred even when they have been violated. A sacred grove is still a sacred grove, even if an intruder has camped out in it. But transgression can change theater space into something else, as happens especially in games. Suppose an outraged fan plunges onto the field and fatally stabs the young man who has been playing wide receiver. The moment the fan crosses onto the field, he has interrupted the game, and the young victim is no longer playing wide receiver. There is no game at all now, and he cannot be playing any part in it. So if the fan intended to kill the receiver he has failed; he has succeeded only in killing a young man. The fan cannot intrude on the game, because once he intrudes, there is no game for him to intrude on. Some forms of mimetic theater are more tolerant of audience transgression; actors who know how to improvise can incorporate outsiders into their performance. But when this happens, the intruder is transformed; the moment he crosses the line he belongs on the stage. So this case too supports the rule that theater does not tolerate intrusions; either it stops, like the game, or it transforms the intruder, like the improvisation.

Sacred space other than theater space is protected by strict rules, and those who break the rules must pay a price. Violated space may require purification, such as the ritual Oedipus's daughters must carry out after he realizes where he has been sitting. But theater space is theater space only while theater is going on, and theater can go on only while the space is inviolate. The reasons for not invading most sacred spaces are religious; the reasons for not invading theater space are practical: invasion usually stops theater before the measured time has passed. Theater may have begun in spaces made sacred by holy ritual, but in a secular culture the holiness is no longer felt. Simply, it is a necessity of theater that its space be protected.

Actor transgression

Actors cross the line frequently, in all kinds of theater, and they get away with it because audience members usually know to stay in their place. But not always. I have heard that a woman playing Dionysus in *Dionysus in 69* once challenged individual men in the audience to drop their sexual inhibitions, along with their trousers, and take her then and there. She was crossing the line, but no doubt she felt safe in doing so, relying on the audience to know better than to cross the line in return. But on one night (so goes the tale) a man from the audience did start to lower his trousers. The actress fled the theater. Actor transgression always carries the risk that the audience will reciprocate, and the experience of theater will come to a halt.

Imagine this. We are watching a play that seems to have a conventional plot about people being arrested and held, abusively, on suspicion of crimes, in some country where such things happen. Suddenly the action on stage is halted. The real police are here, roaring in from the lobby with guns drawn. Well, they look and sound like real police, but they are actors, and their names appear in the program. The chief says, "Sorry to interrupt, folks, but we have been informed by a reliable source that there are subversives in the audience. Stay in your seats. If you are innocent, nothing bad will happen to you. We are only arresting the guilty. When we're finished, you all can get on with the play."

Then the police arrest a few people from the audience. There is screaming on both sides, a woman who resists arrest is clubbed down as an example to others, guns flash into hands, billy clubs are raised. After a brief tumult the police leader announces they have done what they came for: "Folks, you can sleep better tonight. We got all the bad guys who were here. Carry on with your play." Later we see the police and the detainees taking a curtain call, and we are reassured. But we might never have seen the detainees again.

This is certainly theater, and if it is well done it catches you in a web of pity and fear you will not easily forget. It warns you not to rely too much on the line between being a spectator and being caught up in the action. Today you watch injustice being done to others; tomorrow you find it done to yourself.

Here is an extreme example of this. Suppose the white citizens of a town have gathered to watch a lynching. At first, they feel that they are at a safe distance from the violence being enacted under the tree. After all, they are white, and the danger (they believe) is black. This lynching (they feel) confirms their safety and reaffirms their sense that no matter how frail or slow the official law might be, what they call justice will still be done promptly in this town. Moreover, because this is a theatrical event, everyone who might infringe on the town's code is supposed to be frightened into submission. Black people especially are expected to see the danger of being noticed by whites. And so the white townspeople watch in some satisfaction.

Suddenly there is a change. More ropes are thrown over branches in the grove. The armed men are not following the script. Now they are wading into the white crowd and grabbing people. A single man in middle age who has shown a trace of effeminacy, a woman who had protested the lynching, the man who wrote to the newspaper to complain about the schools. Soon they too are swinging from the branches. They had thought they were in the audience, but they learned too late that the space around a lynching is not sacred and its boundary is not untouchable. In matters of punishment, only the law can make a sacred space, and this isn't law.

In some cases, performers expand the sacred space by acting outside its original boundaries, and we shall see that they may even be able to share their sacred space with the audience. But that is not what is happening here. What distinguishes a lynching from lawful punishment is the absence of sacred space altogether. The event I imagined only pretends to have boundaries. The ancient lesson that only law creates a scared space around punishment is recorded in Aeschylus's *Eumenides*; without procedural law, the cycle of violence and reaction to violence could go on forever.

Lynching is still a kind of public theater, even though it does not occupy a measured space. But it is horrible. Its moral wickedness is obvious enough, but its long-range results are not so well known—for example, how the mutual fears exacerbated by this theater fuel a culture of racism lingering for generations after the formal lynchings have come to an end. This is a theater that cannot be trusted to stay in its own space. Such theater can be terrifying.

Collusion

And theater can be fun. In comedy, the joker often gets in cahoots with the audience. He leers or winks at them as he delivers a jibe at the expense of his straight man. By this behavior the joker lays down a line on the stage, with his straight man on one side of the line, and him (with the audience) on the other. The joker has erased the line between himself and the audience, and they are now in collusion against the straight man. We have seen this effect before, when we in the audience were watching an audience on stage and recognized our community with the stage audience. Laughing together, we and the joker form a community that excludes the straight man. We share the joke with each other, but not with him.

Laughter tends to sop up the emotional energy that might have gone into pity or fear, so when we laugh at the straight man, we will not be able to feel for him. Empathy is out. Even without actual laughter, an audience in collusion will have little truck with the big emotions of theater. That was Bertolt Brecht's insight, and it led him to develop "alienation effects." These are communications between stage and audience that remind the audience they are seeing an enactment on stage and that they should direct their feelings at the real conditions of their own lives, rather than at the actors or their gestures on stage. And the feeling Brecht is angling for is not pity or fear but outrage.

Brechtian theater devices have become so common we hardly notice them. The false proscenium is removed. We see the lighting bars and know that the set is artificially lighted. We see the way the flimsy sets are propped up, so that we may have no illusions. The actors comment from time to time on their roles; they cultivate a narrative style of acting, as if they were telling the story from a distance, rather than becoming one with a character in the play. The scenes have titles, like chapters in a novel, and these are displayed or spoken.

All this serves to put us, the audience, on the same side as the actors, sharing their attitudes toward the action that is being represented. The line between watcher and watched remains clear enough; Brecht does not blur his boundary, but he does hope to overcome it. He wants us all to be in this together, audience and actors, so that we all understand, together, that war and exploitation have the consequences shown on this stage. That (he wants us to see) is why we must find a way to bring war and exploitation to an end.

Altar calls

During the high point of protest against the war in Vietnam, in 1971, student leaders set up an event. In the largest auditorium, a series of speakers will address issues related to the war, culminating in a talk by the one student on campus who is known to be a veteran. This will have all the marks of theater: there will be something worth watching, there will be people who have come to watch, there will be a defined space for the performers—a rostrum with one microphone—and there is already a plot to measure the time: a list of speakers.

The speeches proceed in the order planned, each raising the emotional intensity to a higher level. At last the young veteran takes the rostrum. He is passionate as he tells of death and mismanagement. As he closes, a student leader seizes the microphone. "You heard what he said. Now let's take over Nassau Hall." This isn't in the plot. It's not theater, but it is a splendid surprise ending. I am chagrined, however. I am the veteran. I came to speak about the war, and my enemy is not in Nassau Hall (where the deans work) but in the Pentagon, where the generals have failed to set humane priorities for the conduct of the war.

And so the theatrical part of the afternoon's event comes to an end. The faculty and many of the students go home. But a good-sized crowd storms out of the auditorium and occupies Nassau Hall. They have all become participants in the event, and they have become outlaws as well. By following the call, they have committed themselves to action. They have changed themselves from students to activists. The young revolutionaries themselves are surprised to find themselves in this role. I am with them, feeling that whatever penalty they incur should fall on me as well, since I gave the speech that whipped them up to the point of metamorphosis. I didn't call for the change, of course; a student leader did that. But the audience would not have followed him if I had not raised them to a certain emotional pitch.

This is an example of an altar call, albeit a secular one. When an altar call is artfully sounded on a wave of emotion, it transforms an audience. Nothing that can happen in the theater is more exciting or more dramatic. Theater that aims at the metamorphosis of the audience culminates in an altar call that usually comes as a surprise.

In church or revival meetings too, an altar call is a call to change yourself, to cross the line that marks off the inactive watchers and join the active participants in holy ritual, or to become actively committed to the life of faith. If everyone heeds the call, everyone is part of the ritual. Then the audience has vanished or, rather, has been transformed into something else. Its members have taken roles in the event they came to watch. So now there is only the event itself, and it is no longer theater because there is no one to watch. Sometimes there is no need to make the call; the experience is enough by itself to transform the audience. This is theater that has escaped into another form of human experience. But as we heed the altar call, and as we banish theater, we do not wipe out the sacred space. We have become entitled to enter it, and it is all around us.

At the end of *The Laramie Project*, the actors distribute candles to the audience, and fire dances down row after row in the darkened auditorium. We don't need to be called; we don't need to leave our seats. The final scenes themselves have changed us all from spectators to mourners. The actors too have been changed; there is no make-believe in their grief. Like us, they really are grieving. The candles are only a visual sign of an inward change that none of us could have escaped. In this moment of shared sorrow, we are all in sacred space.

SEVEN

Mimesis

A man stumbles blindly onto a platform, leaning on a heavy staff and guided by a young woman. Stepping beyond her, he takes his seat on a small riser. That really happens in front of us, but it's not very interesting in itself. We have seen blind men before, and we'd rather not think too long about their difficulties. So we would, normally, take brief notice of this event and turn back to our own affairs. Could a dramaturge make this riveting for an audience?

Mimesis makes the difference. Let's suppose the old man is not the actor listed in the program, but Oedipus, and the young girl is both his half-sister and his daughter, Antigone. And let's suppose as well that the staff is the weapon with which he killed his father many years ago, and the riser on which he sits is the sacred mound at Colonus, where no unsanctified mortal may set foot. Now the scene is interesting, and we want to know what happens next.

Mimesis is one of the tools that the art of theater uses to make human action worth watching. It is only one of the tools of theater because, as we have seen, theater is not always mimetic. But mimesis has been a central theme in philosophy of the arts ever since Aristotle's *Poetics* made it the genus within which he distinguished poetry—tragedy, comic, and epic—from other art forms. Mimesis is also the subject of the most important work in art theory of the last fifty years, Kendall Walton's *Mimesis as Make-Believe*.

"Mimesis" is a Greek word that has come into English because we have no other word to capture its entire range. "Imitation" comes close, "simulation" covers part of what it means, and so does "make-believe." Mimesis includes some kinds of representation and even of expression. Its dark side contains various forms of pretense, fakery, and deception. "Copying" and "doubling" may also apply to mimesis. So large a stable of rough equivalents in English—you might suppose that mimesis is hopelessly vague. But it admits a fairly precise definition, one that will help us understand the heart of mimetic theater, and much else besides.

Mimesis and ordinary life are not divided by clear boundaries. Our lives are laced with mimesis. In new situations, we often learn how to behave by copying others. Around our students, we pretend to be wiser than we really are; around us, our students pretend to have done their reading. To each other they pretend to have more worldly experience than their brief lives so far could have given them. We are often told to live authentic lives. Authenticity ought to rule out pretense and imitation, but to live without any form of mimesis would be impossible for a human being, and what starts as imitation may lead to an authentic change.

Let's start with examples of mimesis from ordinary life to illustrate three different uses of mimesis: modeling, complicity, and duplicity.

A small boy struts across the room behind his father, and when he speaks he deepens his voice as far as he can. If he can be like his father, he expects that he will have the authority his father has, and so he does his best. In this case, mimesis is educational; the child learns to be an adult by imitating one, and, if all goes well, he will pass from imitating grown-ups to being grown up soon enough. I call this *modeling*.

On Halloween a teacher wears long vampire teeth into the kindergarten classroom; the children run from him, squealing, as they would if he really were a blood-sucking monstrosity, and he chases them as if he really were a vampire. This kind of mimesis aims at pleasure and is shared. All who are present join the game of make-believe. I refer to this as *complicity* in mimesis.

A hunter has learned to sound like a moose in heat, with the help of an apparatus. He hopes that a male moose will come at his call, and he will shoot the amorous beast. His form of mimesis aims to manipulate the natural world; it is not meant to be fun for the moose. Nevertheless, the hunter's call best illustrates the core meaning of mimesis because it brings out clearly the *duplicity* that is common to all cases. I use the word "double" as a technical term in the theory of mimesis. The hunter's call is the *double* of the call of a female moose.

Not all mimesis is done by human beings: Septimus, the young veteran in the street where Mrs. Dalloway is buying flowers, hears an explosion and freezes, transported back to the trenches where shells fly and his friend is blown to pieces; the car that backfired harmlessly turns a corner and is gone. The same example illustrates the general point that not all mimesis is intended to deceive. The backfire is the double of a wartime explosion, but no one intended to startle the veteran. The boy who struts like his father does not mean to deceive, nor does the teacher with the vampire fangs. Yet all of these are mimesis.

7.1 Defining Mimesis

Here I give an account of the classical concept of mimesis—the one employed by Plato and Aristotle in their work on the arts. On this basis we can sustain the conversation over the centuries with these thinkers and their successors.

On classical theories, when mimesis occurs it usually takes the place of something real. By doing this, it has real effects on the world. Medicine is mimetic of natural healing (Aristotle says), but it really heals. Poetry is mimetic of the teaching of wise people, but (Plato complains) it really changes people's beliefs and behaviors.

Mimesis is a way to make things become real, and the art of theater often has this aim—to make something become real—as we have seen. My examples illustrate several varieties of mimesis, but they all have this in common: there is an original. For the small boy, it is his father; for the teacher's game, it is the vampire's hunt; for the hunter's call, it is a female moose; for the backfire, an explosion in the trenches. The original does not have to be real; it may belong to an imaginary world, such as a world of fiction or of myth.

Each case also has something that is not the original but does some of the work that the original would do if it were around. The child impresses, as his father would, though not nearly as much. The vampire game makes the children run and scream, as they would if a vampire were after them. The moose call brings the moose. The backfire terrifies Septimus, like the explosive round that killed his friend.

Mimesis is an activity by which one thing produces at least part of the effect that another thing would naturally produce. Let "M" stand for the actor or agent of mimesis and "O" for the original or object. Then mimesis occurs when M acts enough like O that M produces part of the natural effect of O. Let this be the general account of mimesis.

In one special kind of mimesis, the activity produces its effect through creating a mimetic object—as when a painter creates a painting of a tree. The painter is doing what nature does in making something that looks like a tree—a tree, after all, does look like a tree. So the painting itself has part of the natural effect of a tree: it looks like one. But the painting cannot actually perform mimesis; the painter did that.

Essential to the idea of mimesis is a theory of natural causation. A certain sort of thing naturally has a certain effect, and it is not quite natural for anything else to have that effect. When the ancient Greeks said that art is mimetic of nature, they had in mind arts like medicine. The body naturally heals, but when medicine causes the body to heal, this is not quite natural, because the medical art has intruded on, and taken advantage of, a natural process. Predators have naturally evolved to eschew poisonous beetles, but if a nonpoisonous species has evolved to take advantage of the situation, then predators will avoid this nontoxic species as well, even though their doing so is only a by-product of the original natural process. Mimesis does not have to be unnatural, but it does have to be secondary to a natural process.

For mimesis to occur, the mimetic cause must differ from the original one, and its link to the original is usually something like resemblance. A mimetic *cause* works through resemblance to the original, but the mimetic *effect* is the same for the mimetic cause as for the original one, as far as it goes, and that is rarely all the way. The veteran hears the car backfire and reacts as if it had been gunfire—except that there is no trench for him to leap for and no friend to warn. The children run from the teacher and squeal; so far, so good: they would do that if they saw a vampire. But in this case they laugh, as they would never do if running from a real danger. By "as far as it goes" I mean this: a mimetic effect needs to match only part of the effect of the original. The moose actually heaves himself on the scene, drawn by the desire for sex, just as he would if called by a female, but he need not mate with the hunter who made the call. Mimesis has occurred, even in the absence of the full effect.

I have given examples of three kinds of behaviors that fit the general account of mimesis: the hunter's call is a case of *duplicity*; the children running from the vampire-teacher are engaged in *complicity*; the small boy imitating his father is learning by *modeling*. These overlap. In theater, for example, the same mimesis may aim both at the deceptive effect of duplicity and the pleasure of complicity. But all cases of mimesis involve duplicity, since all produce doubles of originals. That is why they are the same in definition. But when human beings intentionally do mimesis, they may have different principal aims: in duplicity they aim mainly at mimetic effect, in complicity at mimetic pleasure, and in modeling at education.

7.2 Modeling

Learning is a pleasure for human beings, as Aristotle tells us, and mimesis can be part of that in two ways. The first depends on duplicity. A picture of a lion is a lot safer to be around than the lion herself, but we can still learn a lot about lions by studying the picture closely. Of course, the picture cannot teach us everything that the lion itself could teach us, but that is the point of mimesis after all: it gives us only part of the effect of the original.

The second way to learn from mimesis is by modeling. An agent of mimesis takes on some of the attributes of an admirable person in the hope of becoming more and more like him or her, as in the case of the small boy with his powerful father or the small pitcher who dreams of the major leagues. Modeling takes an agent through mimesis to a new reality, as we saw in the case of the boy growing up; a new way of appearing becomes a new way of being. We have all become the people we are by modeling ourselves on others—at least in part. Years after taking a class, you will probably forget the lesson the teacher was trying to give you, even if she was a great teacher. But if she was, you will not so easily shake off the influence of her example. We model ourselves on powerful examples unconsciously.

Conscious modeling raises a moral issue. On moral grounds, we should choose good originals, but actors do not have that luxury. Actors who perform many roles are likely to take a variety of originals to be their models, but no one actor can actually come to be a variety of people, and the attempt to be various may be damaging to your moral character. How can you hope to have a stable and reliable moral character if you keep turning into different people as a result of modeling? Even if you play only one part in your acting career, a moral question remains: What if it is not a good part, or if it is not appropriate for you? How does it affect a man to play a woman's role? a free man to play a slave? anyone to play a villain?

Plato was afraid that acting could change people for the worse, and that was one of his objections to theater. He was right to raise the question. Because modeling aims to change people, and often succeeds, modeling in mimetic theater carries a certain risk. But modeling need not have such effects, as countless actors have shown in their lives. No one who has played Iago, to my knowledge, has therefore betrayed a friend.

This kind of mimesis has nothing to do with deception. Modeling is not meant to fool anyone; no one thinks for a minute that the small boy is a man, nor does the boy expect anyone to do so. But he does hope to become more and more like his father until, eventually, he truly is a man like his father. Modeling also has the common aim of mimesis—to have at least part of the effect of the original. The small boy wants people to take him as seriously as they do his father, but he does not want them to expect him to do everything his father does, because he can't. In the same way, an actor playing a dangerous murderer models herself on the murderer in the hope of becoming that way on stage. She also wants to have part of the effect on an audience that such a murderer would have: she wants to horrify them. But she does not want them to shoot her down or call the police or take any of the other actions they would take around a dangerous murderer. Both the boy and the actor are asking for some measure of complicity from those who watch them; modeling overlaps with complicity.

7.3 Complicity

Mimesis in theater often demands complicity from the audience. Complicity occurs when those who are affected by mimesis help it along through an effort of imagination, through make-believe. The children run from their beloved teacher when he is wearing vampire teeth only as part of a game of make-believe. The children know perfectly well who he is, and they are delighted by the game. Audience reaction in mimetic theater almost always involves complicity to some extent. We come to the theater knowing that we will see actors performing; we may even know who they are behind those masks and costumes. Even mimetic theater has a place for nonmimetic behavior, however. The members of the Chorus in the *Bacchae* are young men impersonating foreign women, but when these young men enter the orchestra they are really singing and dancing. Moreover, they are doing this in praise of Dionysus, whom they and the audience really believe to be a god, and what they are singing is probably a real hymn. Mimesis and reality overlap.

Keep in mind that complicity does not undermine the effects of mimesis. The children make believe that they are frightened, but they still run and squeal; they really run and squeal. Because real things really do come from any sort of mimesis, we cannot answer Plato by simply saying, "Oh, relax; this is only make-believe." A game of mimesis could lead to violence, and often has. People who use mimesis wisely consider where it leads. Mimesis of terrible actions may lead to real emotions, and real emotions normally lead to real actions.

Also keep in mind that the theater of presence is supposed to summon a divine presence into the space it makes sacred. Dancers may feel they actually come to be possessed by spirits, with startling consequences. They may have started out in mimesis, inviting the complicity of the audience, but they have gone beyond that altogether, and they are no longer themselves playing parts. They are something else now, and they invite belief now, not complicity.

I said at the outset that complicit mimesis aims at pleasure. Being really terrified is painful and debilitating, but audiences have fun rather than pain with the kind of terror they experience in mimetic theater. Joining in a game of make-believe is fun, and that is what you are doing when you are complicit in mimesis. The emotions we seem to feel in mimetic theater—even the painful ones such as pity and fear—these are part of the make-believe that is shared by actors and audience. Mimesis can transmute agony into pleasure.

7.4 Duplicity

Duplicity is common in nature. When a harmless insect resembles a poisonous one in appearance it may have one of the effects on predators that the poisonous one has: it will frighten predators off, even though it would not poison them. The harmless insect is a double of the poisonous one. A double is not identical; if it were, it would just be what it is the double of. But it isn't. This beetle is not poisonous; the one it looks like is.

Duplicity also occurs between human ingenuity and nature. For example, the ancient Greeks thought that medicine was mimetic of the natural healing process—same effect, different means, as we saw above. Medicine serves as a double for nature when it produces the same effect as nature would if it could. There is no intention to deceive any person in such cases, but something like deception does take place: the medicine in effect fools the body into responding as if the natural process were taking place.

Plato has two families of objections to the tragic theater of his day. The first concerns mimesis; the second, emotion, which I treat later. Plato has three worries about mimesis: two about duplicity and one about modeling. First, he complains that poets play the part of wise men and so enjoy the respect that belongs to the wise; but (unbeknownst to themselves) they are not wise. Philosophers actually are wise, although poets may not know it. So poetry in fact serves as a duplicitous mimesis of philosophy. Poetry has part of the effect of philosophy in that it causes people to honor it and follow it as a guide in their lives. But not the entire effect. A boy who hears performances of Homer may model his actions on those of Achilles, but, as Plato points out, Homer never won any wars or founded any cities.

Philosophers have not been very effective either; they haven't had much of a chance to win wars or found cities. But the effect of philosophy would be reliably good for those people who take it as their guide, if the philosophers are truly wise, whereas the effect of poetry varies. Poets do not actually know how to improve people's lives, with the result that sometimes their poems may be good for their audience, sometimes not. There's no telling. All poetry was performed for audiences in Plato's day, so this complaint is about a kind of theater that presents poetry, which is only sometimes wise, as if it were a vehicle of wisdom, and does so to a crowd that cannot tell the difference between wisdom and its false image.

The second of Plato's complaints about mimesis is technical and cannot be understood apart from his theory of reality. Plato holds that we can achieve knowledge only by focusing our minds on what is most real. Because what is most real is not accessible to our senses, we must shut off our seeing and hearing in order to approach what is real purely through our minds. His complaint about poetry is that it presents mimetic images in place of their originals, so that poetry lovers try to learn from images instead of from reality. This is rather like the moose coming to mate with the hunter in place of the lady moose who is grazing at the next pond. The hunter intervened in the moose's natural mating process; in the same way, a poet may intervene in the natural learning process with disastrous results, says Plato.

Suppose you want to learn how a good doctor talks to a patient. You could learn something by following a good doctor on her rounds; but suppose instead of doing this you watch medical shows on television. You will learn how to behave the way an audience expects a doctor to behave, but you won't be able to tell how much of the actor's behavior actually belongs to a good doctor and how much the actor or writer has made up. The person you are learning from, after all, is not a good doctor but a good actor. We must learn from the originals, if we want to learn how things really are.

Here Plato adds a wrinkle: the good doctor you follow on his rounds is not perfect; sometimes he screws up, and you cannot make yourself a good doctor simply by following his example. You need to focus your mind on something else—what it is to be a good doctor—which he is modeling for you, albeit imperfectly.

So here's the Platonic picture: the original of good doctoring is not found in any hospital but can be approached only through the mind. The best doctor in the hospital is modeling good doctoring for you. Plato would say that her relationship to good doctoring is mimetic; her example can show you some of the things a good doctor does, but not all of them. Because you see her only in particular circumstances, you won't know what to do in other cases unless you know why she does what she does. Her example may also show you some personal mannerisms—things a good doctor does not have to do. To sort all this out, you would have to know what it is about her that makes her a good doctor, when she is behaving as a good doctor, and for that you need to know what it is to be a good doctor. Plato would say that to make good use of her example, you would have to go back behind the example to what it is an example of, to good doctoring itself, and understand that. So if you are learning only from this particular doctor's example, you are letting mimesis substitute for reality in your learning process.

Now go back to the aspiring medico who is learning from the television series. That series is modeled on the good doctor we have been talking about. So if you let that be your guide, you are letting a mimesis of a mimesis take the place of the original. That is what Plato means by saying that poetry presents material that is twice removed from reality. The original reality would attract you, so that you would want to learn from it, and everything you would learn by studying the original reality would be true. But of course we human beings don't have clear access to the original reality, and that is why perfect knowledge eludes us. The best we can do is to focus our minds on the examples that seem closest to reality. But poetry can only pull us away from the examples closest to reality.

Reality does not always teach us what we need to know, however. A drawing of human anatomy supports a first lesson on this subject better than a dissection, because it selects for emphasis what must be learned first. Selectivity, as we shall see, is one of the main advantages of mimesis; a selective account of the sack of Troy could be more powerful emotionally than an eyewitness experience of the same event.

7.5 Mimesis of Virtue

I made up the good doctor example, although I think Plato would welcome it. Plato's prime examples come from the virtues, things like justice and courage. There are two sorts of doubles for these moral qualities. Fearlessness looks a lot like courage, but it is not the same. Fearlessness can be stupid, as Plato has Socrates point out, but courage is always good. So if you were taken in by this duplicity and cultivated fearlessness, you could ruin your life through stupidity. Not so courage; if you cultivated true courage, you would never go wrong. Common usage often does not distinguish courage and fearlessness the way philosophers have done. When you hear people say that it is sometimes wrong to have courage, they mean it is sometimes wrong to be fearless. But "fearless" and "courageous" do not mean the same thing. It is never wrong to be courageous, as the ancient philosophers used the word. The double of courage takes people in, all too easily. We should sharpen our weapons against duplicity.

Justice illustrates the second sort of duplicity. Many human codes of law seem to embody justice in our lives. But all of these, being human, are imperfect. Suppose the law tells you to return what you borrowed on demand. But what if you borrowed a weapon from a man who has since then become dangerously insane? Then justice requires you to keep the weapon. No code of law perfectly embodies justice, because no code of law could account for all the exceptions to a rule like the one about borrowing.

Plato holds that the original of justice is out of this world, beyond even the boundary of heaven. This is the transcendent Form of Justice, and even the laws that seem most fair are merely doubles of that Form. You could learn a lot about justice by examining the Form of Justice if you had access to it; but, since no human law ever embodies justice perfectly, you could never learn the whole truth about justice from studying human laws, and doing so would make you liable to picking up false opinions. The consequences of mistaking a double for the original are momentous, according to Plato, and they can lead to great evils.

As we have seen, Plato charges that duplicity occurs twice in the production of dramatic poetry. Poetry may treat justice, but (Plato believes) it bases this treatment on such things as laws and customs. Now law in human life is the double of what justice truly is, because human law is not always truly just. So we should study justice first, not law. The worst thing we could do would be to study theater. Justice or law in the theater is the double of law in human life. So theatrical justice is removed from the original transcendent justice by two successive acts of duplicity—by putting a double twice in place of an original. Poets are easily taken in by their own duplicity; they think that they are wise and that their products are instructive. If so, they are not conscious deceivers, but they are the more dangerous for that.

No sooner had Plato made these criticisms of mimesis in poetry than defenders began to speak out. His pupil Aristotle was probably the first; many famous philosophers and poets have followed him into the fray. But Plato's core argument is sound, as the example of the good doctor shows: you shouldn't learn medicine by watching TV serials, and you can't learn it well even by watching good doctors at work. You have to think about what it is to be a good doctor. How else would you even know which doctors to watch?

After granting Plato his argument about learning, however, we can still defend poetry. One strategy is to show that we can make good use of poetry without trying to learn everything about the real world from it. Mimesis is enjoyable in itself; perhaps the pleasure of mimesis should suffice. But you can learn safely from experiencing mimesis, as long as you know that this is what you are doing. You may learn a lot about lions from a plush toy accurately shaped like a lion. But you need to know that it is a toy, and you need to have other sources of knowledge. Someone needs to tell you that lions are dangerous predators. Otherwise, you might learn from your toy that it is safe to cuddle a lion in your bed. Theater should be the same. If we know it is mimetic, and if we know some of the truth, theater should not lead us to false beliefs. This is how most of us seem to profit from experiencing mimesis. Our knowledge serves, Plato tells us, as an inoculation against being led astray by mimesis.

Another strategy is to argue that the best poets are closer to understanding reality than we are; far from working at two removes from reality, the great poets, owing to their genius, have special access to reality. These great poets, of course, are not writing for TV, and their views may be too hard for us to understand, especially on good and evil. To make matters worse, they are dead, and we cannot ask them what they meant or engage in the kind of discussion with them that might really illuminate their great subjects. I side with Plato here; we are better advised to trust our own critical minds, rather than the work of the poets, in approaching the truth about such things as good or evil.

A third strategy is to show how theater can provoke us to use our critical minds, often by engaging our emotions. If a performance of *Electra* leaves you outraged at what passes for justice in that play, that could make you think more deeply about justice than you had before, and so the experience would lead you away from law and custom toward the kind of philosophical reflection that Plato values. Electra has a just cause in calling for her mother to be killed, but that strikes us as horrible, so what does justice really require of her? The old rule used to be that you should help your friends and harm your enemies, but Electra's mother is both her friend (by family ties) and her enemy (by killing her father). The old rule fails. In this play, the failure is disturbing enough to make us think about what justice actually requires. Must it require this ghastly matricide?

A fourth strategy is to show how the experience of mimesis can train our emotions in good ways. This strategy is attributed to Aristotle in his *Poetics*. I argue for a version of it in part II of this book. We are better people, I believe, if we can train ourselves to pay attention to human action—to care about what those around us are doing. But caring about real people is different from paying attention to mimesis on the stage, so this strategy sets up a series of problems I have to address.

7.6 Mimesis by Music

The Greeks generally held that a piece of martial music—for us a John Philip Sousa march—could be mimetic of courage. They had in mind not songs or poems set to music, but music as such, abstracted from words—they meant rhythms and modes, pure music. People often say, wrongly, that music communicates emotions. Surely, music does something with emotions; but it is nonsense, I think, to say that what music does for emotions is to communicate them. Suppose Schumann was in love with Clara, and when he wrote a certain piece he was feeling this particular love, his love for her, and we, if we have read the program notes, feel as we hear the music that Schumann was throbbing with his love for Clara when he wrote what we hear. But we came to that not by simply listening to the music but by reading the program notes and then listening to the music. Clara is not mentioned in the music the way she is mentioned in the notes. Words do things music cannot do. There is nothing in the music that can possibly refer to either of the lovebirds.

Now there is no love anywhere that is not someone's love for someone. Perhaps the music conveys a lovelike feeling that has no subject and no object, but such a feeling is not an emotion, and it certainly is not love. Music cannot communicate emotion because it cannot refer to subject or object, and (as we shall see) emotion by definition has both of those. Music may communicate moods, and often does, but moods and emotions are not the same things. What is it that the Sousa march does? It invariably brings an audience to its feet, stomping, leaping, shouting. Much of this is a purely physical response, I think. If there is a cognitive component—if you connect your response to patriotic sentiment for the United States, this is due to knowledge you acquired outside of the music, or perhaps through association, not from the music itself.

Now real individual courage in the face of the enemy might also bring me to my feet stomping and yelling, fearless of defeat, proud of my fatherland, and all the rest of it. The Sousa march has generated in us the physical symptoms, internal and external, of those emotions. Take away all our thoughts and associations; music still has a purely physical effect on us because we ourselves are musical instruments. We vibrate in tonal sympathy with music, and our bodies take on its rhythms. If, as the Greeks believed, the physical part of courage is felt as a rhythm, then music and courage can have the same physical effects on us. That is why music is mimetic of courage. But it cannot generate the emotion of courage. How could it? There is no trumpet note that means the good old USA, no drumbeat that signifies the hated enemy. It is not the music that tells us this tune is about the "Star-Spangled Banner." Music cannot convey the subjects and objects of emotion, although experiencing music often feels just like having an emotion. Why are people reluctant to accept this? Perhaps they don't think of pure music; the music they have in mind has words to be sung, program notes to be studied, or associations to be dredged up—and any of these can carry emotions. But pure music can carry feelings that are often powerful, even though they are not directed. A clever propagandist or melodramatist can then direct these feelings to objects in the vicinity. Think how fascists used music. That, I think, is how music tends to work in theater. In film and television, its most calculated use, music sets the tone for emotion, while pictures provide the objects. A film audience is swept away on a tide of fearful feelings at just the moment when the filmmaker presents an image of the object he wants them to fear. And then the fearful feeling becomes a full-fledged emotion, a feeling with an object.

Now take away the filmed image of the object of fear. What is left between music and audience? The music has had an effect on the audience that would naturally have been caused by real fear. Only this is not fear. The audience does not feel like running. What would they feel like running from? They have not seen anything to fear or to run from, and so they are not afraid. This is mimesis as I defined it above: one thing's having an effect that naturally belongs to another, music's having an effect that naturally belongs to fear.

Aristotle says he knows that music contains likenesses of virtue and vice because he observes that our characters are changed when we listen to music. Why should this prove his point? In a little-read text, he gives a sketchy explanation of the likeness of melody and rhythm to character. Melody and rhythm are motions, and so are actions; both kinds of motion, when perceived, set up corresponding motions in the mind of the audience. So far this would seem to explain only the likeness of music to actions. Where does character come in? Actions are both indicative and formative of character: the music that corresponds to a given type of character simulates that character in the listener by setting up appropriate motions in his soul. Listening to heroic music, I feel heroic rhythms pulsing through my soul, and these are just the motions I would feel if I were a hero engaged in an heroic action, and these are the motions to which, if I had an heroic character, I would become accustomed. This music, then, is like a heroic character—it does for me what it would do for me to have that character; and if I listen to such music regularly, my soul will become accustomed to motions of that kind, and I will in fact develop a heroic character.

7.7 Mimesis in Theater

Mimesis in theater (unlike music) is directly related to emotion. Mimesis calls up emotions and other feelings in an audience, and these resemble what we would feel if we actually experienced the events that are staged. Real events are the originals, and actions on stage are the doubles. The effects that are caused equally by the events and their doubles are feelings. Mimesis in theater is making the action lifelike enough that it packs an emotional wallop.

Mimesis in theater crosses the line between fact and fiction. History—a record of facts—can be staged so well that it has a powerful mimetic effect, and we feel as if we have witnessed the actual events. Fiction—a made-up story—can be staged so badly that all we feel is boredom. We have seen actors at work, but they did not move us to any feelings related to the actions they are staging. Mimesis in story telling also crosses this line. True stories can be more effective than ones that have been made up. If a teller of a story has the gift of mimesis, however, she can affect us almost as deeply as experience itself, whether her story is true or false. But if a storyteller has no gift for mimesis, he will put us to sleep.

That, by the way, was how Plato wanted most stories to be told—without the power that could come from mimesis. Mimesis drives a wedge between our minds and reality, as I showed earlier. It also evokes strong feelings, and Plato feared the effect of strong feeling on the mind. He wanted to protect the student philosophers in his ideal state from the effects of mimesis, so that they could evaluate everything they heard on a purely rational basis. Plato was correct in thinking that mimesis overrides rational belief, whether in the theater of tragic plays or in the theater of the Athenian law court. In a law court, you could be convinced rationally that the accused is innocent, but then succumb to the prosecutor when he stages such a gut-wrenching performance on behalf of the alleged victim that you are moved to compassion and vote for conviction. (It was everyone's nightmare in ancient Athens to be the accused in such a trial.)

Made-up films and re-creations of true events are often more compelling than documentaries; historical novels are more gripping than transcripts of events. As a teacher of writing, I tell my students, when they are describing events, to make me feel like a spectator of those events, but I do not really mean that. I have been a spectator of terrible events, and I know that the effect is usually numbing. Had I been present at the death of Priam, what would I have felt? What would I have done? So much going on, so many refugees, so many bloody boys with swords. I cannot say that I would have wept for Hecuba at the moment or felt moved to comfort her, had I been beside her at the death of Priam. I hope that I would have felt moved, and that I would have tried to do something to help her.

The First Player in *Hamlet* cannot help Hecuba; he can only weep for her as he tells her tale. And his weeping is surely different from that of a true eyewitness. The Player entertains us with his tears; the eyewitness would shock us and perhaps make us run for the exit. The presence of survivors can be unbearably heavy, if what they have survived is horrible.

Suppose, by the magic of time machines, I could either place you by the side of Hecuba or bring back a video documentary from the fall of Troy. The magic of mimesis could aspire to approach either of these levels of immediacy. You could have this particular scene on tape, blurry, but unmistakably true, like the Rodney King beating. Or you could actually be there. But if you were there, what you would see would be even more blurry and confusing than the film. Worse, the acting would be poor. The figures would rush through the scene in the haste of violence, without giving you a chance to see what is really going on. The blow that kills Priam would not be visible at all; it would happen so fast that the expression on Hecuba's face would probably be blank. And you would be so distracted by fears for yourself, as well as by the general tumult, that you would not be able to pay attention to Hecuba's situation. The documentary film would be a little better; at least it could focus on Hecuba, and you would not be scared out of your wits, at least not for your own life. But the film would suffer from the flaws of the actual experience—poor acting, bad timing, poor lighting, etc.

We do not know how to watch terrible events in real life. That's because, luckily, we do not get to see very many of them. It's also because we do not have the ability to see the whole thing; we cannot take a god's eye view. Mimesis can allow us to have the experience that a good watcher would have of the fall of Troy—if there were, among humans, a good watcher for such an event.

The closest you could come to being a good watcher for Hecuba's experience would be from a well-staged mimetic performance, either on stage or on film, with the First Player's speech a close second. The art of mimetic theater can bring out the full emotional meaning of this scene for the audience. Moreover, the art of theater could stage Hecuba's scene in a context that would allow us to see it as emblematic of the plight of women in war. To our pity for Hecuba we would then add a sense of outrage at war itself, fury that boys be given swords and not taught when to stop using them, despair that the hatred of one people for another should lead to such scenes.

Powerful mimesis of an action may bring up a stronger and better response than the original action would have done, because mimesis selects for emphasis just those features that would (in real life) give rise to emotions. At the same time, it somehow blocks out those features of the scene that would move us to take action.

This illustrates the selectivity of mimesis. In mimesis, the agent produces certain effects of the original but not others, and may do so more strikingly than the original. In theater, a compelling performance is mimetic of the actions it represents—it does to its audience only part of what the actual events would do. And that part the audience will be able to experience more vividly than they could the whole. A mimetic performance does not try to have every effect the original would have. If it did, it would move beyond mimesis to extreme theater. But that extremity could be too much for us. Mimesis makes us good watchers—as good watchers as we can be for this event.

For the theater crew, selectivity is essential. Part of the job of the theater is to make sure the audience knows it is watching a play, so that no one runs out to call the police or rushes onstage to prevent the murder of Priam. The clues you must give an audience, so that they may be good watchers, are culture-specific.

Sometimes, however, you should not be a watcher at all. Extreme theater, such as lynching, is not mimetic in its main thrust. The young man under the tree is a make-believe criminal in someone else's game;

but the game is truly deadly, and he will die if someone does not save him. You ought to do what you can on his behalf. If you do not stop being a watcher, you will be an accomplice in a crime.

Audience members in mimetic theater are complicit in the mimesis. Audience members know they are watching a mimetic play, and they know how to behave as an audience at this kind of theater. They know, in their complicity, that the action belongs on the stage, separated from them by an indelible but invisible line, and they are not, and cannot, be part of that action.

So far I have treated mimesis mainly as part of the art of making human action worth watching; but it is part of the other twin as well, of the art of finding action worth watching. Good watchers know how to be complicit in mimesis. Mimesis is a bridge between the art of watching and the art of being watched. Good mimesis makes good watchers.

PART TWO

The Art of Watching

Small children are slow to learn the art of watching as it is practiced in formal art theaters. Children learn by doing, and nature has made them too active to be good watchers for the two or three hours required for an art theater performance. Parents like to defeat nature when they are exhausted by the activity of their children. Drugs would do it, but television is cheaper and less toxic: cartoons, videos, films are all used to deactivate children. But this does not make them good watchers.

We rarely practice the art of watching alone. In theater, we do it collectively, laughing together, gasping together, and unconsciously sharing our deepest emotional responses with those around us. In a highly active audience we experience the kind of effervescence that Durkheim observed at religious rituals. Even when you stop to watch construction workers through a slit in a fence, you probably do so because you see others watching also. Watching alone is anomalous in theater. A crucial part of the art, then, is knowing how to be part of a community of watchers—how, in other words, to watch *with*. Communities formed through watching carry on after the time of a piece of theater has been measured out. Football games help students become engaged members of the college community; churches traditionally brought villagers into harmony.

The art of watching is different in different cultures. European-based art cultures discourage active watching and try to keep an audience still and silent in the seats; other traditions and other forms of theater allow for more activity. A football audience in Texas is very active indeed, but they are still an audience that is expert at the art of watching football. The children I know best learned to watch Shakespeare (and to love the plays) while romping on a lawn outside the open walls of the barn at the Winedale Historical Center, where students perform in summertime.

A good watcher pays attention; this is the common thread in all the different cultures of watching. But what it is to pay attention will vary. A good watcher of *Antigone* knows how to respond emotionally to the scenes, with pity and fear and some kind of empathy for each of the main characters. When things go badly, she does not call the police. A good watcher of the house next door—one who frames his neighbors' doings as a kind of theater—would be right to call the police if burglars appear on the scene. A good watcher in the theater of presence knows when to drop the attitude of a spectator and join wholeheartedly in shared activity inside the sacred space.

Emotion in theater belongs to what I will call "spectator emotion," which is distinguished from other kinds of emotion by its inactivity. Emotions generally move those who feel them towards action, but there is little action a spectator can take without becoming a participant. Yet emotion has a large place in the experience of theater, as does empathy, which involves emotion. Understanding theater also involves emotion. And empathy, to complete the circle, includes a kind of understanding. Laughter works differently from emotion as I understand the two, but laughter also has a place in empathy.

The art of watching is as important in life generally as it is in theater. Learning to pay attention to others is basic to living ethically. Mindfulness of others is important, but it is not enough. You could be mindful and still not emotionally engaged; and if you are not emotionally engaged, you will not be moved to take action. Of course, you might do the right thing without being moved to do so, but that is unusual and scarcely human. To live well as human beings, we need to be moved in good ways by emotions that are about others.

And about ourselves. At the summit of the art of watching is audience recognition. For tragedy, part of the art of being watched is staging a scene in which a main character such as Creon sees himself for what he is and takes responsibility for what he has done. A good audience is capable of doing this for themselves—to see themselves for the human beings they are and take responsibility for their part in the ongoing drama of being human. This is so important to us that, more than anything, it justifies my claim for the necessity of theater.

A good watcher knows how to care, and caring involves emotion. So we will begin there, with a fundamental question: Can we, as mere spectators, feel genuine emotions about what we watch?

EIGHT

Emotion

> What's Hecuba to him, or he to Hecuba, that he
> should weep for her?
>
> —Shakespeare, *Hamlet* 2.2, lines 559–60

The actor turns pale; tears come to his eyes and his voice chokes. The audience shift in their seats, uneasy at first over the emotional demands the actor is making of them, but soon they are responding to the anguish in the actor's voice. Eyes are beginning to grow moist. Someone reaches for a handkerchief. A young couple in the second row grasp hands reassuringly. And before long there is, as they say, not a dry eye in the house.

And what is all this about? For whom are they weeping? For Hecuba. Long-dead, far-away, mostly fictional Hecuba, described here as witnessing her husband's death. In other words, for nothing. There is no Hecuba here, no Hecuba ever in the lives of these actors and their compliant audience. And yet, for this moment, all of them seem to care about Hecuba. The First Player is showing his skill, before Hamlet and his friends, with a scene from a play about Dido and Aeneas, in which Aeneas tells of the cruel death of old king Priam and the grief of his queen, Hecuba.

"Oh what a rogue and peasant slave am I!" exclaims Hamlet, ashamed of the weakness of his own reaction to a real outrage, when this actor could, merely "in a fiction, in a dream of passion, force his soul so to his own conceit."

Hamlet cannot force his soul anywhere near a passion over his father's death. And yet he is not dead to emotion. How could he be, when he is furious at himself? Grief rises slow and hard in Hamlet, as in many of us, and he flashes out more easily at himself than at his enemies. He is starved for emotion—not just any emotion, but the emotion that would make him feel like doing what he feels he needs to do now.

Hamlet does not have the emotion that would be in harmony with his life. His father is dead, the murderer is king and sleeps with his mother—but where are his anger and his grief? Somewhere, but not pointed where they should be pointed. Making emotional harmony a habit—having emotion in harmony with the needs of a life—is what the ancients called virtue. Putting emotion in harmony is the main work of a human life.

Putting emotion in harmony is also the business of theater. The art of watching asks an audience to set aside their everyday passions, as far as possible, and call up the feelings that suit the performance. Our actor in this scene from *Dido and Aeneas* is a professional, Hamlet's First Player. He knows how to express grief for Hecuba whether he feels it or not, and he has the trick of inviting the audience to experience consonant feelings as well. But he depends on the skill of his audience; he expects them to have learned how to watch the sort of melodrama he performs. After all, such melodrama is familiar to most people in his time and place. Traveling troupes of players have carried it throughout the realm.

A good audience that is attuned to the Player's style of acting will never be distracted or bored during his performance. They will never respond in the wrong way—never laugh at Hecuba's misery, as they might if they heard the same overwrought speech from a beginner, or if they had no experience of the Player's form of acting. Today's good audience might laugh at yesterday's death scene, but they will not laugh at today's. Successful theater is a collaboration between performers and audience, and the two groups must share—or at least be willing to learn—a culture that allows them to practice the same art from different sides of the line.

8.1 Boredom

Hamlet is bored. He takes no pleasure in his usual amusements. "How weary, stale, flat, and unprofitable / Seem to me all the uses of this world!" Even a visit from his former schoolmates does not raise his spirits. He tells them: "Man delights not me, no nor woman neither..." He does not even know how to find his own life interesting. That is why he contemplates suicide. Worse, perhaps, he does not know how to find Ophelia's life interesting, which is why she really does commit suicide. Hamlet's boredom is deadly.

The radical boredom has been called by other names, "melancholy" being the term of art in Shakespeare's day; "depression," with a different meaning, comes to mind in our own time. Its cause in Hamlet's case is the crisis in which he finds himself. He has erected a monstrous dam to hold in his grief and anger, because he does not have the power to express them. And this dam, with the maelstrom of emotion pent up inside it, prevents him from engaging with people around him. Poor Ophelia.

Hamlet's boredom is radical because it makes all things flat for him, and it keeps threatening to disconnect his mind entirely from the world. Most of us who teach have known about a student who has succumbed to radical boredom. We never actually knew him, because he did not come to class. He did not figure out why he should get out of bed in the morning, why he is in college, even why he is alive at all.

The boredom we have to fear in theater is not so deadly, and most cases of boredom are not so radical. The boredom I actually face in class is merely about my lecture. I may see that a student's eyes have glazed over during my lecture. She is no Hamlet. Far from being flat and stale, the world of her experience is scintillating with delights. Simply, she is fascinated by something else. Her mind is not adrift. Sex is drawing the wind like a full sail; plans for the evening, hopes for friendship, dreams of games and encounters—all these tug at her mind and give it steerage way. She is not uninterested in life, but she is bored by me.

Imagine an audience of people who feel nothing about *Dido and Aeneas*. They do not care what happens; their minds wander to the business of the day (or night), and losing track of the twists and turns of a play's action they are soon taking pleasure in nothing if not their own thoughts. They may fade away in the interval; worse, they may even rise from their seats and exit noisily during act one. They are bored by this play.

Boredom is *at* something; it is what philosophers call intentional. Being bored by *Endgame* is not the same as being bored by the friend who brought you to the play. Nor is it the same as thinking the play a trifle. Indeed, I have thought *Endgame* a work of deep significance and still, at the same time, been bored by a performance of it. Boredom is privative: it is the absence not of thought but of emotional engagement.

The problem I have with this staging of *Endgame* is that I do not care what happens on stage.

Boredom is not caring about something you should be caring about. In theater it is usually a double failure. When that student is bored at my lecture, she blames me for not saying anything worth hearing. Meanwhile, I find her at fault for not knowing how to hear my lecture as the fascinating tour of ideas that it is. But why speak of blame in this case? I have been pleased enough with my own lecture, and I have left her free to enjoy a delicious daydream. We have both tasted pleasures enough for an hour. But not at what we came for. I did not lecture in order to please myself, and she did not come to class in order to daydream. We have both failed.

Boredom is emotional disengagement. The opposite of boredom is emotional engagement, and the short word for that is "caring." Like boredom, caring is intentional; it is about something. My happy student cares about many things, but not about my lecture. Hamlet and my melancholy student (remember the one who never got out of bed?) cannot find anything to care about. When the art of theater succeeds, the watcher knows how to care about *this* performance, and the performer knows how to make *this* performance worth caring about.

"Caring about" can mean several things, so I must be clear. By "I care about Hamlet" I do not mean "I am in love with Hamlet." True, we care about the people we love. We experience our love as emotion when we fear for them in danger, rejoice with them in success, or are angry on their behalf when they are injured. But that is not what I have in mind for theater; you do not need to love the characters in the play you watch, and my student need not love either me or my subject in order to pay attention in class. Quite the reverse; a student with a crush on the teacher may misunderstand the class entirely, and an audience in love with an actress or a character will make poor watchers for the others on stage.

"I care about you" might also mean "I have sympathy for you," but that too goes farther than I wish to go. I might have no sympathy for the villain Iago, but still I care about him in the sense that I want to know what happens to him. I want to make sure he is punished, and I will not be emotionally satisfied until he is. Hatred too is a kind of engagement. I care about Iago.

The art of theater produces an audience that is emotionally engaged with characters who are carable-about. When I care, I stay to see how the play turns out because I want to know. A good performance calls up emotions that will hold me to the plot until its complications are resolved. Simply, I feel like staying till this performance ends, because only then am I free to disengage my emotions from it. If I am forced to leave a closely fought game before the end, I will be on emotional tenterhooks until I hear who won and how they won; then I can arrive at the joy or misery that brings my active engagement with this game to an end.

A good watcher knows how to care.

8.2 Why Care?

We are watching the First Player speak the part of Aeneas, as he tells of Hecuba's shriek of horror at Priam's death, and we see him give way to tears, crying for Hecuba. As a Trojan, Aeneas ought to be close to Hecuba. Engagement with Hecuba is part of his birthright, and it has turned out to be a painful legacy. Hecuba is suffering the worst fate she could imagine: her home pillaged, her husband slaughtered, her grandson thrown from the high city wall, and herself enslaved.

Caring about another person sets you at risk of pain. The people you care about may suffer a fate as horrible as Hecuba's, or they may simply sicken and die. Worse, they may turn out to be vicious; imagine caring about someone who grows up to be a serial killer. If you want to avoid pain, give up caring altogether and you'll be safe. But terribly isolated. To experience a full human life, you must take the risk of caring about other people. Still, why not give up caring about characters in theater or related arts? That would reduce your pain without isolating you from real people.

Not caring about Hecuba would be easy enough for you, who have no connection with her. When confronted with a new character, you make a choice whether to care or not. The road of caring is rough with surprises, taking us through a minefield of potentially painful feelings; the road of not caring is smoother and, literally, more carefree. The art of theater points us down the rougher road. So why should we take it? Why care about Hecuba?

If Hecuba were my cousin or my dinner companion, she would more easily command my sympathy. But as it is, she is not here at all; she is long dead and at least partly fictional. Mimetic theater calls us to care about people represented on stage, but my question about caring is not specific to mimesis. Why care about the quarterback in the big game? He is nothing to me, except insofar as he is playing this role in the defeat of our hated rival. Or suppose I am attending a wedding, bearing witness as a dewy young couple exchange their vows. Why should I care about them?

If you don't care, you won't watch, and if no one watches, none of us will have theater at all. Generally, you have to care about one or more of the main characters in order to watch a play attentively. If I am staging a play for you about Hecuba, I want you to care enough about *her* to stay through to the end. What happens when no one in the audience cares about Hecuba? The play fails, as plays fail all too often. So the art of theater must help the audience see why they should care about Hecuba.

We can give a number of general reasons for caring. It is good for us to be able to care about other people; our lives will be richer for caring, and more praiseworthy. In theater, the emotions that arise from caring may be therapeutic: laughter is often said to be medicinal, and the painful emotions of pity and fear may lead to a healthy catharsis. Perhaps having appropriate feelings in theater is good practice for real life, so that people who are good at watching are also good at living.

General reasons for caring, however, are useless in life or in theater unless they are brought home to you in your current situation. You need a reason why you, in particular, should care about Hecuba right now, while watching this performance. If the play is well done, it should give you the reasons you need, and if you are a good watcher, you should find those reasons sufficient. I am not supposing that you work through a conscious process of reasoning; in the usual case you do not. Caring is about where you peg your feelings, not about premises and conclusions. But it is something you do, not something that happens to you. Caring is to your credit, because it reflects the way your mind works.

Caring about Hecuba carries a price for us; we will suffer, to some extent, along with her. So we have a number of ways of protecting ourselves against caring—of watching in ways that make no emotional demands on us. Consider what I call the "technical dodge." Perhaps you are interested in how the art is practiced by those who perform, and you watch *Dido and Aeneas* to see how it is performed. You observe that certain scenes have emotion-engaging properties: this one is sad, that one triumphant, the other frightening. You can recognize these properties without allowing your feelings to be engaged. In fact, if your feelings are engaged, you probably will not be detached enough to recognize those properties. In that case, at most, you will be interested in techniques of staging, and once you have assessed them you will have no reason to see how the play ends, and you can happily make an early exit. But good watchers at a good performance would hate to leave before the play ends. That is why good watchers care about more than technique; in Hamlet's chosen scene from *Dido and Aeneas*, they care about Hecuba.

Then there is the personal way of dodging engagement in theater. Suppose you stay to the final curtain only because you are taken with the actress playing Dido, your former student, and your attention is fixed on her (rather than on the character she plays); then you will not be a good watcher of the play, though you will not be bored. The emotion you bring to this performance aims outside the theater space, and so it is not what is wanted from a good watcher. Good watchers of mimetic theater know how to be complicit in mimesis. If you are being a good watcher, you play in your mind the game of thinking that this woman you are watching is Dido, rather than your former student.

Or suppose Hecuba reminds you of your mother, who is elderly now, and who has seen the cruel death of her husband. Thinking about your mother, you resolve to send her a postcard tomorrow and immediately you feel better. Again, you have felt a genuine emotion while watching the play, but it is a feeling that leads outside the play, and in this case takes your mind off the stage altogether. Good watchers put their mothers out of their minds during the time marked off for the play.

A strong example of the personal way of dodging engagement with theater is the response of King Claudius. Remember the play Hamlet sets like a trap to catch the conscience of the king? Stung by the opening of *The Murder of Gonzago*, King Claudius rises, calls for lights, douses the performance, and goes off to pray. You may want your life to be affected by the play about Hecuba as deeply as *The Murder of Gonzago* affected Claudius, but you surely do not want to stop the play in mid-course. Claudius would be the audience from hell, far worse than an audience that is merely bored. Good watchers do recognize themselves in the play, but not the way Claudius does. Good watchers watch the play to the end, and they pay primary attention, the whole time, to what is on stage.

The third way of dodging engagement is laughter. Suppose you find Hecuba's suffering grotesque and burst out laughing. The play is ruined. Laughter usually banishes care, as we all know; and this is one reason comedy is harder to sustain than drama. Generally, if you care about Hecuba, you will not laugh at her fate. Good watchers, attuned to the style of this play, know when to laugh and when to cry. We may find caring ways to laugh, so laughter does not always dodge engagement. But it often does.

There are many other dodges that bad watchers may use. Generally, a play fails when the watchers do not engage emotionally with the characters and action of the play itself. The best watchers may carry into the theater real emotions directed at real people, and these may be tangled in the web of their experience of a particular performance, but they still pay attention to the performance. Good watchers are alert to the reasons for caring that are furnished by each performance, and these reasons give the unique answer to the question why we should care about this performance.

"Reasons for caring" may strike you as an odd expression. Caring is like love; both are about emotions, and both set us up for having emotions that are connected to certain people. Many thinkers say that emotions just happen to us; we can't give reasons for having emotions, these critics might say, any more than we can give reasons for being in love.

We can give reasons for being in love, however, though these probably do not tell the whole story: She's beautiful, she's brilliant, she knows how to laugh or tell a joke, she makes me feel wonderful, and, most important, she loves me back. And we can give reasons for caring about action in theater. Suppose your friend whispers in your ear, "This is boring. Let's go get a beer." You could give him reasons to stay. One set of reasons would look like this: "But the lead actor is my daughter; she'll think I hate her if I leave early," or "But this football team represents my school; I have a duty to support them to the bitter end." These are external reasons, because they depend on relationships I had before joining the audience of either performance.

Contrast these with internal reasons. Suppose you have no tie to either team, but you are won over by the heroic efforts of the underdogs: "These guys have been playing their hearts out, and now they are only seven points down, with five minutes remaining in the last quarter; they could still pull it out. We have to stay to see how it ends." That reason depends on a stake in the game that I developed because of what happened in the game, which has chanced to have an excellent plot.

Many reasons are mixed, combining internal with external factors, as when you stay to the end of the game both because it is a good game (internal) and because you are partial to one of the teams (external).

External reasons are worst for theater. I pay attention, all right, when my daughter is playing Hamlet. But this way of holding my attention is not theatrical. For one thing, I would pay attention to my lovely daughter whatever she might be doing. It needn't be *Hamlet*. For another, this reason is unique to me; no one else besides me cares about this performance because he has a daughter who is playing Hamlet. But the art of theater seeks to make action worth watching for its whole audience, not merely for one person. That is why good theater is part of the glue of community. When a number of people find reason to pay attention to the same thing in theater, they are learning to care about the same thing. They are not merely individuals, each present in the same space for a different reason. They are a community, and they are together in their caring.

Beauty is a reason for watching, but not for caring. At the ballet, no child of mine is dancing; there is no contest between my team and theirs, and very little suspense. I am not waiting to see if two males collide while leaping. But the dancing is so beautiful that I cannot bear to see it end. Beauty is internal to this ballet, but it is not unique to theater. Beauty in a sunset can hold me as tightly in its grip as that beauty in dance. Now I watch the color spread across the sky, rippling through high trails of clouds and fading from salmon pink to amethyst and then to pearly grey. This too I cannot bear to leave before it is over, but it is not theater.

Other internal reasons for staying to watch are intelligence and humor: I watch in the hope of gaining wisdom or in the delight of my own laughter. These too may be found outside theater—beauty in any lovely face, humor in a written text or cartoon, wisdom in a philosophical treatise. More confusing, they may be found in members of the audience next to me—in the face of my beautiful date, in a joke she cracks about the show, or in a brilliant comment she makes to me in a whisper. But these are all distractions. They are not reasons to care about theater.

Theatrical reasons for watching a performance to the end belong mainly to plot and characterization, and these are almost always reasons for caring. We care about characters when they themselves have something to care about. Hamlet will come to care passionately about the wrongs done to his father, and his caring draws us in. Caring about Hamlet, as he cares about his father, may be make-believe for us, but it is real enough to count as practice for caring in real life.

Mother-hating Electra invariably engages an audience. Even when we are horrified by the depth of her anger, we are engaged on her behalf.

She is not the only character in Sophocles' play whom we care about; when Clytemnestra hears of her son's death and reacts with a mixture of pain, relief, and joy, then we are engaged on her behalf as well.

We are hooked by O'Neill's *Long Day's Journey into Night* from the first scene, when we see how closely James Tyrone is watching his wife Mary. He fears she is taking opium again behind his back. He is a drunken skinflint who has poisoned the life of his elder son and has made a foul start on the second. But we hardly remember to breathe while we watch the tormented Tyrones on their journey in the fog to a few shreds of drug- or drink-induced honesty. Why do we care about this miserable family? Because they care about each other, because they love each other. Even though they love each other to death, we cannot watch them unmoved.

Good plots are reasons for watching theater even when we don't care about the characters. A plot can keep us caring about events, by stringing our emotions onto what happens next, as the plot works steadily through complication toward resolution. Some plots keep us in suspense, like the cliffhanger football game, but some plots do not, like those of *Oedipus Tyrannus* or *Hamlet*. We know the endings of those plays already, but we still long for resolution, and we can't bear to leave until the play has given us the promised release. Musical works often have such a plot. We are not staying to see whether the violins outplay the violas, as we might if this were a contest; we are staying to hear the musical complexities of this piece march through one gorgeous complication after another to the final cadence.

If we did not care, we would have no emotional bond to be released by the end of the performance. So theater depends on watching, watching depends on caring, and caring depends on emotion. Yet some thinkers have believed that no true emotion could be had in theater, while others have argued that, although it can be had, it should be kept at bay. Both groups are wrong. To see why, we need to frame a general account of emotion.

8.3 Engaging Emotions

When I hear martial music, I am excited. Is that excitement an emotion? When I hear something like gunfire, I am startled, although I do not know what caused the noise or where it is coming from. Is that startle response an emotion? Once, during what may have been a night attack (but luckily wasn't) I remember being terrified without having any idea what the threat was. The symptoms of this terror were a surge of adrenaline that shut down my mind and froze me to the spot. Were these physiological symptoms an emotion?

If you answer any of these questions "yes," I have no quarrel with you; the word "emotion" has been used in those ways. Besides, all of these stories feature feelings of one sort or another, and everyone agrees that emotions are feelings. But not all feelings are active enough to engage us with other people; caring has to be about someone, and the emotions that go with caring for someone must also be about that someone. So we need to define of emotion that way—as a kind of feeling with a lot of aboutness in it.

If you prefer, you may call this only one *kind* of emotion, but remember that I have selected this kind because it is what the art of theater must aim to produce—emotion that is engaging, that makes us want to watch something in particular. Of course, theater may play on our moods or on other feelings that are not about anything in particular, but theater does not have to do this. What it does have to do is to make us care. Emotions that are truly engaging satisfy four requirements.

First, an emotion is a feeling that someone consciously has, so for every occurrence of an emotion there is a subject who feels it—the subjectivity requirement. Emotion shares this feature with every kind of feeling. But the second requirement—action—marks off the emotions we are interested in from everything else. An emotion must move its subject toward at least one specific action—that is, it should make the person who feels the emotion also feel like doing something. Fear, for example, makes you feel like running away from something; shame, like vanishing from the spot so that someone will not see you; disgust, like being sick; pity, like giving comfort; regret, like reliving and repairing your life; grief, like weeping.

The action you feel like taking, when you have an emotion, does not have to be doable. In fear, I feel like running away even when I am trapped. In regret, I feel like reliving and repairing an episode in my life, even though I know that time is irreversible. In anger, during a game I am watching, I may feel like running out on the field and hobbling the enemy quarterback. But I know this is forbidden.

Although it need not be doable, the action you feel like taking needs to be specific. In a full-fledged case of fear, I feel like running away from that particular lion who is advancing toward me, looking as if she has just caught sight of a long-deferred luncheon. Fear tells me what to run away from. Panic might make me lose control of myself and run into the lion's jaws, but panic is not fear; indeed, it is not an emotion at all in my restricted sense. That is because losing control of yourself is not an action, and emotion (as I understand it, following a long line of thinkers) is a feeling that moves us to actions.

Third, the action requirement entails that emotions be connected with objects of which we are aware. This is the intentionality requirement. In this case the object is the lion; that is what you fear and feel like running away from. But panic has no object; that is why we often call it blind. Because actions must be connected to objects in the world, emotions must be connected to such objects as well. Here is the lion that has put fear into me, and she is the lion I feel like escaping. If the lion threatens my child, then my fear has two objects—the lion, which I fear, and the child, for whom I fear, and whom I feel like rescuing. This second object seems to vanish in the usual case in which I am afraid only for myself, but we need to keep the possibility of a second object in mind, especially for the emotions involved in loving or caring. The first object is what the emotion is directed at, the second is what (or whom) the emotion is about. So emotions pick out objects, and their ability to do so is called "intentionality" by philosophers.

Generally, caring about someone is having a disposition to feel emotions that take her as second object. Love is one kind of caring; hate is another. Loving Mollie is having a disposition to feel certain emotions that have Mollie as their second object. When Mollie does well, I rejoice at her success, and my joy is about her, on her behalf; when she is in danger from a lion, I fear the lion, and the fear is about her, on her behalf. Hating Mollie leads to emotions that are about Mollie also, but not, I would say, on her behalf. If I hate Mollie and I see her fall in a mud puddle, I rejoice, and my joy is about her. Suppose, however, that I care only about myself; in that case I would always be the second object, and all my emotions would be about me. I would rejoice at Mollie's success or failure only insofar as I felt that these affected me.

The possibility of caring for others supports the possibility of altruism; if caring for others is impossible, then so is altruism. Emotion in theater is parallel to altruism: it also depends on the possibility of caring for others. If Mollie is a character in a play, she is nothing to me except insofar as I care for her, and if I don't care about anyone but myself, I won't care about anyone on stage. Good watchers in theater are practicing the emotional skill that makes altruism possible.

A standard occurrence of an emotion, then, is a feeling for which you are able to specify four things:

1. Who has it?   Subjectivity requirement
2. Towards what action?   Action requirement
3. What is it directed at? Intentionality requirement (1)
4. About whom?   Intentionality requirement (2)

On my definition, emotion carries a kind of knowledge about the world. My emotion cannot pick out objects of which I am ignorant. Intentionality implies awareness and judgment. If I feel fear as an emotion, I am aware of this THIS LION, and I believe that she is the thing that is making me shake and want to run. The same fear carries a judgment: "This lion is DANGEROUS to me." (That judgment could be wrong; that is why we are able to speak of "false fears.")

8.4 From Tonal Sympathy to Caring

Feelings we pick up from music or from other people without knowing what is going on belong to what I call "tonal sympathy." Tonal feelings are the kind that may be due to music or to general features of a situation. They have no objects, and therefore they may satisfy only the first requirement, subjectivity. Think of the feelings we pick up from other people directly, in the way that one cello's C string vibrates with another's. Tonal sympathy feels a lot like emotion, but it is missing the cognitive features of emotion, and for this reason it either frustrates us or invites us to supply objects for them, so that we may experience complete emotions.

Coming home from work I open the door on a scene of immediate tension. The one-year-old is loud, fussy, and agitated—and so is her mother. One breath of the disturbed air in our house, and I too am agitated. I have no idea why the baby is feeling this way, but I find myself with similar feelings. Other people's babies merely annoy me when they are fussy; I cannot say why this one's feelings affect me so deeply. The world has gone out of joint for me because it has gone out of joint for her. But I have not picked up an emotion from the baby: there is nothing at which I am angry or of which I am afraid. For all I know the baby has true emotions, but she is unable to share them with me.

To be technical: my feeling fails to satisfy the first intentionality requirement, and therefore it fails to satisfy the action requirement. Because I don't understand my daughter's feelings, I have no idea what to do. I am frustrated because, like Hamlet, I cannot act on the feelings I have—in my case, feelings I have picked up from the baby—in Hamlet's case, the anger he has picked up from a ghost of unproven reliability. My caring is incomplete because it lacks the knowledge that emotions carry with them, and because, therefore, it cannot lead to action. Hamlet knows more than I do about his situation, but not enough to act. He knows he is angry at the guilty person, but he is not sure that his uncle is guilty, so the judgment part of his emotion is blocked by ignorance. I am blocked at a lower level, because I am completely ignorant of the cause of the baby's distress.

In our ignorance, Hamlet and I have strong feelings, all right, but in our ignorance we don't find anything we feel like doing in response to these feelings. Without action, what would be the use of caring? Without at least an inclination to act, Hamlet and I are deprived of full-scale emotion. What we feel, therefore, is not really caring, though we would like it to be. That is why Hamlet-type situations are so frustrating. And so, to the agitation I pick up from the baby, I add my own frustration at being unable to act. Worse, I have been stymied in my attempt to care.

There is another person in the house, however, the baby's mother, and I love her to distraction also. She has feelings too, but I am not picking them up as emotions. She feels responsibility for the happiness of her child and she is simmering with anger at herself for not being able to help the child, an anger that flashes out at me. Anger, like lightning, frequently shrivels objects adjacent to its main target. "What has either of us done to cause this particular mess?" I ask myself. "It is no use her being angry at me." But now I too am angry, at her, and so I have at last achieved a genuine emotion. It is an emotion very like hers—it is, after all, anger. It is, in fact, more like her anger than I realize at the time, since she and I are angry at the same person—her. But although I share her emotion, I am not at this moment caring about her.

What is missing in all of these cases is knowledge: I do not know why the baby is fussy, and I do not know how my wife feels about this;

in particular, I do not realize that the object of her anger is herself. Caring about her can only happen when I learn what is going on with her—in this case, I need to learn the objects of her emotions. Fast forward eighteen years. The baby is now a freshman at a fine university, one that challenges bright students with tough courses. The young woman, my wonderful daughter, is on the phone with me. She is tense and agitated. So, naturally, am I, at hearing the tremor in her voice. But this time she can tell me why: her English professor has given her a C on a paper (the first C in her life) without any indication what is wrong or how to improve. My daughter is upset with herself, angry at the professor, and afraid for the future. I, hearing this, and knowing what I know, am not in the least upset with her or angry at her professor. I know that high school graduates will flounder at first in a college-level writing class, and I know that students never think their writing teachers have explained how to write an A paper. I know, what she does not, that she has the ability to be an A student at this place. Still, I do not know how she will be affected by this disappointment; and I have known students in her situation go into irrevocable tailspins. So I am afraid for her future, as she is, although my fear is different from hers, and although the action I am moved to take—reassurance and helpful questioning—is not the same as the actions to which her emotions lead her.

Now this begins to look like caring. I know enough, and I am close enough to my daughter, that I feel for her a true emotion, one that meets all four conditions: (1) It is mine and not hers, and (2) it moves me to action. (3) There is something I feel like warding off—her meltdown—and (4) there is someone on whose behalf I have this feeling: her. Also, I have the knowledge I need for my emotions to have these objects. The differences between my daughter's knowledge and mine preclude my simply sharing her emotions; nevertheless I am heedful of most of her feelings in the case, share some of them, and am moved to take appropriate action. That is caring in practice, a disposition to emotion that is now active.

Caring for my daughter is easy. I do it every day. But caring about Hecuba is more difficult, even if I am persuaded that I ought to care about her. Because Hecuba is a character in a play, I can't know much about her, and because she and I are divided by sacred space I cannot take any action that would affect her. So my attempt to care about her will be defeated, apparently, by failures to satisfy knowledge and action requirements.

8.5 The Knowledge Problem

There is not much truth in fiction and precious little we can do about what happens in fiction. So it appears that fiction defeats emotion because fiction cannot satisfy the action and knowledge requirements. When the content of theater is fictional, (on this view) we would not be able to have emotions about it, and so we could not possibly care.

Noël Carroll has put it this way:

1. We are genuinely moved by fictions [in theater].
2. We know that [what moves us by fiction in theater] is not actual.
3. We are genuinely moved only by what we believe to be actual.

And knowledge implies belief. If you know the event is not actual, you can't believe that it is. The problem looks clear enough: To solve it we have to deny one of those three points. Some say that we are not genuinely moved in theater, others that we believe, for a time, that the stage world is actual, and Carroll wants to say that we can be moved without believing that what moves us is actual. This formulation of the problem leaves me dissatisfied, however, because I do not know what any of it means. The word "moved" could apply to a wide range of feelings aside from emotion; "actual" is true of much of what is staged even in mimetic theater (the chorus in *Antigone* are actually praying), and "believe" could cover a range of commitments, including make-believe. We could defuse the bomb of Carroll's problem by specifying the meaning of any one of these terms.

My solution would be to deny sentence 3 as stated: we may be genuinely moved by what we believe, *in the sense of make-believe*, to be actual. Nothing in my definition of emotion requires that the objects be outside all worlds of make-believe. Much of our emotional life is animated by emotions with objects that are not real. Indeed, Macbeth is genuinely frightened by his vision of Banquo's ghost, and the ghost could be a creature of his imagination.

To solve the knowledge problem along with Carroll's puzzle, I need to show that we can have knowledge about objects that belong to make-believe, and this knowledge must be comparable to the knowledge I have about my daughter and her college education. I must know about the fictional Hecuba in her fictional context—a context that stretches beyond what is explicit in the play. I need to know something about Trojan family life and about the customs of victorious Greek armies, if I am to know what defeat and the death of her husband mean to Hecuba. We know such things about many plays we watch, as most playgoers will agree, so I will not tackle the philosophical problem here, but I am confident that this is not a serious difficulty.

The best alternative solution to the knowledge problem is to deny that genuine emotions occur in theater at all. This solution is due to Kendall Walton, whose book, *Mimesis as Make-Believe*, became an instant classic in its field. He would deny sentence 1, holding that the actions of a play are make-believe and so are the emotions directed at them. Think of a child who runs away giggling when her father pretends to be a wolf. Her fear is make-believe, and so is ours (Walton believes) when we are frightened by events on the stage of a theater.

Walton's concept of make-believe does solve the problem for the theater of make-believe. But not all theater works through make-believe. Some people in a ritual do believe in the presence of the god, for example, and the art of theater sometimes aims at that kind of presence and that kind of belief.

Suppose you are staging the play about Hecuba. Do you want me, the audience, to make believe that I care about her? Perhaps that make-believe caring will be enough to keep me glued to my chair, in shocked suspense, waiting eagerly for the denouement. Certainly, make-believe is sufficient for the child in the game of wolf; she cares about her daddy, and this game is one of the ways father and child act out their love for one another. Their love for each other—not make-believe—grounds the caring that keeps her and him in the game together. But there is rarely anything like that love in the theater; usually the actors are strangers to us. Good watchers of a play do not make believe that they are paying attention to the play; they really do pay attention. The less make-believe they have in their caring, the more real their attention will be.

Caring about Hecuba is not child's play; it has moral significance, and it is a kind of caring that we find outside theater. The characters in a play—the persons with whom we are expected to share feelings—are always in conflict with one another and sometimes are felt even to be in conflict with us. The original for Hamlet's Hecuba comes from a deeply moving play, Euripides' *Trojan Women*, which summoned its audience's feelings on behalf of a woman who was felt to belong to actual history. Hecuba was not nothing to the Greeks; she was queen of the city against which the Greeks had waged their most famous war. She represents the human side of the great enemy. Caring for the enemy in defeat is one of the moral triumphs of ancient Greek culture.

8.6 The Action Problem

A deeper problem lurks behind the one about knowledge. Knowledge seems to be a problem only for fiction, but, as we have seen, theater is not always fictional, and even nonmimetic theater poses a problem about action. How can you have genuine emotions about a football game, when there is nothing you can do about the way the game is going, apart from expressing your feelings with cheers or groans? Let us state the problem this way:

1. We have genuine emotions at what is presented in theater.
2. We are not moved to action by what is presented in theater.
3. We have genuine emotions only when our feelings move us to action.

Sentence 1 reports what I take to be a fact in need of explanation. Sentence 2 seems to be true in what we might call normal theatrical conditions. But we need to qualify it. What I see on stage might make me feel like leaving the theater; it might also make me feel like being sick; it might even make me feel like stopping the action altogether for the safety of the actors. These actions would all occur offstage, outside the sacred space of theater.

But I cannot be moved to take part in the action that is presented on stage. I do not run onto the field to hobble the enemy quarterback, and I do not leap to the stage, sword in hand, to save Hecuba's husband from the bloody boy who is poised to cut him down. But I feel like doing those things. The problem is to understand how emotion can make me feel like doing something which I will never do (and, as we will see, which I cannot do). If I am in the grip of real emotions, why do I stay in my seat?

The problem has nothing to do with fiction or mimesis. It is as real a problem for the football game as it is for the play we are imagining about Hecuba. In either case, if I were actually moved to take action, several things would have gone terribly wrong. For one thing, I would have interrupted the performance, perhaps forever. For another, I would have shown that I am not a good watcher for this event, because I do not know the rules of watching. I will have violated the sacred and inviolable space of theater. More precisely, it is no longer sacred once I have crossed into it, and so I have erased the line that formerly marked this space. And without its own inviolable space, this is not a performance at all.

Suppose that I am outraged by the failure of the defense on our football team, and I resolve on the next play to try to sack the enemy quarterback myself. I plunge onto the field and rush toward a player named Matt Leinart, who has been playing quarterback for the enemy team. But at the moment I cross the line, the game is interrupted, and Matt Leinart is no longer playing quarterback in the game. There is no game. The game is defined in such a way that I can take no part in it; at most I could sack Mr. Leinart, but outside the game it is pointless to sack the young man. He would now be simply an athlete attacked by a fan.

The same goes for Hecuba and her husband's assailant. There is an actor playing the killer, and I could block that young actor, but the moment I cross onto the stage he is no longer playing that part because there is no longer a play for him to be playing a part in. He is simply an actor obstructed in playing his role. The play has been interrupted, at least in the normal course of theatrical events.

For a watcher to be engaged in the action shown in theater is a conceptual impossibility. So how can I be engaged emotionally when I cannot possibly be engaged actively? This problem is not unique to theater. Grief and regret almost always make me feel like doing the impossible. I cannot change the past. Fear and anger often make me feel like doing things I cannot do in the circumstances. The bully is too big; I cannot fight him. The precipice is too close; I cannot leap aside from the snake.

The supposed problem evaporates when we realize that emotions merely make you feel like taking action. They need not also make you actually take those actions. The third sentence is false as stated. The spectator attitude recognizes sacred space; that is what makes it a spectator attitude. As a watcher, you feel that you would break a spell if you engaged in what you are watching, and in most cases you are right.

Real life, however, calls us to know when to take a spectator attitude. When an old man is attacked by muggers, people who are watching from a nearby street corner may well take a spectator attitude. But they are wrong to do so. There is no spell here to break; there is only an old man who needs help. It is a kind of idolatry to treat the mugger's street corner as sacred space. It is entirely profane, and the street between us is not a boundary. Good watchers know what lines to cross and when to cross them.

8.7 Feeling for Hecuba

A blood-smeared boy stalks refugees across the stage; his sword, held low, is quick, stabbing, efficient. A woman crouches in the shadows, lank white hair tangled over her wrinkled breasts, spider lines on her face scrunched in horror. She reaches up, catches the old man by his tunic and tries to pull him back beside her. He is standing, straining to pull his bent back into a straight line. The arm he puts out to protect her is trembling; folds of skin wobble on brittle bones. His eyes are sharp, glaring at the boy. Again Hecuba tries to pull Priam down, opens her mouth in a wordless entreaty, and the red blood sprays her face. The boy moves on down the line. Other women shriek, but Hecuba's mouth is still open, silent.

And you in the audience, your comfortable dinner half digested, shifting your fanny in its soft seat, what do you care about Hecuba? Pity for the old woman? Fear for her future? Horror at the implacable boy with the sword? Outrage at this terrible war? Yes, all of that, if the scene is well played. Your feelings for Hecuba are real; they have kept you glued to your seat, they brought you back after the interval to see what would happen to her. They will keep you there until the play achieves some sort of resolution (unless the curtain falls first).

You are the one who has those feelings, and they are genuine emotions. They have objects—the boy with the sword, whom you fear, and Hecuba, on whose behalf you feel the fear—and they make you feel that some action must be taken: the boy punished, Hecuba comforted. But you also feel that these actions are not yours to take; they belong to the stage, and you do not. Indeed, you cannot. You wait and watch, hoping that someone else will do what you feel must be done. The emotion is intense, as intense as anything you might feel outside the theater. But it is fairly short-lived; it may not outlast the measured time of the performance. You are feeling this for Hecuba, for Hecuba who is nothing apart from the play-world of this stage, and nothing to your active life, though she may haunt you afterward in your dreams. But now, while your mind is on the stage, she is everything to you.

NINE

Empathy

My wife and I are watching Alice as she makes her wedding vow to Charles. She is radiant, proud of her bride's beauty, and full of joy, though shadows of apprehension cross her face and her eyes brim with tears. Charles is radiant too, proud of himself and of his bride. No tears show on his face, but he too is lit with joy and shadowed by fears. My wife and I feel for them both; we remember our own wedding, and so we feel for ourselves as well. Our hands meet and we squeeze to share the thought, "I remember. This is how it was. This is how it is. I wish them the best, I wish us the best. And for all who take such vows, I wish the best, and we all wish this together."

The wedding room is steaming with empathy. The watchers feel empathy for the principals and for each other, while the principals feel empathy for each other. Weddings are so much part of our common experience that we cannot escape empathy while watching one. Few of us know enough to feel much empathy with a sacked quarterback, but all of us know, or think we know, enough to feel empathy for a bride or a groom.

Good watchers pay attention because they are emotionally engaged with what they are watching, and the best kind of emotional engagement is a form of empathy that involves understanding.

9.1 Defining Empathy

The word "empathy" was brought into English to do a precise task, but this task was soon forgotten, and contemporary usage treats the word as a rough synonym for "sympathy," although some language experts try to distinguish them.

In its original use, "empathy" referred to a process by which properties related to the emotions of an observer are assigned to an inanimate work of art. Looking at a dark landscape, you "feel into" it the melancholy you would feel if you were a mountain on such a dark and stormy day, and you say the landscape is brooding and melancholy. But neither the mountain nor the painting of it is really either of those things. Mountains don't brood.

The same process can be applied to human objects. To see why Napoleon invaded Russia, you identify with Napoleon; that is, you imagine that you are going through what he did; and so you try to learn his motivation through a kind of make-believe. The result is an enhanced historical understanding.

In both of these uses, the subject of empathy assigns emotions (or emotional properties) to an external object—a person or a landscape. These are emotions she supposes she would have on identifying herself with that object. Strictly speaking, the emotion does not belong to either the subject or the object. Instead, the emotion in question belongs to the subject's make-believe.

Suppose, for contrast, that I arrive at a gallery deeply mired in melancholy, and I project my melancholy onto every painting I see. That is not empathy, but projection. The feeling is mine, and I am somehow projecting it onto the paintings. In empathy, however, I am not simply laying my own feelings on the paintings. I am putting myself into the painting, through an act of imagination or make-believe, and observing my emotions under those special conditions. When I assign these to the painting, that is empathy in the original usage. And similarly for Napoleon.

The more common usage of the word these days is for something like sympathy. We say we have empathy when we feel the emotions of another person as directly as if we were that person. (I will try to make this notion more precise in a moment.) If my sad story brings a tear to your eye, we compliment you on your empathy. An older generation of philosophers would have called this "sympathy," but recent usage tends to use "sympathy" for a more calculated response: I hear your sad news, I understand it, and I am moved through that understanding. This is the sympathy we express to the bereaved. In expressing sympathy, we make no claim to feel what they feel, just to know what they feel, and to care about it. Sometimes, by "sympathy," we mean a specific emotion that we express in sympathy cards and at funeral homes.

In theater, empathy occurs when a spectator feels what he supposes the hero feels, owing to some sort of fusion in the spectator's mind between him and the hero. The German playwright Bertolt Brecht complained that empathy in theater would block the kind of critical thinking he wanted his plays to provoke, and so he aimed at a theater without empathy.

If I am right in the previous chapter, however, the art of watching calls for emotional engagement on the part of the audience. Brecht's goal would be impossible, then, if it includes making the theater a zone free of emotions. That would be an absurd goal; Brecht should have no reason to drive emotion out of theater. True, certain kinds of emotion defeat critical thought, but emotion as such does not. And the most powerful sorts of understanding involve emotion, as we shall see.

9.2 Brecht's Complaint

When Plato criticized theater, one of his complaints concerned the effect of theater on the emotions; he feared that theater had an effect on the emotional faculties of an audience that would undermine moral education. This complaint was revived by Rousseau, who was convinced that effective comedy must depend on, and foster, vicious dispositions of the human heart. Both of these thinkers held that there was just one way for a play to affect an audience, and it was bad. Brecht thought there were two ways, and the bad one was the one for which he did not write.

Actually, as we will see, there are many more than two ways for theater to engage the emotions. Different kinds of theater aim at different kinds of engagement, and this provides a useful classification scheme for theater. Complaints that theater inhibits critical thinking or moral learning may be justified against some kinds of theater but not against others. This result alone would make it worthwhile to mark off the kinds of theater; such an analysis would be useful as well for explaining the history of theater.

Different approaches to theater seek to engage the emotions of an audience differently. The same emotion can be engaged in different ways. Suppose an audience is moved by fear for the hero's life; this fear may affect them more or less directly, depending on their relationship to the hero. A primitive model for what I have in mind is the distinction Brecht made between what he called dramatic (or Aristotelian) theater, which works through empathy and identification, and epic (or Brechtian) theater, which does not. I propose to root out the basis of this distinction, expand it into an analysis of the whole range of possibilities, and apply it broadly to classifying the kinds of theater.

Brecht's distinction

Brecht was trying to say what was innovative in his own plays. While earlier theater (he thought) presented characters that were matter for empathy, Brecht's epic theater was supposed to distance its audience to the point at which empathy was impossible, so that, freed from emotional engagement, they could think critically about what they saw. By "empathy" Brecht evidently had in mind an emotional state incompatible with understanding. Brecht thought that an empathic spectator could not take a critical attitude toward a character or the character's situation because he—the empathic spectator—would feel on his own behalf what he supposed the character to feel.

> The dramatic theater's spectator says: Yes, I have felt like that too—Just like me—It's only natural—It'll never change—The sufferings of this man appall me, because they are inescapable—That's great art; it all seems the most obvious thing in the world—I weep when they weep, I laugh when they laugh.

> The epic theater's spectator says: I laugh when they weep, I weep when they laugh.

To avoid empathy, Brecht employed his famous distancing effects; more to the point, he went out of his way to make his protagonists unappealing. The most famous example is his revision of *Mutter Courage und ihre Kinder*. During the world premiere at Zurich in 1941, audience and critics were moved by Courage's maternal strength and courage. This was not the effect Brecht had planned. Therefore, for later productions, he rewrote crucial scenes so as to make Courage less motherly and less an object for empathy. In the first version Mother Courage was at times distracted by other people's needs (a sick sergeant in scene 1, a horde of wounded civilians in scene 5); but in the later Berlin versions she is moved to action only by greed, which is now her salient characteristic. In later versions she does not show her maternal side till after the loss of her last child (scene 12). Her greed distracts her from keeping a watchful eye on her children, and so at the end she has lost all of them, in different ways, to the war. Never mind that her greed would be necessary to save her children (if she could save them at all in her situation); her greed is not an attractive emotion, and it is meant not to be shared but to be outrageous. Brecht's point is that she cannot be anything but outrageous in the situation he depicts.

Brecht intended his plays to provoke and not to obstruct critical thought. He wanted his audience to be free to choose their attitude toward what they see. Aristotelian theater would not leave them free, he thought, but would disarm their critical faculties by infecting them with empathy. Aristotelian theater makes you accept what you see as inevitable, as due to the working of a tragic machine. Acceptance comes with the appropriate feelings of pity and fear.

In Brecht's ideal theater the audience would be free to think that situations like those presented on stage are not inevitable—that they can and should be prevented. In place of pity and fear, Brecht's audience should feel outrage, anger, and an urgent desire to change society for the better.

On its face, Brecht's concept of epic theater is bad theory and worse theater. But Brecht's theater can be electrifying, and his theory, which counts Plato among its ancestors, is worth careful consideration. Especially in this book. My long rumination on the art of theater began with puzzling about Brecht. Empathy seems central to the practice of theater, even Brecht's theater. How could he have taken against it so strongly? Obviously, Brecht did not go wrong in practice; in theory he seems to have erred, but I will show that his theory is vague enough that we can save it by clarification.

Saving Brecht's theory

The theory is bad because it is fuzzy about what it counts as empathy. Although he tries to treat empathy as a single concept, Brecht uses the word to cover a host of different things he wishes to banish from his theater: carrying the audience away emotionally, drawing them together into a collective entity, inducing them to share feelings with a character, or calling them to identify with a hero. These are not the same thing. I can be carried away emotionally without feeling anything like empathy; I can share your feelings without identifying with you; indeed, I can identify with you and not share your feelings. Brecht either has one thing in mind imperfectly described, or he groups many things loosely under one concept. Either way, he is sloppy about what empathy is.

His account of empathy might mislead a careless reader into thinking that Brecht sought to avoid emotional response altogether in favor of a cool, calculated understanding. But Brecht does want an emotional response, and a very heated one at that. Far from disengaging the emotions of his audience, he wants to reengage his audience with their sense of outrage at the horrors of war and capitalism. But there is a kind of emotion he wants to avoid, and that is the sharing of emotion with characters on stage. We can't complain that Brecht downgrades emotion, but we can complain that he is not clear enough about the difference between what he wants and what he does not.

Brecht's distinction is of the utmost importance for the art of theater, because it points to a difference between good watching and bad watching. The art of watching at its best is thoughtful and critical, and the emotions it cultivates do not interfere with understanding. My goal in this chapter is to save what is good in Brecht's theory.

Saving Brecht's theater

I do not need to save his theater. He did that for himself. Anyone who tried to make theater an emotion-free zone, or to eliminate empathy altogether, would fail in the art of theater. Unless we care about what we see, we will not be good watchers of theater, and, as we have seen, caring is a disposition to have emotions. In fact, if we don't care, we may not be watchers at all.

Fortunately, Brecht did not wipe empathy out of his plays. Audiences do feel a kind of empathy for Mother Courage, even in the revised version. She cares enormously for her children, she is driven by this care to keep all her thoughts on business, and we are drawn into this care like twigs into the center of strong current in a stream. We admire her for carrying on in the face of endless troubles; we are impressed when she is able to hide her grief in the heartrending silent scream at the sight of her dead son (scene 3).

Brecht must have felt this in creating her: she is a model of the two-faced survivor that Brecht himself became in the suspicious atmospheres first of McCarthy's United States and later of East Germany. Audience engagement with Mother Courage must account for the success of the play. Something like this, of course, must be done for any play, if it is to be a success in the theater.

To his credit, Brecht's theory is more complex than it seems at first. He did not want to rule out empathy entirely. The effect he wants from his theater is supposed to come from an empathy that is engaged and rejected at the same time. Brecht was too good a playwright to let his practice in the theater be sunk by the weight of a narrow theory. But how his theory escapes narrowness he did not explain.

We shall have to ask whether a theoretically adequate distinction of the kind Brecht wants could be made to apply to the working theater. I begin by distinguishing three ways by which theater may engage emotions: I call them congruence, identification, and cognitive empathy.

I use Alice's wedding to illustrate these three kinds of engagement in theater. For this wedding, I have selected watchers who have different responses to the same event. Actual performances in theater may lead to mixed responses in the same watchers. *Mother Courage*, for example, evokes identification as well as understanding from attentive audiences. The uneasy tension that results is part of what makes the play an adventure to watch, holding us in suspense as to our own responses: Will we relax into identification, or will we hold back and think? In watching the play we are liable to surprise ourselves. Courage's firm resolve lures us toward identification, but the contradiction in her life drives us back again. She is tough-minded, and we would like to follow her in that; but she is driven for her children's sake to foster the war that destroys her children, and there we cannot follow her.

9.3 Congruence

Come back with me now to Alice's wedding, which was awash with empathy. This time we have our eyes on a second woman, whose emotions are quite similar to Alice's. That is because she too is a bride, and she too is proud of her fresh-eyed beauty, her lovely dress, and the special arrangement of her hair. She is full of joy shadowed by apprehension. She too is saying her wedding vow today, and she is saying it to Charles.

I forgot to tell you: this is a bigamous society, and double weddings to a single groom are common here.

Barbara's emotions feel exactly like Alice's, as they should. They are similar people, same age, same background, and they are undergoing exactly the same event. But no one would suppose that the similarity of their feelings is a sign of empathy. Far from it. Neither one is thinking of the other, except as a rival. Barbara may fear Alice, but she has no feelings on behalf of Alice. She does not feel *for* Alice. In the language of my theory of emotions, neither bride serves as second object for the emotions of the other. Emotional pairing such as Barbara's with Alice is what I call "congruence" in emotion. We have a pair of emotional responses that are congruent because they feel the same, have similar causes, and are directed at similar first objects and parallel second objects. But neither response serves as a cause for the other. Barbara does not feel as she does because of the way Alice feels. The two causal chains, leading to the two emotional responses, are independent.

This double wedding ceremony illustrates the fullest possible emotional congruence. It may strike you as bizarre, but don't forget that many men who marry one person have deep commitments elsewhere—to work or to sports or to family—and many a bride has felt she was assigned a role in competition with her mother-in-law. So Alice's wedding is really not so very strange to us. And, as theater, it illustrates a goal that should now be familiar: theater of presence seeks to make a second bride of every member of the audience, drawing them into the meaningful heart of the action as principal participants, and giving them the same role as that of the original leading performer.

A slightly weaker case of congruence occurs between Charles and either of the two brides. He too is proud of his beauty and his finery, pleased at landing such eligible partners in marriage, filled with joy, and somewhat apprehensive. But his fears are different from theirs, as he is taking on a different kind of responsibility. In this case of congruence, the analogue in theater is audience participation through roles different from those of the original performers. An altar call might summon us to double Charles's role; then it would bring the audience into the ceremony and thereby into an emotion-based relationship with each other and with the original performers. Such a mass wedding is bizarre, but we can imagine it: we would all be getting married to Alice and Barbara.

A weaker altar call would summon us to be bridesmaids or grooms-men, and this would lead to a still weaker form of congruence, which is far more common in current-day participatory theater. When a pro-duction aims for audience involvement, it usually does so by giving the audience a minor role in the action.

When emotions are congruent, they are shared in the absence of what is called "identification." Neither bride is identifying with the other, and Charles is surely not identifying with either of them. If a bridesmaid starts to identify with the bride, that changes the picture, and her response is no longer congruent, because it is not independent of Alice's.

Theater of presence transcends theater, or, you might prefer to say, returns us to the ritual roots of theater. Either way it leaves behind the art of theater, because theater of presence does away with watching and being watched. Everyone is, in effect, a second bride or a second groom in theater of presence.

The weaker forms of congruence are compatible with theater, however. Bridesmaids and groomsmen are present as designated wit-nesses, and in their ceremonial roles they are exercising the art of watch-ing. But they are still in line for congruent emotional responses: They too are nervous about their clothes, proud of their good looks, joyful, and a little worried.

Congruent responses are generally unconducive to a critical under-standing. Since all present are actively engaged in the performance, no one is in a good position to observe and evaluate. If Brecht knew of such a theater, he would have recognized it as an extreme case of the sort of theater he rejected—a theater in which the audience's emotional engagement precludes critical thought.

So far I have covered only the kind of congruence that comes from active participation in an event that started as theater. There are two forms of congruence that require no active participation at all, and these are far more common in theater—theater of memory and tonal sympathy.

Theater of memory

Now imagine Delores in the third row at Alice's wedding, recalling her own ceremony twenty years before—her pride, her excitement, her apprehension, all congruent with Alice's feelings at the moment. But Delores adds her own grief; bigamy has given her the short end of the stick; her married life has been a steady and inescapable misery. And so she is now grieving for Alice's future in a way that Alice cannot. Delores is locked in a cycle of memory and experience. Alice's wedding—this piece of theater—offers her nothing to break the cycle. Nor does she bring to this wedding any of the mental tools that would allow her to rebel against its tradition.

Often at real weddings, a long-married watcher is carried back to the scene of her own wedding and feels again the excitement and love she felt then. Much the same can happen in mimetic theater. Tina Howe's *Painting Churches* carries an added emotional punch for the large part of any audience who have had to face the senility of parents. Such watchers are carried back to the emotional scene of their own anger, frustration, and misdirected love, and so they feel emotions similar in form to those of Howe's protagonist, but in relation to their own parents.

Memory-based responses are congruent up to a point; but they are complicated by the variety of memories that impinge on them. A watcher at a wedding, if she remembers her own, may find her remembered excitement clouded by subsequent disappointments and tempered by regret. And some of Howe's audience may have learned to accept a sort of situation her protagonist finds outrageous. Or perhaps they have learned to insist on changing situations that Howe's protagonist (like most of us) feels forced to accept.

Though strongly moved by the performance, such an audience is still capable of some critical understanding. Like Brecht's ideal audience, they may laugh when the protagonist cries, and cry when, at the end of the play, our protagonist laughs. But, Brecht would complain, this audience is unlikely to think that the situation ought to be, or even could be, changed. What shows on the stage matches their recollections; the play makes us think that this is how life is, that it is always the same.

When theater touches us through memories that arouse congruent emotions it is in danger of reinforcing the idea that life must be as it is shown on this stage. Audiences enjoy congruent feelings in the theater of memories because they are comforted by it. It shows them that they are not alone and encourages them to think that what they have suffered could not have been avoided.

"You see?" Delores says to herself as she watches this scene that recalls her past. "It is happening to Alice and Barbara too. So it was with me. We are all in this together." But Brecht wanted his audience to believe that life could be otherwise. It does not have to happen that way.

In fact, Delores could take a critical attitude toward bigamous weddings if she had the strength to do so. It is just that the theater of memory makes it easier for her to accept life as she knew it.

Tonal sympathy

Imagine now that Alice's wedding is taking place on a cold day. Edward, a traveler from abroad, has taken refuge from the wintry weather in the church. He is sitting in the very back row, straining to understand what is happening. He does not speak Alice's language, but he has the emotional equivalent of highly sensitive antennae—as dogs and babies often do—and he is picking up the excitement in the room. Right now, as Alice is taking her vows, all eyes are on her, and Edward is feeling some of what she feels—the captivating mixture of joy and apprehension that makes her upper lip quiver and brings a tear to her eye. But Edward has no idea what is going on in this building; his home culture, happier in many ways, does not celebrate such weddings. His response is congruent to Alice's, but in the absence of the relevant knowledge, Edward cannot actually share emotions with Alice. His feelings feel like hers, but they cannot have the same objects; indeed, as Edward is experiencing them now, these feelings have no objects at all, and so they are not emotions. Part of Edward's response is no more than a certain mood, but he may also have headless or decapitated emotions—feelings in search of objects, rather like verbs in search of subjects. If he supplies his own objects for these feelings, then he is experiencing emotions, but these may not be relevant at all to Alice's feelings or to her situation.

The model for tonal sympathy is the action of one violin string, when plucked, on another string nearby. If both are tuned to the same note, or if one is turned to a harmonic of the other, then the second string will vibrate along with the first. Pure tonal sympathy is most familiar to us from our response to music, but lighting and dance may also be used to call up moods or headless emotions in an audience. Plot and character provide objects for emotion, and so our response to them is rarely tonal. When mimetic theater arouses tonal sympathy through music or lighting, it uses plot to supply heads for the headless emotions that result. The music in melodrama creates an atmosphere of dread; the villain provides the object for that dread. In any event, the art of theater rarely aims at tonal sympathy. Edward is not the ideal audience for most purposes. Edward is in effect only a sounding board on which Alice's wedding is playing. The art of watching requires us to be more than sounding boards, and for this reason good watchers are familiar with the language and customs of a performance tradition.

Brecht had tonal sympathy in mind when he rejected dramatic theater for seeking to "carry away" its audience. He was right to suppose that a tonal audience would be carried away by a wave of feeling that would render it unable to think for itself at all, let alone think critically. But, for the same reason, a tonal audience cannot be swept into any emotional response at all to what is presented on stage.

Emotions have a cognitive component, and this is missing from tonal sympathy. Emotions know what they are about. So when theater engages emotions, it does not merely sweep an audience away on a wave of feeling. Instead, it teaches them where to direct the feelings it imparts. Brecht would be right to question the value of tonal sympathy in theater, but tonal sympathy is at most a by-product of the Aristotelian theater he was trying to replace. Any form of congruence supplies too weak a connection between the watchers and the watched; it leaves the watchers turned inward, concentrating on their own emotions. The art of theater aims at a deeper connection, one that will sustain close and careful watching from the beginning of its measured time to the end. And this requires the watchers at Alice's wedding to be engaged with her.

9.4 Identification

Let's try again to find good watchers for Alice's wedding. We are looking for people who are paying attention to the wedding because they are emotionally engaged with Alice.

Fantasy

Frederick, a friend of the groom's family, is watching intently. Tears streaming down his cheeks show how deeply affected he is. You and I can't say exactly what is going on with Frederick, because nothing very exact is going on. Frederick is confused. He is identifying with Alice. By that I mean that Frederick is lost in a fantasy in which the differences between him and Alice have blown away like leaves from a tree. In his sweet fantasy he is dressed in white splendor, seething with pride and excitement, while he swears his wedding oath to Charles. In some secret part of his mind he has been wishing for this consummation for some years now, but he would never admit it, not even to himself. He is not in love with Charles, as far as he knows, even though his pulse rises deliciously in his presence.

Frederick's feelings, then, are very similar to Alice's; indeed, they are exactly what Frederick takes Alice's feelings to be. But they are not congruent with Alice's feelings. That is because Frederick's response is based on factors unknown to Alice—Frederick's perception of Alice along with his fantasy about Charles. He has unconsciously shaped his response to bring his perception and his fantasy in line with each other. Alice's true feelings are not relevant to Frederick.

Little Ginger, one of Alice's cousins, is in much the same state. She too identifies with Alice, but her fantasy is fully conscious. She has long been playing bridal games, and she has been dying to be a real bride. Now she is almost swooning with excitement as she imagines herself in Alice's shoes. She is like Frederick in every respect except that she knows she is dreaming. Like Frederick, she has a fantasy that elbows Alice's real feelings out of her mind.

A watcher identifies when he merges his fantasy with the action he is watching in such a way that he—the watcher—is playing the primary role. Fantasy identification is limited in the scope of its emotional engagement; both Frederick and Ginger are missing important parts of the scene. Neither can imagine that Alice would have any grounds for apprehension, and so they attribute all of her visible symptoms to an excess of excitement or joy. They leave out the fear, which has no place in their fantasies.

Frederick's fantasy is playing out just below the conscious level, so it is sneaking in underneath the gaze of Frederick's censor, which would never allow him to play at being married to Charles. So in many cases we indulge fantasies in the theater that we would not entertain at the fully conscious level. Theater embodies fantasies that we would not have the courage to shape deliberately in our own imaginations. These censored fantasies may be loving, like Frederick's, but more often they are brutal.

Ginger's fantasy, being conscious, is more romantic. In a similar way, audiences are inclined to identify with the heroes of survival plays, and identification is a factor in the success of *Mother Courage*, and of any play in which a hero comes through a trying ordeal. I am that hero, for the measured time of theater, and I exult in my power to prevail.

When the art of theater aims to merge with the fantasies of its audience, it sets strict limits on plot: it may not go beyond what fantasy would allow. Frederick's fantasy, for example, must pass unseen by his inner censor, so it must not be too explicit. We would ruin the story for Frederick if, at the end of the ceremony, we revealed that Alice is a young man in drag. That is not Frederick's fantasy at all; his fantasy is not about dress up but about being something that, at the conscious level, he knows is not possible. Many recent films about male bonding have exploited such covert fantasies, celebrating the closeness of handsome men or boys to each other with no explicit revelation of its homoerotic ground. Revelation kills fantasy.

Revelation could ruin Ginger's fantasy easily. Suppose that, at the conclusion of the vows, Charles turns his back on Alice and envelops Barbara in a steamy embrace. That was not Ginger's story at all; Ginger *was* Alice, and she was marrying for happily ever after, before this terrible thing happened.

Romantic fiction of all kinds, including theater, steers carefully away from the shoals of revelation. Romance ensures that the boy gets the girl and that the hero survives the ordeal. To kill off the hero is an unpardonable sin; only the weak may be killed off in romantic theater, and the weak must be minor characters with whom we are not invited to identify. As for getting the girl—to deny the consummation of love in marriage, as Shakespeare does in *Love's Labor's Lost*—is to raise the audience's engagement above fantasy to a level that is more thoughtful and more critical. If *Love's Labor's Lost* were simply a romance, the ending it has would ruin the play. But Shakespeare almost never confines himself to a single genre, and in *Love's Labor's Lost* he is not serving a romantic fantasy.

Theater that aims at fantasy identification not only accepts the limits of the watchers' fantasies; it also allows its watchers to see the action it presents with a blurred and uncritical eye. Such theater grafts the watcher's fantasy onto the root of the performance, so that what blooms in the watcher's mind belongs to the stock of his fantasy more than to the performance. That is what Brecht feared in the case of *Mother Courage*: He does not want to allow the audience to graft their survivor fantasies onto his play. If they do, they will not be able to see the harsh world he is trying to present to them, which (he believes) is the world they inhabit stripped of illusions.

Imagination (reflective identification)

By one account, empathy occurs when you consider what it would be like to be someone else, so as to learn what she must have felt. In order to distinguish this from what happens in fantasy, I shall call this identification "reflective." It occurs in our responses to both history and fiction, and it amounts to asking and trying to answer a counterfactual question: "How would I feel if I were she?" Our ability to do this depends on a combination of information and imagination.

On asking the "how would I feel" question, a thinker tries to flesh out the "if I were she" hypothesis with information from what she knows about the character—either from history or from the text of the play. In the case of fantasy, by contrast, dreamers do not pause to ask such questions or weigh the different answers; even if they did, they would be prevented from looking at sources of information about their heroes, since they can accept from the play only what embodies their fantasies.

Reflective identification raises a number of theoretical difficulties, which we do not need to explore here. The art of theater does not seek to engage an audience through reflection, because this belongs not to watching but to thought. Reflective identification helps us to understand the script of a play, or, after the curtain falls, to evaluate what we saw earlier. We do not ponder counterfactuals while gripped by the sonnet scene in *Romeo and Juliet*; we do not ask, "How would I feel if I were Romeo?"

While watching, we do not reflect on what we are watching, unless our emotions are not engaged. But this does not mean that our cognitive faculties go dark when our emotions light up. Not all thinking is reflective. An emotion has a cognitive element that is not reflective, and so theater can engage us emotionally and intellectually at the same time and about the same things. A good watcher is alive with thoughts and feelings intertwined. But theater offers many temptations for bad watching.

9.5 Bad Watching

Bad watching occurs when (a) the audience is not emotionally engaged with any of the main characters (so that they have no reason to pay attention for the measured time) or (b) the audience is engaged in a way that distracts them from the action they are watching (so that they are never really paying attention at all). Theater that aims at bad watching is bad theater, because it undermines both sides of the art of theater. Bad theater limits what the performers can do and how the audience can respond. Bad theater is bad for us because it infringes on our freedom in acting and in watching. Bad theater shrinks the range of human possibility that we can readily imagine. It is both false about us and damaging to us.

Congruent emotion leads to bad watching because it carries the audience away on a wave of feeling that swamps their ability to perceive accurately what they are watching. A second bride is no more able than the first bride to perceive accurately what is happening in her wedding or to think critically about it; moreover, she is unable to engage emotionally with the first bride.

Theater of presence is the kind that tries to turn us into something like second brides at a wedding. Theater of presence makes us bad watchers because it makes us performers. Suppose the young people watching Socrates refute Gorgias are drawn into the philosophical process, answering questions for themselves; they may stop paying attention altogether to the Socrates-Gorgias story. But that is not a bad thing; they are becoming philosophers, and they could not do that in the role of watchers. Or suppose some young people are summoned to the front of the church, at the last moment, to be groomsmen and bridesmaids. Their parents will be better watchers, but they will have the special pleasure of having participated in this wedding. Sometimes you should try only to be a good watcher. But there are times when you should forget watching and join in the action.

Theater of tonal sympathy aims at the most familiar kind of congruent response. Music, lighting, and the tone of the actions force a certain kind of response on the audience. But that response is not engaged with the characters, and it tends to distract the audience from paying attention to the action that is presented to them—except in the way that has already been determined by the music, lighting, and tone. You cannot ask, "Is this really a heroic moment?" The music has settled that question for you. This theater intends to deprive you of choice and thought. In effect, it sets out to make you a bad watcher.

Identification leads to bad watching in a different way. The theater of identification indulges watchers in a trip that they—the watchers—have already mapped out. The audience of this theater will endure no risk of being taken to unfamiliar ground. So the performers have no freedom to challenge the watchers or to deviate in noticeable ways from the fantasies that they expected their audience to bring with them. This theater has nothing to teach its audience. It cannot shock them with surprise revelations or reveal dark and unexpected secrets. All this theater can reveal is the details by which it works out the expected ending. We know from the start of a mystery that the killers will be loathsome and that they will be caught; we only do not know who they are or how they will be caught. We know from the start of a romance that the boy will get the girl. We await with eager suspense only the sweet details.

Theater of identification does not permit dramatic irony; that is, it does not permit the audience to know more than is apparently known by the lead characters. "No man is a hero to his valet," and no audience in this theater may know as much about its hero as a valet would know. Neither a valet nor an omniscient audience can be engaged through identification. Fantasy thrives on possibilities; it would die on the dry ground of certainty. This mode of theater cannot provoke an audience to critical thinking about its characters or their situation; it surrenders its characters to the engines of fantasy, so that if a watcher thinks about anything, it will be about his own idealized self.

To take a critical attitude toward a character, you need to know more than he does. Brecht always tries to see to it that his audience is aware of the self-deceptions of his protagonists; this is not simply to make them unattractive but to put them outside any fantasy we could have of ourselves. We know too much about his characters to share their illusions—more than *they* know about themselves, and much, much more than we would ever like to know about ourselves.

To be emotionally engaged with a character—to care—you need to leave a certain distance between you and that character. In theater of identification, you do not care about the hero as much as you care about this new merged entity—yourself in the hero's role. Identification in fantasy fuses spectator and character, and so betrays the relation of watcher to watched that is the essence of theater. Good watching calls for robust attention to the action that it watches. You must, in short, know what is going on.

9.6 Cognitive Empathy

We have still not found the ideal watcher for Alice's wedding. We wanted someone who is paying attention to the scene because he cares about

Alice. All these watchers we have examined so far are caring more about themselves than about Alice, either because they have injected themselves into the scene through identification or because their feelings are only congruent with hers, and therefore bounce back upon themselves.

"Who cares?" you might ask; "Whether Frederick watches Alice for her own sake or not; he is still watching either way. Why isn't that good enough for theater?" I would answer that Frederick is not watching Alice very well at all. He is not aware of her apprehension, he is not open to all the twists and turns that the plot might take, and he is in danger of drifting away into fantasy altogether, and then he will not even be watching badly. Moreover, even when he is watching, he is unable to understand what is really going on with Alice. Lost in fantasy, his mind can't find its way to the truth about Alice's plight.

So we try again. Henry is present at Alice's wedding as a friend of her family. He is over forty, unmarried, and knows too much to slip away into fantasies of married bliss. He has seen what it means to have children, and he knows how often couples must face illness, death, poverty, or divorce. He also understands the joy that wells up in the best of marriages. All this he brings to Alice's wedding, and against this background he experiences a set of emotions different from all those we have reviewed so far. First, all of his feelings are definitely about Alice. Second, his feelings are different from hers, and different from any feelings he imagines that she might have. She is too young to know what he knows, and too much in love to face all of the fears that Henry has on her behalf.

Drama

Henry is the best watcher we have found so far. He is paying attention to Alice for her own sake, and his emotions are informed by an understanding of her situation that is superior to her own. He is thoughtful and emotionally engaged at the same time. He will pay attention throughout the ceremony, and his mind is not closed against anything he might see. In later years, Henry will be a good friend to Alice, come what may, because he knows how to pay attention to her for her own sake. In a good watcher like Henry, ethics and art make the same demand: pay attention to others for their own sake.

Henry is an excellent watcher. Any kind of theater that invites an audience to be like Henry is also excellent. It is the theater of Sophocles and Shakespeare; it is an art so powerful that it drew the attention of Aristotle in his *Poetics*. Its most famous genre is tragedy, but it is known these days mostly by the simple word "drama."

Contrast drama with two other forms that theater can take. Theater of presence tries to cast its watchers as second brides in a ceremony, but that's to take them out of the context of theater altogether. Theater of identification truckles to the fantasies of its audience but cannot win them over to watch the truer human action that falls outside fantasy. Henry does not participate, and he does not dream. He watches.

Henry's mode of engagement with Alice is an example of what I call cognitive empathy—the experience of well-informed emotions on behalf of another person. Another word for this is "understanding"—a specific sort of understanding for which well-informed emotions are necessary. Henry's level of understanding is informed by general truths about the world that seem to him invariable. He is well informed about what Alice should expect from her wedding, but there is something important he does not know. Weddings do not have to be as horrible as this one, but he has seen no other kind.

Social criticism

What sort of watcher could realize that life does not have to be this way—that men don't have to bring outside commitments to a marriage, and that women do not have to accept it if they do? We need to imagine a watcher who finds this scene to be outlandish.

Irma is an exchange student living with Alice's cousins. She comes from a culture in which bigamy is illegal; where she grew up, a marriage like Alice's and Barbara's would be seen as an abuse of women. When Irma realizes what is happening to Alice, she is outraged. She whispers loudly to her hostess, "How can you let this happen to Alice?" Her hostess does not answer; everyone but Irma accepts this wedding as part of the normal course of events.

Irma is teeming with emotions that are about Alice, but these are competing with her anger at the cultural system which, she fears, will destroy Alice. She is the ideal watcher for the theater of social criticism because, unlike Henry, she is prepared to think critically about the kinds of events she watches. The theater of social criticism tries to turn us all into foreigners in our own land, so that we can see the patterns of our lives with the eyes of a tourist.

Brecht intends his epic theater to have this effect. "Epic" is a misleading term, however. The theater of social criticism is in fact the theater of irony and satire, with roots as deep as Aristophanes. Its finest writer in the early modern period was Molière. Such theater seeks to impress its audience with a sense of the incongruity of what it represents. In *Mother Courage*, a mother is driven by mother-love to set profits above her children's lives; this at the same time repels and attracts an audience. In other hands, it would be comic. But Brecht's final effect, driven home by the mother's lullaby for her dead daughter, is not incongruous but pitiful, and the play ends in a deeply charged dramatic understanding.

The conclusion of *Mother Courage* brings out the maternal warmth in what began as a repulsively greedy character. Brecht would have done better by his lights to do the reverse, as he does in *The Good Person of Setzuan*, in which economic pressures change an attractive character for the worse. The effect Brecht wanted is most powerfully realized in the earlier, and more comedic, *A Man's a Man*, which shows the transformation of a sweet young man into a killing machine.

Alice's wedding, if performed as a play, would be a heavy-handed satire of marriage à la mode. In the world of this play, we would all be visitors from a far-off land. But we would not be entirely secure in our outrage against Alice's customs; we would suspect that our own are not so very different, and our empathy for Alice would be informed by our own experience of marriages that have shortchanged the women involved in them.

9.7 The Art of Empathy

Theater that seeks knowledge-based empathy like Henry's or Irma's is the most theatrical, because it produces situations in which audiences are drawn to watch performances most intently. As we have seen, the kinds of theater that do not let you learn (those of presence and identification) are precisely the ones that do not let you watch but instead divert your attention to your own situation or to your own fantasy. The nature of theater is to be watched; when it cannot be watched it cannot be theater in the full sense. So if you want to experience the complete art of theater, you must be fully capable of empathy with the chief characters. Empathy involves emotion, and, as we have seen, emotion depends on knowledge. It follows that empathy also depends on knowledge.

The knowledge that grounds your empathy with Alice is knowledge about Alice. You cannot empathize with Alice unless you know what is going on with her. You could share Alice's emotions without knowing anything about her, but that would not be empathy in the full sense. If you are still tempted to think that empathy is sharing another's emotions, think again about the second bride at the wedding. She shares the first bride's emotions, but we would not say that her experience is empathy, because it has nothing to do with Alice.

Theater can be watched in many ways. Good watchers have mastered the art of empathy for the characters they are watching. They never feel compelled to take a certain attitude. They watch, think, find the attitude that they judge is right, and in so doing learn about the action they are watching. Bad watchers are distracted by their own roles or their own fantasies; they are ignorant about what they are watching, and, in consequence, they are incapable of empathy.

Plato and Brecht, though far removed from one another in time and philosophy, still had virtually the same complaint: that theater arouses emotions which disable the power of reason in those who watch. They are right about something: there are kinds of theater that manipulate audiences through emotions and disable their powers of reason. The most familiar of these is melodrama—what I have called the theater of tonal sympathy—which we know best through its imitation by filmmakers.

Plato and Brecht are wrong about many things, however. They are wrong about emotions. They do not understand how emotions depend on understanding. And they do not appreciate how understanding depends on emotions. We use emotion to understand our world, especially the people in it. There is no understanding of people without empathy.

9.8 Pleasure

Theater is supposed to be pleasant for the audience. Otherwise, why would anyone choose to attend? But empathy often requires us to feel the pain of other people. So if good watchers must be good at empathy, and theater shows actions that are sad, how can good watchers take pleasure in the experience? If you are enjoying Alice's wedding, you are not a good watcher. The good watchers all find it excruciating. How can they enjoy an excruciating experience?

Pleasure in tragedy is an old problem. Aristotle gnawed at it in the *Poetics*. Tragedy, he writes, aims at arousing both pleasure and the emotions of pity and fear. And these emotions he defines as kinds of pain. He never explains the pleasure he thinks tragedy can give, but it seems to have something to do with mimesis and the learning that mimesis yields.

The problem may not be as serious as it seems. Pleasure is not the only attraction of theater. People went to Alice's wedding not for the pleasure of it but to support Alice. Football fans attend a game even when they know their team will lose, even when they expect a painful time of it; they do so not only to support their team but also to be together. We did not look for pleasure when we went to see *The Laramie Project*. But we were well rewarded by the experience, especially by sharing it with the rest of the audience.

The best theater is not the theater that gives us the most pleasure. But a good watcher takes pleasure in watching well, just as a truly generous person takes pleasure in generosity. Pleasure is not really the goal of anything we do, but pleasure is never far away from human action. We take pleasure in achieving just about anything we set out to do, and this would include watching Alice's horrible wedding, if that was what we wanted to do. The goals we set, and the pleasure we take in them, are clues to character. Good people make good watchers because good people take pleasure in empathy.

Besides, pleasure is not excluded by pain. Real football fans will enjoy the game, even though they hate losing, and so for the other examples. Still, few people would choose to attend Alice's awful wedding unless they were family or friends and felt obliged to do so. In that case the main pleasure available to them, if they are good watchers, is that of feeling part of a group. And this is no small pleasure, even if the group is united by pain. Another pleasure they may have is aesthetic: Alice's wedding has a beautiful narrative shape, and it will have a conclusion that is satisfying in its own terms. Add to this beauty the beauties of music, fine language, spectacular clothes, and radiant young people. Alice's wedding may bode ill for her, but it is a beautiful thing to see.

Suppose that we try to play Alice's wedding as mimetic theater, to attract and please an audience. I don't think any doctoring would make this a good play (although it has been a helpful example for my purposes). But suppose we play it for laughs. Laughter is delightful. Or suppose we play it for understanding. Aristotle is right about this: we take great pleasure in coming to understand things. Either way, we should play it for the pleasure of dramatic resolution and other beauties that can arise in theater; and, if this is mimetic theater, our watchers won't be as pained at the end by worries about Alice's future, as they would be in a real wedding.

If I were to write the play about Alice's wedding, I would aim for all three pleasures—laughter, understanding, and beauty. I would have Frederick and other watchers on stage. I would introduce well-timed revelations to defeat their fantasies, and every revelation would get a laugh. Then I would bring on Delores, the battle-scarred veteran of a wedding like this, with a narration or voice-over, in aid of understanding. In the end, I hope the audience would leave refreshed by laughter, satisfied by a neat ending, and tingling with a growing understanding about the joys and perils of commitment.

If you have mastered the art of empathy, you will take pleasure in empathy for the understanding that empathy brings, and for the rueful, community-sharing laughter that attends empathy. Good performers know how to give watchers many delights, and good watchers know how to take pleasure in hard things.

TEN

Laughter

As soon as Juliet realizes what is going on at Alice's wedding she bursts out laughing uproariously. Now something has to change. Perhaps the wedding is interrupted for only a few minutes; Juliet is the only one to laugh, and someone ushers her out of earshot, so that the solemnity of the occasion can be restored. Perhaps, however, this will put an end to the whole proceeding. Juliet's laughter is infectious; others pick it up, and soon the whole audience is screaming with laughter. Either way, the event has gone sour for Alice. She will never forgive Juliet for spoiling her special day. Imagine a young bride trying to pledge her troth for life while the walls are echoing with abusive guffaws! She will not have the witnesses she needs, because they will not be paying attention to her.

Alice is not the only one who loses by Juliet's laughter. Juliet has missed an opportunity for empathy. She can't very well feel any emotion for Alice while she is laughing at her. Fear, joy, pity—all the emotions she might feel for Alice are blocked by laughter. If laughter blocks emotion, it also blocks empathy. And if Juliet infects the other watchers with her laughter, as could easily happen, they too will have no chance at empathy.

Juliet's laughter has been fatal to both parts of the art of theater, both to the art of performance and to the art of watching. And yet Juliet was not wrong to laugh. The wedding was absurd, and it deserved to be interrupted. Some events ought to be hooted off stage, and this was one of them.

Laughter is no enemy to theater, however. Laughter joins the community of watchers more closely together, and it links audience to performers as well. Great works of mimetic theater almost always call for laughter. Good watchers can laugh at the Watchman's verbal antics in *Antigone*, at Dionysus's cleverness in the *Bacchae*, at the porter's drunken monologue in *Macbeth*, at Hamlet's mockery of Polonius, and at just about anything in Beckett's *Endgame*, even though this play shows the last hours of the human race.

When you tell me a joke, you hope that I will laugh spontaneously, without choice or premeditation. Above all, you hope that I will not laugh out of mere politeness. And yet a polite laugh is better than nothing. When you attempt a fine dive and execute only a belly flop, you hope that I will not laugh at you, and yet you know that I may not be able to help myself. Laughter seems outside our control; the more sincere it is, the harder it is for us to control our own laughter. As performers, too, we lose control of the laughter of our audience insofar as it is sincere.

Successful theater is marked by laughter, and so are dismal failures in theater. Moss Hart knew he finally had a success when an audience laughed through the last act of his first play. The Duke and the Dauphin in *Huckleberry Finn* knew they had a flop when the audience roared with the wrong kind of laughter. Theater aims at the kind of laughter that spells success. That is one reason for distinguishing between good and bad laughter. The other reason has to do with ethics.

Ethical character shows in the way you laugh. It is bad to laugh at people in a way that excludes or degrades them; it is kind to include all those who are present in your laughter. You are laughing well if you can tell a Polish joke to a Polish friend so that she can laugh with you comfortably or even add the joke to her own repertoire. You are doing poorly if she is hurt, whether she shows the pain or not.

The more spontaneous your behavior, the more it reveals about the kind of person you are. That is why you are not entirely responsible for the ethical character you have. Your parents had a lot to do with it, and so did the culture in which you grew up. It is not your fault if you grew up around racist and ethnic humor. But it is to your credit if you now find racial jokes disgusting or downright dangerous. A philosopher who follows Aristotle would say that although you are not responsible directly for a particular episode of helpless laughter, you are at least partly responsible for the way you are about laughter—for the ethical character that your laughter reveals.

There are times to laugh and times to grieve, and there are ways of grieving and ways of laughing. Good watchers in theater laugh at good times and in good ways, and good theater pieces call for laughing well. Outside theater too, a good life is characterized by good laughter. Laughter can be a shared delight or a slashing sword. It can even be both at the same time: when we are insiders we share the cruel delight of laughing at those we take to be outsiders. Imagine the brotherhood's living room, where older members show images of nerds and other campus misfits and teach new members to ridicule them. Or visualize a circle of light from candles, in which a group of distinguished guests gather around a polished table—all members of the same political party—and share a laugh at the stupidity of their nation's president at the time, who has never been one of them. It is only human. This is a way we come together; we know how special we are by the laughter we share at those outside our group.

Laughing at outsiders is not the only way we can come together. Let's sort out the various roles laughter can have in theater.

10.1 Laughing Badly

In theater we can laugh too much or too little, and we can laugh in the wrong way. We laugh too much if we laugh at the wrong lines; this can ruin any event in theater. Toward the end of Euripides' *Bacchae*, Agave cradles the severed, bloody head of her son in her arms and declares that she has slain a wild lion. If we do not stage the scene with great care, a modern audience will laugh and spoil the effect. The worst sort of misplaced laughter is the laughter that drives performers off the stage. If Alice runs from the room, weeping, her wedding has been ruined. When, in *Love's Labor's Lost*, Holofernes runs offstage on the edge of tears, his part of the play has been ruined. The audience has been cruel, but he did not play his part effectively. The watchers and the watched are both responsible for keeping laughter in bounds.

We laugh too little if we miss jokes, and, when this happens, it is usually the fault of the performers for failing to connect with the audience. Performers may also fail to realize the potential of a scene

Beckett imagines the last minutes of the human race with a gentle humor that allows us to arrive at resignation rather than horror. And this is good, because horror tends to dampen our perceptions; if we watched in total horror we would not notice the details of the small losses that add up to the end of all things, and we would be deaf to the sad and sprightly poetry of his speeches. Laughter helps us be good watchers by softening the horror, so that we can, over time, digest the entire awfulness of it.

Laughter helps us watch *Endgame* closely in a good production, but it does not give us a good time. And it shouldn't; there is nothing pleasant about the end of the human race. The event could easily be made too horrible to contemplate, and yet Beckett's light touch makes it, through laughter, just barely tolerable to watch. Beckett does not make it hilarious or seductive; he observes the delicate line that reveals the horror without making us feel it too deeply.

Laughing together in the audience we recognize that we share an understanding of what we are watching. Laughing with characters who are troubled, we recognize that we are not so very different from them. And all this is good. But when your lover trips and falls, and you laugh, are you laughing in empathy or ridicule? You had better be clear, or she may not forgive you. Laughing-with is often hard to distinguish from laughing-at. Confusion of the two causes trouble among friends and ambiguity in theater.

A wide-ranging satire produces a result that is equivocal in another way as well: it can make us laugh at both sides in a quarrel (just as tragedy can make us feel empathy for both sides). In the *Clouds* of Aristophanes, for example, we laugh equally at the old and the new learning—the "superior" and the "inferior"—during the great debate toward the end of the play.

Sometimes laughter is crossed with other feelings, and when this happens the tension between laughter and emotion makes us hold back from both and ponder the situation. The last scene of the *Clouds* shows the Athenians burning down Socrates' school, incinerating the students alive. In a good production of the *Clouds*, this should be both hilarious and horrifying. You can laugh and cry at the same time, but you can't laugh it up while murder is being done. When drawn toward conflicting attitudes, watchers must stop laughing and start thinking.

Satiric theater does little to determine the final attitude of its audience and therefore does much to encourage critical thought. Laughter frees watchers from the tyranny of tonal sympathy, so that they may take whatever view they choose of the situation. Laughter banishes the more mindless forms of emotion; this is well known and has given humor its reputation as handmaid to rationality.

10.3 Comedy and Tragedy

Genre is a matter of pedigree. You know what you will get when you buy a puppy of pedigree, but you might enjoy a dog more if it had the power to surprise. Dog lovers know how to love a dog without assigning it to a breed or a mix of breed, and, truly, the finest dogs I have known defied categorization. So it is with theater. The great playwrights have never been content with a single pedigree. Sophocles and Euripides already had comic and tragic traditions to draw on, and they drew on both, though their works were performed at tragic festivals. Many of Shakespeare's plays are beguiling mongrels, and Molière, whose work defines a modern strand in comedy, stretches the limits of comedy in more than one direction.

Defining comedy or tragedy has no place in the art of theater. We need no boundaries in order to make human action worth watching, or to find it so. True, performers and audience should share the ability to tell the difference between a time to weep and a time to laugh, but no one need know whether *Much Ado about Nothing* is a comedy or whether *Death of a Salesman* is a tragedy. We weep and laugh in both plays.

As a matter of history, however, we can speak broadly about the different trends of comedy and tragedy. And this is worthwhile: when separated, the two genres speak for different kinds of wisdom, and these seem irreconcilable. But comic and tragic strands are often twisted together. We have comic characters and moments in ancient tragedy, such as the Watchman in *Antigone*, who runs humorous rings around his king, and the scenes in *Bacchae* that show Dionysus toying with his young cousin in a way that is both cruel and comic—not unlike Hamlet's mocking of Polonius. The most famous comic figure in modern tragedy is of course the Porter in *Macbeth*. Then there are the problem plays of Shakespeare, such as *Measure for Measure* or *Troilus and Cressida*, which seem to hover between the two genres, and recent plays like those of Beckett, Chekhov, or Brecht, which place themselves in the comic tradition while treating tragic themes of loss and absence.

Unmixed comedy covers a broad range including bitter satire, rollicking farce, love-conquers-obstacle romance, and honesty about the human condition. We have Touchstone's clowning at the light end of a comic spectrum. At the other we could put the performance of Gethin Price in Trevor Griffiths's *Comedians* (1976), whose gags evoke the laughter of alienation and despair. Historical strands of comedy curl into even the darkest plays of Ibsen, and they provide the main structure for Beckett.

The tragic tradition implies a certain moral order; things go dreadfully wrong in tragedy, but we have the comfort of knowing at the end that order has triumphed. Murder has come out, the guilty have suffered, the heroes who rose too high have been brought low. And we, who are not heroes, and who have no chance of rising too high, are not directly threatened. In tragic recognition, tragic figures rediscover their own humanity, while we in the audience are allowed to believe that we have never forgotten ours.

Tragic heroes have a past before the curtain rises, and this explains the predicament in which they act. That is why they can take responsibility for what has become of them, as they do in the most effective recognition scenes. Comic heroes have no past they can remember; all their predicaments are generated on stage before our eyes. They seem ambushed by the absurdity of human life. They never understand themselves or take responsibility. Comedy leaves us to recognize comic characters for what they are and to see that they are us. Tragic characters are doomed, and so they have no future. We never learn how comic characters turned out to be the way they are, so they have no past. But they are often promised a future, such as a happy marriage, though this is a future we would not want to see on stage. Tragedy takes place in a world ordered for our understanding; comedy pictures an episode of order pulled by a magician's wand from a world without meaning.

We weep at miseries we understand; we find comfort in weeping with understanding. But we laugh at the absurdity that defies our understanding, and laughter is a greater comfort.

ELEVEN

Understanding Theater

Three friends, a rabbi, a priest, and an atheist, attend a performance of Beckett's *Endgame*. They have never seen the play before, and they know nothing about Beckett or about any of his works, so they are here to experience the play without preconceptions about what they are to see. Tonight Hamm and Clov and the trashcan parents will face the end of all things before a fresh audience.

This has been a superb production, and the actors are in good form tonight. The actors and director have understood Beckett's script very well, and they know how to bring out humor and despair at the same time. Afterward, the director interviews the three friends to see how well they understood the play.

The rabbi says he was the first to laugh when Clov forgot his ladder and had to go limping back to retrieve it, before the first line of the play. The atheist was shocked at the rabbi's peals of laughter. "It wasn't funny," he expostulates. "That poor cripple, his mind going, his world slipping away from him—how can you laugh at a thing like that?" "But it was funny," says the priest. "I couldn't help laughing. He was playing it for laughs, wasn't he? You atheists take everything too seriously." "God himself would laugh," says the rabbi. "Now that I can't believe," says the priest. The director writes all this down.

"What did you feel when Hamm asked for his painkiller?" asks the director. "Did any of you feel like laughing at that?" No, not even the rabbi had laughed at that. The atheist was reminded of his mother, who had begged to die lucid but had breathed her last in a haze of drugs pumped into her by her well-meaning children and attendants, who hated to think of her in pain. At Hamm's first call for painkiller, the atheist was struck with sudden grief for his mother and sank into the bottomless despair of knowing that, in the end, a person's wishes mean nothing. The rabbi, whose parents are still full of life, reports that he didn't take the painkiller issue very seriously. "He didn't look like a man in pain," he says, and the director nods. She and the cast had decided there was enough pain in the script, without adding much in performance.

"But I almost laughed," said the priest. "When I preach about the last things, my people tune out. They don't want to think about the end at all; they are looking for ways to anesthetize themselves. I saw this as a play about people's reluctance to face the radical contingency of this world."

"I agree," says the rabbi. "People don't want to face the end of human life. The painkiller represents your religion, of course, because it promises good things for the faithful after Jesus returns to judge the quick and the dead. We are more honest in our beliefs: we face the pain and try to laugh about it."

The atheist turns to the director: "Did any of us understand the play?" he asks. The director nods. "You all did," she says.

"Impossible," says the priest. "None of us had the same reaction. Understanding should be the same for all. But this play is impossible to understand. Each of us brings his own life experiences and his own ideas about death to this play, and we can't help it."

"Right," says the atheist. "This play invites us to have many different ideas. They may all be equally good, taken by themselves. But they can't all be right about the play. If the play could really be understood, it would allow only one correct understanding. We three—if we have understood anything, it is not the play. We have understood the life experiences that we brought to the play. At best we have understood ourselves. We have not understood *Endgame*."

Behind the atheist's judgment lies a long tradition of philosophers insisting that understanding is about the truth, and the truth is the same for all. If two people disagree on a matter of truth, at least one of them must be wrong. But understanding theater is not simply a matter of assessing truths about a play. It requires emotions as well as beliefs, and these emotions arise in a complex relationship between actions presented on stage and the lives of the watchers. To understand *Endgame* you have to understand yourself and the play together.

So the atheist is wrong. They can all three disagree and still understand the performance equally well. But none of them has achieved a final understanding of the performance, any more than they have arrived at final understandings of themselves. When you have solved a puzzle, you may close the book and put it away. But understanding theater is not like solving a puzzle. After the performance is over, it may linger in your mind, and your feelings about it may change on reflection, even as you yourself are changing.

The disagreement about *Endgame* grew out of two kinds of difference. Because they have different beliefs, the three watchers understand the symbolism of the play differently. And because they have different life experiences and different emotional dispositions, they respond differently at an emotional level. We shall have to see how these differences are compatible with understanding.

Some differences, on the other hand, rule out understanding, because some interpretations are just wrong. *Endgame* is not about a birthday party or a wedding. All watchers of *Endgame* should agree that the play shows four people facing the end of all things. No other human beings are alive. Nothing happens outside their shelter. At the end they have no food, no medicine, and not even a catheter to help an old man urinate. Clov cannot sit. Hamm cannot stand. They have nothing left to do but to speak. If watchers miss these points they have misunderstood the play.

Action is the stuff of theater. The art of performance aims to make its actions understandable, while the art of watching aims at understanding those same actions. After the performance, a good audience can correctly describe the series of actions that forms the plot: After a football game, you should be able to say who won and roughly how they did it; after *Antigone* you should be able to say who died and why. You have to follow the plot if you are going to understand the play, but following the plot is not the same as understanding the performance.

An audience that understands the play does more than follow the plot: during the play they have been emotionally attuned to the events that are staged. That is, they have experienced appropriate feelings and responses. A good audience feels pity or fear at actions that are sad or threatening, and bursts into laughter at actions that are hilarious. But attunement is not all. An intelligent audience reflects on a play, and students are often required to do so.

11.1 Reflecting on Theater

After the play, an audience that has watched with understanding may take time to reflect on what they have seen. Before the play, we might prepare by reading the text and making sure we know what it means. And the performers, if they are any good, will have taken some pains to understand the play before rehearsals begin. Because this takes place after the performance is over or before it begins, it is not as theatrical as emotional attunement. But it is still about theater.

Interpreting text

Scholarship is essential to interpreting a text, but this is more than an academic exercise. The performers must know what their words mean, if they are to convey that meaning to the audience. For old plays like *Macbeth* or really old ones like *Antigone*, we depend on people who know the language and history of the period that gave birth to the play.

History matters more than you might think. You'll miss part of the point of the *Antigone* if you do not know that leaving rebels unburied was not uncommon as a punishment for the crime of waging civil war. We tend to love the young firebrand who gives her name to the play, but we need to know that her culture does not entirely support her point of view. And it may help with *Macbeth* to know that it was written at a time of rising fascination with witches and an increase in the brutal hunting down of eccentric women.

As for language, the point should be obvious. You need a good translation of *Antigone*, and for *Macbeth* you need to know something about Elizabethan usage. If the actors understand the lines, they can go a long way towards helping the audience. If the audience cannot make out what the lines mean, there is little hope that they will understand the play. I have seen Greekless audiences take away a fair understanding of a play performed in Greek, however. Like the foreigner who came in from the cold at Alice's wedding, we snatch at every clue we can to understand a scene with lines that are opaque. When we have no idea what is going on, we may manage at best a weak emotional attunement, what I have called tonal sympathy.

Reading symbols

Remember the painkiller in *Endgame?* It has run out, and our few survivors must face the end with whatever consciousness is left to them. The priest saw the painkiller as a symbol of people's ability to forget the radical contingency of their lives, and so not to take his religious teaching as seriously as he would like. The rabbi went the opposite direction: "It is your religion," he says. "The promise that your church makes to its members is a kind of painkiller, but it has run out. In the last hours of the human race, religion will have no solace for us."

This disagreement is not about *Endgame*; it is about religion, a matter of great importance to this audience. If the rabbi and the priest are busy decoding symbols during the performance of *Endgame*, they are not watching the play, or at least they are not watching the play very well. Hamm is pleading for his medicine, a drug on which he depends, and that should be enough for an attentive audience. Afterward, perhaps, the audience may ask whether the drug stands for something outside the play. This could be part of a reflection about the author's intention, which is nothing to do with theater as such. But it may also be a reflection about the meaning of the play for these watchers, as they try to bring it home to themselves, to connect it to their own lives. We should not be surprised to find that the rabbi and the priest bring *Endgame* back to different homes. They do not live in the same place.

Bringing it home

You do not understand a piece of theater unless you see how it bears on you, until you bring it home to your own life. Because we are all leading different lives, bringing a play home will be different for each of us, and it will result in a different understanding. The philosopher Arthur Danto writes:

> The thought I want to advance is that literature is not universal in the sense of being about every possible world insofar as possible, as philosophy in its nonliterary dimension aspires to be, nor about what may happen to be the case in

just this particular world, as history...aspires to be, but about each reader who experiences it....Each work is about the "I" that reads the text, identifying himself not with the implied reader...but with the actual subject of the text in such a way that each work becomes a metaphor for each reader: perhaps the same metaphor for each.

This is an exciting proposal. It would accord equal value to different understandings. For our atheist, *Endgame* is a metaphor for his mother's death; for the priest, it is a metaphor for his despair over the erosion of religion. Same play, same metaphor, perhaps, but different meanings.

Bringing a piece of theater home, however, is not as easy as you may think. Even in reflection after the play is over, you may lose the play altogether as you turn your thoughts to yourself. You may all too easily destroy something by bringing it home. Our atheist was very close to losing *Endgame* when he let it remind him of his mother's death. How can you bring the play home with you and still have it breathing and full of life?

The most blatant case of killing a play by bringing it home occurs in Shakespeare's *Hamlet*, during the play within the play. Hamlet has designed his production of *The Murder of Gonzago* to bring home to his uncle a certain truth about his life, and he succeeds so powerfully that his uncle puts an end to the play. This is King Claudius's moment of truth, but it has nothing to do with the play.

When Claudius understands Hamlet's production of *The Murder of Gonzago* he understands the mind of his nephew, and, if he did not do so before, he understands what he has done—his brother's murder, the rank offense "that smells to heaven." In understanding these things, besides, he is struck with emotions that take him out of his seat in the theater and bring him literally to his knees. And this appears to be what it is for Claudius to understand the play, for if he had not left his seat, and not fallen to his knees, desperate to pray but unable to do so, and later if he had not banished his nephew—if he had not done all of that, we would not agree that he had understood the play. Somehow, we would say, he missed the point. Perhaps he was distracted by a kiss from Gertrude, or perhaps he fell asleep or let his mind wander to affairs of state; perhaps he was watching Hamlet's crude behavior with Ophelia. But no, Claudius did not miss the point.

Still, I do not think that he has understood the play. It was not the play but his sense of guilt that brought Claudius to his knees, and this was no part of the play or its production. Understanding no doubt happens in the theater, as Claudius's example shows; but what he understood was not a work of theater. Claudius has understood his own life as it was represented metaphorically on stage, and he has understood Hamlet's purpose in staging the play. But all this is outside theater.

Good watchers of theater will not bring what they are watching home while they are watching it. If they did, they'd stop paying attention to the play. But they will want to bring the play home later on, in reflection, and when they do this the play and some truth about their lives will be in their minds together, like the elements of a living metaphor. The use of "dough" for money has long since lost its life; it just means "money." But once upon a time it presented the staff of life and money together to the mind. So it is when a play is brought home alive.

A pair of lovers goes home after watching *Romeo and Juliet*, and the play is with them for months afterward, in their loving and in their fear of loss. An ambitious man goes home after watching *Macbeth* and harks back to the play as he asks himself how far his ambition might take him. A young woman watches *Antigone*, and the image of the rebel lives with her for days as the embodiment of standing up against authority, but she also keeps alive the image of Creon, the thoughtful ruler who is trying to do right but does not listen well to young people. She thinks about how this gap between youth and age widens in the play, as it does in her own life, and asks herself how it might narrow. She has not brought the whole play home—it is far too rich for that—but she has brought enough home to grow in understanding, both of the play and of herself.

11.2 Attunement

I cannot tune my cello to every kind of noise. Many noises are confused, cacophonous, and there is no tuning to them. An orchestra starts with the clear tone of the oboe, not a jumble of sounds from the street. In the same way, not every piece of theater can be understood. Some plays or performances are incoherent. Suppose a director instructs the cast of the *Bacchae* to play Agave's mad scene simply for laughs. There she is, with the head of her son in her hands, exultant in her demented belief that she has killed a lion with her own hands. The scene is absurd, horrible, fascinating. But this director has rendered it only laughable. If the audience responds to the situation as they understand it, they will have to miss the director's cues to laugh; if the audience simply laughs the scene away, they will misunderstand the situation. So there is no understanding this scene as it has been performed. It makes no sense.

Emotion-engaging properties

Theater puts actions on stage. Both the actions and the characters who take action have what I call emotion-engaging properties. By "emotion-engaging property" I mean such properties as being scary or amusing or boring or shocking (for events) or being charming or hateful or admirable (for characters). These properties belong to actions and characters whether or not we recognize them; these properties belong to characters and actions whether or not a given performance represents them as having those properties. Playwrights and actors and directors can make mistakes, as they would do if they represented a loathsome person as being admirable or a gruesome scene as a light joke. The possibility that plays can be wrong in this way raises a special problem for the understanding of theater.

To be understandable, a play must show its events as having the emotion-engaging properties they actually have: a funny event must be funny, a pitiful one must be sad, and a frightening one must be scary. Many events have complex emotion-engaging properties, and these can be understood by those capable of complex responses. That is why there are such things as dramatic irony and black humor, and why these are not failures of consistency. Still, a playwright or director can, by mistake, give to his events the wrong properties, as did the director who made the gory scene from the *Bacchae* into a sick joke. Confronted with such a choice a wise audience should see that the scene does not make sense and not attempt to understand it as shown. Persons as well as scenes may have complex emotion-engaging properties, and these may be misrepresented even by the person himself. Someone who seems a charming villain calls for a complex understanding; but someone who seems a truly admirable villain defies understanding. In real life, we demand to know him better before trying to understand him; in theater, we simply reject him as badly drawn.

Emotion-engaging properties raise philosophical questions that I will not pursue here. They are not like "straight" or "curved," which seem to belong to the natures of things. They are not even like "red" and "green," which seem to emerge in human perception. These properties emerge in human emotional response. I wish to claim, nevertheless, that these are not subjective. The whole world may laugh at Agave's scene, but it is still gruesome. People who watch well may be very rare, but they will find the scene gruesome, and they will pity Agave. They are better watchers than those who merely laugh at her.

Good watchers respond to what is there, laugh at the humor, weep at the suffering, and so on. Bad audiences laugh in the wrong places. But who is to say what is there? The majority found the scene funny, but I claim that it was gruesome and pitiable. Who is to decide between us, and on what basis? Emotion-engaging properties cannot be measured with a stick or a thermometer.

The measure of emotion-engaging properties in theater is the good watcher. Being a good watcher belongs to ethics, and so, in the end, we find that emotion-engaging properties are themselves irreducibly ethical.

Watching well

How well you watch shows how good a person you are. Following a tradition that goes back to Aristotle, I take it that your goodness belongs to your character, which consists in your ability to respond with emotions that lead you to act well. A good person is one who is generally moved by emotion to do good things. An ability to respond well in a certain sort of situation is called a "virtue." Courage, for example, is the virtue that enables us to do the right thing without being deterred by fear. Aristotle describes courage as the balance point between too much fear on the one hand and too much confidence on the other.

Before all else, a good audience respects the people it watches by granting them the honor of being worth watching. At the same time, this good audience is prepared to laugh at the people it watches when they are ridiculous—without giving up the respect that made them watchers in the first place. A good balance between respect and laughter is the aim of *reverence* in human affairs, and reverence is the primary virtue of good watchers. There can be no watching without it. (I have written at length about reverence in an earlier book [2001a].)

The second virtue of good watchers is compassion or *humanity*, as I prefer to call it, which we show by feeling pity for those who suffer. The third is *courage*. A good audience fears for those it sees in danger, but not so much as to want to prevent them from doing what is right.

Pity and fear are the emotions Aristotle associated with tragic theater. As these are kinds of pain, Aristotle left us with a famous question: How can we take pleasure in a performance to which our main responses are painful pity and painful fear? This has been much discussed, by me among others, but here I will only point out that understanding is itself a kind of pleasure, and these emotions play a role in understanding.

The fourth virtue is *justice*. We feel our sense of justice as a surge of anger when the people we watch are treated outrageously. We are furious at the villains, and with good right. Public trials and executions are forms of theater in which this anger is answered and allowed to subside. The same often happens in mimetic theater; the pain of anger is resolved by punishment. So all of those who put out Gloucester's eyes in *King Lear* come to bad ends, and this we find most satisfying. But Brecht's plays leave us with an anger unresolved; we feel that "there must, there must, there has to be a way" to make things right for the good person of Setzuan. But that is not available in society as we know it.

The virtues are so closely related that some philosophers count only one of them, and others provide much longer lists. But these four cover the main responses that theater engages—respect, laughter, fear, pity, and anger. There are more emotions than these, of course, and virtues I have not named may be assigned to temper them, but the important idea here is that good watchers respond virtuously to whatever it is that they watch.

Attunement of an audience to a theater piece depends on the ethical character of the audience. Watchers are attuned to a piece of theater when their responses match the emotion-engaging properties that people of good character would find in that piece of theater.

The paradox of attunement

I said earlier that a good audience feels pity or fear at actions that are sad or threatening, and bursts into laughter at actions that are hilarious. But our rabbi laughed at a moment that made our atheist weep during *Endgame*. This play is not unusual in showing us actions that are both sad and hilarious; one good watcher may laugh at the hilarity, while another grieves at the sadness. Attunement apparently is not the same for all of us, and that is absurd. If two violins are tuned to the same oboe, they are tuned to each other; why then, if two watchers are attuned to the same performance, may they be out of tune with each other?

A relativist would say that the rabbi and the priest are both right, because both are true to their personal experience, and there is nothing more to go on. The relativist would deny that the scene has emotion-engaging properties. There is nothing more to this story, the relativist would say, than the emotions that people in the audience actually feel.

But there is more to this story. The business with the ladder was both humorous and pitiable, like much in Beckett's plays, and it has these two properties whether you are aware of them or not. Suppose you disagree: "No," you say. "It wasn't funny." I can't persuade you to be amused, once you have missed the point of a joke, but I can show you how this scene falls in a tradition of stage gags leading to the sort of humor found in Beckett. I can give reasons to believe that the scene has the property of being funny. And you might concede that it is presented as a gag, even though it is not one that amuses you. You may go on to say that you are pleased with yourself for not being amused by this gag, because you think that, in an ethical sense, it is not funny. Good people would not laugh at it. In this discussion we are arguing first about the scene and then about ethics, but neither of us bases our case on the nature of our personal responses. There are facts—some of them ethical—under dispute.

What shall we say then about the atheist and the rabbi? The director said she thought they both understood the play. I can make sense of this without falling into relativism. The scene fascinates us because it has conflicting properties, humor and pathos. Both atheist and rabbi have been attuned to properties that the scene truly has; they disagree because they have been attuned to different properties, and they were attuned to different properties because of attitudes they brought with them to the play. Both of them really do understand the scene, up to a point. Far better, however, is the understanding of the priest, who is sensitive to both humor and pathos; in him humor and pathos resonate with his sense of the absurdity of human life apart from God, and he holds back from both tears and laughter, in awe at this reminder of the human condition.

11.3 The Web of Understanding

Understanding an event, whether historical or fictional, whether present to us in life or re-presented to us on stage, is always the same thing, according to the theory that I am proposing: Understanding an event is responding to it with appropriate emotions, and these emotions are intentionally linked to that particular event. That is why it was one thing to understand the scene in *The Murder of Gonzago*, and another for Claudius to understand his killing of his own brother. These are different events, and understanding them is constituted by different emotions. It does not follow, however, that the two understandings are not linked. Claudius's understanding the scene does lead to his understanding of his life, and, no doubt, if his life had not been overwhelming, his self-understanding would have contributed to his understanding of the play.

All of our understandings are woven together in a web of capacities for emotion, and this is why we set a high value on understanding events even in fiction. When I understand the death of Ophelia I gain not because this is exactly the same thing as understanding some event in my own life but because a growing power to respond to the plight of frightened and abused women enhances my ability to understand both the play and the events around my life. Understanding an event is good in itself, but it is good also as evidence of an enhanced capacity to understand other events.

Here is a personal example of how this works. I have seen Shakespeare's *Henry V* on more occasions than I can specifically remember, and I have read it and studied the text. For years I felt the pride of an anglophile at the conversion of naughty Prince Hal into a noble warrior king. This pride was so strong in me that I overlooked the seamy side of English Tudor jingoism and felt no whit of horror at Henry's threatened massacre at Harfleur. Shakespeare's bloodthirstier contemporaries probably felt less horror than I do now at such scenes; still, this speech of Henry's is remarkable even in Shakespeare. Here is what Hal promises the people of this town if they do not surrender:

> If not—why in a moment look to see
> The blind and bloody soldier with foul hand
> Defile the locks of your shrill-shrieking daughters,
> Your fathers taken by their silver beards
> And their most reverend heads dashed to the walls;
> Your naked infants spitted upon pikes
> Whiles the mad mothers with their howls confus'd
> Do break the clouds…

> What say you? Will you yield and this avoid?
>
> (Shakespeare, *Henry V,* act 3, scene 3, lines 33–42)

How could I have heard this with pride and excitement, as just another episode in the life of a warrior prince? But I did. In fact, I was so swept up in the mood of Henry's heroism that I felt the wooing of Katherine by Henry at the end of the play to be delightfully romantic. I was so proud of Henry, and I felt she was so lucky to have him, that I felt none of the shock I now feel at witnessing what is really a rape scene, a symbol for the brutal conquest of France by England. I did not misinterpret the scene. I knew he was forcing himself on the young woman, but I did not respond as one should to such a scene. There are clues enough that the princess is being forced by arms and rhetoric and the power over her of her father. But these passed me by.

I missed clues also when I heard the St. Crispin's Day speech, which left me enthralled and inspired. Here is how Henry encourages his captains when they feel their numbers are too few to face the French:

> If we are marked to die, we are enow
> To do our country loss; and if to live,
> The fewer men, the greater share of honor.
> God's will, I pray thee wish not one man more.
> . . . .
> This story shall the good man teach his son;
> And Crispin Crispian shall ne'er go by,
> From this day to the ending of the world,
> But we in it shall be rememb'red—
> We few, we happy few, we band of brothers...
>
> (Shakespeare, *Henry V* act 4, scene 3, lines 20–23 and 56–60)

When I hear that speech, now, forty years and a nasty little war later, I am angry and dismayed at seeing a shallow and violent young man manipulate his elders. I still hear the ring of heroism too, and I am excited by it as I always was; but I now smell evil in this plausible prince. Now I ask myself, "Did Henry really treat his soldiers as brothers?" And Shakespeare gives us the answer: he did not. Once the battle is over, he deals with Williams from a distance, almost with contempt. And this was not what he had promised for his "band of brothers."

At the end I heard from the final chorus that this battle was all in vain. Then it washed over me. How could a victory be in vain, when it was so glorious? I did not know enough to hear this theme.

I think that now, at last, I understand the play. It is not, as I used to think, a simple celebration of English patriotism, to which the appropriate response is enthusiastic pride. Nor is it, as Sam Johnson saw it, an inconsistent rendering of a half-converted prince, sometimes sweet Hal and sometimes sour. Instead, the play represents the defeat of France by an irresponsible boy-king, an event that is stirring, exciting, and terrible all at once. The appropriate response is complex and disturbing.

I am able to respond in this way now because of my experience. It is not that I identify with Henry or even see him as a metaphor for myself. I never did anything remotely like sending troops once more into the breach. But in attempting to understand what happened to me in war, I have learned to feel emotions as complex as those required for an understanding of *Henry V*. I might say, "War is like this, war is a universal, the same for me and for Shakespeare." But this is to miss the point. My understanding is not of war in general. I am coming to understand my own war, and in doing so I am developing the capacity to understand Shakespeare's war as well. It is equally true the other way around. When I first heard the St. Crispin's day speech the way I do now it took my breath away, and I felt in the same moment both the enthusiasm of my joining the army and my horror at that enthusiasm. These were different understandings, my understanding of the play and of my life. But each strengthened the other.

A historian would point out that I have not been alone in this. Our culture generally took pride in Prince Hal from the 1940s to the late 1960s, then soured on him after Vietnam. My changing response reflects a changing culture, but it also reflects personal growth. My earlier understanding of the play was forced; I could sustain it only by overlooking much of what I saw in the play. Now I can take all of the play into account.

Of course I was not alone in this either. As it is with individuals, so with those who share a culture. We should not be afraid to say that an entire culture misunderstands a play, if it is denied the experience it would need to support that understanding. If people are generally shocked by Restoration Comedy, for example, then they will not understand it. Those plays are funny, not shocking.

The historian is right, however, to insist that those who saw Prince Hal with pride in their hearts were not making a mistake. There is nothing they could have done that they failed to do. They felt for Hal just what their history had prepared them to feel. So did I. But history can serve us well or badly in preparing us to understand. There is an element of luck in understanding. There are many things I would never have understood if I had not had children. So it is with theater. The more you have lived, the more you will understand.

TWELVE

The Mask of Wisdom

The curtain falls on Fortinbras and a stage littered with corpses. The curtain will rise once more to allow us the release of applause, but then, after the applause dies away, we should ask, as we gather our coats, are we any better for having watched *Hamlet*? We have whiled away a long evening; we have been engaged and entertained; and we have been reminded of a string of famous, half-forgotten lines and speeches. But are we any wiser?

I would like to believe that I might come away from a performance of *Hamlet* wiser than when I came in, with my mind enriched. But what food is there in theater to enrich the mind? Food for the mind should be something like truth, but there is precious little truth in theater, and, if there is any truth in theater, it is easier learned in other ways. What truth is there in a football game, or a wedding, or a funeral? Things happened at these events, but the truth that they happened is not very nourishing. We can learn such things from a newspaper, in any case, without attending the event.

In the case of *Hamlet*, however, these things did *not* happen—they did not happen while we were watching (unlike what transpired at the wedding), and they did not happen at any other time either. Shakespeare made them up. Perhaps we will find some truth in the speeches. Polonius is not entirely a fool; some of his advice is worth remembering. It comes, after all, from an ancient source of platitudes. We have seen how

Creon and his son exchange platitudes during their debate in *Antigone*, and much that they say is true. Haemon is right, a city of one man is a desert; and Creon can be right also, as when he speaks of the need for orderly succession to power in a state. So we might choose to believe only what is wisely said in a play. But we, hearing Polonius, are we wise enough already to know when he speaks the truth or when he is foolish? If we are, then we have nothing to learn from him; we brought our wisdom into the theater and acknowledge it in the characters. If we are not able to tell folly from wisdom, then his speech could do us harm; we might take his folly to heart and ignore his wisdom. But we didn't come to *Hamlet* for the wisdom of Polonius; Shakespeare was the one we thought had wisdom to give us. But what could that wisdom be?

Wisdom is not the same as knowing a bunch of things that are true. You may learn many things that are true from theater. If you watch Tom Stoppard's *Invention of Love* attentively, you will learn the principles of textual criticism as practiced by A. E. Housman, and you will learn them as surely and as accurately as I did from my classics tutor at Oxford University. But I didn't need theater to learn this. The same goes for all didactic theater and theatrical didacticism. Most classes I attended as a student were theatrical in one way or another, since I was supposed to shut up and pay attention most of the time. But the truths that I learned in lectures—their content, we would normally say—I could have learned from books. The theatricality of the lectures added something, but not to the truth of what the lecturers said.

When truth is spoken in theater, theater can show us what it is like to be the person who believes this truth. Polonius is the sort of person who witlessly mingles wisdom and platitudes, and we can see what it is like to be Polonius if he is well played. Great lecturers may embody the truth of what they say, even in a classroom setting, if they show their students what it is like to live as those who believe the things they teach.

Theater does not always speak truth directly, however, and we are looking for what theater as such might contribute to our wisdom, or, I would prefer to say, what our minds can do for themselves on the basis of theater. We are looking for the wisdom that is peculiar to theater, that belongs to theater in all the shapes that theater takes, whenever the art of theater is successful on stage and in the audience. Since the art of theater makes human action worth watching, we should expect this wisdom to be unique to the watching or the performing of human action. What is it about doing the art of theater that could make us wiser?

12.1 The Challenge of Philosophy

Poets in ancient Greece were reputed to be wise. Before democracy, we are told on weak authority, the rulers of Athens introduced Homer and other poets of performance in the hope of improving the common people. During democracy, theater evolved as a treasure of the people: it was both a fixture at certain religious ceremonies and the main source of education for citizenship. Epic and tragic poetry were both written for performance; both represent the art of theater, and together they constitute the wisdom literature of ancient Greece.

If wisdom was the property of poets, however, what claim could philosophers make for themselves? Plato, the first writer who identi-fied himself as a philosopher, would not concede one ounce of wis-dom to poets. If they set down wise words in their poems, Plato held, they were inspired to do so by the gods, while they themselves—the poets—understood nothing of what they composed. In other words, if there is wisdom in a poem, it could not have come from the poet. So when anyone claims wisdom for a poet, he is taken in by mimesis: poets may occasionally have the effect of wise men, by uttering something wise, but they are not wise themselves, and so they are not to be relied on for any real wisdom. Plato therefore insisted that poets of theater only pretend to be wise, and that, far from improving the common people by theater, poets lead them astray. Poets of theater lead folks astray, according to Plato, precisely because they are limited to showing us human action.

The trouble with action is this: philosophers who follow Plato are seeking to understand the nature of justice or other such entity. But these philosophers say that human action is at best a mere imitation of what they are looking for. They are looking to know what justice truly and precisely is, but there is nothing they can look at in human action to find the answer. Their argument goes like this: suppose we find an example in human action of perfect justice. Let's agree that Socrates acted with perfect justice when he chose to accept his penalty rather than to cor-rupt officers of the law. Couldn't we learn something useful from that?

Well, no, according to Plato and those who follow him. Seeing justice in this case will not enable us to recognize justice with certainty the next time we see it. What if, by corrupting the officers, Socrates could participate in the overthrow of a venal tyranny, if, indeed, his very act of bribing them brought to the public eye how important it was to change the system, then what would justice require of him? Recognizing justice in the first case is no help now.

Human actions are messy; they have features that make them seem right in one context and wrong in another. Plato captures this idea with an image: in what we call real life, human action is at best a mimesis of justice. But action on the stage is (in most cases) mimetic of real action; it follows that theater gives us, at best, a mimesis of a mimesis of justice. So we should turn away from theater even more firmly than we should turn away from watching human action, and we should focus our minds' eyes on the nature of justice itself. That, say Plato and his followers, is the road to wisdom. The poets of theater are on the same road, but they are headed the wrong direction, away from justice, toward mimesis.

Plato was no fool, and he was right about this: theater is no place to learn the truth about justice. But then neither is the world in which we live. Justice does not live here; it does not live even in heaven, according to Plato. It can be glimpsed only beyond the rim of heaven, where it is visible only to disembodied souls that are pure enough not to be pulled downward by desires for things of this earth. That is why, Plato says, philosophers must try to die to this world, to practice philosophy as if practicing for death itself.

This earth is no place for the wisdom that would know the true nature of justice; I will not challenge Plato on that point. But this earth is the place for another kind of wisdom, and so is theater. I call this second sort of wisdom "human." It is the wisdom of knowing ourselves. Human wisdom is available here on earth; we do not have to die in order to attain it. We may not even have to leave the theater.

Socrates provided a theater of presence in Athens for the young people who gathered to watch him show that their elders—even the ones with the most brilliant reputations for wisdom—could not answer the vital questions he put to them, questions like "What is justice?" And so these watchers were drawn into philosophy as they learned something about human limitations. They could have picked this lesson up from comedy, but Socratic theater was more immediate, more transformative of watchers into thinkers. It was also dramatic, more tightly focused on the false claims to wisdom that people actually made in the public places of Athens, false claims that affected directly the young men who clustered around Socrates as his audience. And the elders who were refuted, did they gain wisdom? In most cases, they plainly did not. They were deep inside the space of theater, unable to see themselves, and all they knew at the end was that they had been humiliated by a fiendishly clever man. So they went away not wiser but more angry at Socrates and his cleverness.

So it is generally in comedy, on stage or off. There is no scene of recognition for the characters. No one in comedy says, "What a fool I have been! I must change." Only the audience, if they are wise enough, can say to themselves, "What a fool that man is!" And if some watchers are wise enough to learn from this, they will add: "And how similar we are to him! We must take care not to fall into his pattern; it would be all to easy for us to do so." That is comic recognition, self-recognition by an audience. It may occur as well around Molière's stage or Socrates' theater of presence. A foolish audience may leave the theater unchanged, except perhaps for growing in self-satisfaction; they felt superior to the characters they watched, and that was that.

Tragic recognition is available at Socrates' theater as well, but few of Socrates' companions experience it. Among these few was Socrates himself. He knew his limitations. He was the first to call self-knowledge "human wisdom"—the recognition of his own ignorance. He claimed this for himself, with a strangely proud humility. And where did he obtain that wisdom, if not from watching himself in argument, sometimes even in argument with himself? He must have watched his own Socratic theater and seen himself for what he was—a fierce arguer, a passionate seeker after truth, but, in the end, a man with no wisdom beyond his own self-knowledge.

This is the hardest art of theater to practice—the art of watching oneself, self-theater, the art of being present to oneself. By my account, it transcends theater altogether, once it erases the boundary between watcher and watched. It is too much for most of us most of the time, to be self-watchers. That is why we need to watch people other than ourselves; that is why we need theater to give us human wisdom. But here lies a paradox: theater shows only what can be seen, but human wisdom is never visible. People who are humanly wise never make a spectacle of their wisdom. Anyone who tried to do so would be a fool.

12.2 Wisdom in Hiding

Socrates had human wisdom, but most people who knew him did not know this about him. Socrates did not look, or act, like a wise man. He concealed his wisdom so successfully that the people of Athens voted to kill him. A majority in the people's court thought he was maliciously clever, but not wise. They thought he pretended to be ignorant, while actually knowing something very well. They thought him expert at the art of dazzling young people by humiliating their elders. This Socrates, this man they were killing, he was brainy and wicked, they thought, but never wise.

Sophocles, the poet of tragic plays, had human wisdom in a different way, and perhaps this was harder to miss; when he died at a grand old age the Athenians buried him with honors due a demigod. But he, no more than Socrates, fits our image of a wise man. We have nothing from him directly, no wise words we can live by. He designed everything he wrote to be heard from behind the linen mask of an actor who was playing a part, not to come from his own lips, and not to represent his own beliefs directly. Sophocles was honored at his death not for his plays (although they won many prizes) but for his role in bringing to Athens the worship of the healer-god. He was the Receiver, the Host of the god, not the god's mouthpiece. The man they were honoring was good-hearted and religious, thought the Athenians, and prudent in counsel for affairs of the city. But we do not know that they ever thought of him as a sage.

The very wise are different from you and me. If we could find one of them, what wonders we could learn! If only the wise would make themselves known and talk to us! But, alas, we are told they are usually silent. They hold in the fastness of their minds the secrets of life and death, what lies on the other side of birth or death, what it means to live too many years or not enough, even what purposes should shape my life or yours today. You and I could rely on a sage to tell us how to live and what to believe. We could trust a sage to put nothing in our minds but what would be good for us, whether it is true or false. A sage could give us myths to believe that would lighten our burdens or help us play our assigned roles in society, and these would be good. A sage could even cloud our minds to protect us from truths that would torment us or lead us astray, like a parent who knows best what truths a child should face.

We will never find a sage, however, and, even if we did find one, we could not be sure of her wisdom, and, even if we were sure, we could not be able to make her speak. The sage on the mountaintop is a comic image for us now, calling up the laughter that masks despair. Sage-wisdom is not for us. Sophocles and Socrates both knew that. It is only the god who is truly wise, and this they both recognized, in reverence. Human beings who think they are wise with the wisdom of gods are doomed. That is the principal lesson of Sophocles' tragic theater, and it is the principal lesson of Socrates' theater of questioning as well.

The wisdom of sages has doubles, however, and these sometimes take us in. False sages and false prophets pretend to sage-wisdom and ask us to follow them. They may say that they know the mind of God; they may have the grace and powerful presence we associate with wisdom; they may have drawn to themselves a wide circle of admirers who believe that they are wise. And these false sages are often not conscious of being frauds; how could their many admirers be wrong? They believe they are wise, and their first victims are themselves.

The poets of theater did not pretend to be sages, as far as we can tell from our sources. They could not possibly do so; poets of theater cannot misrepresent themselves because they do not represent themselves at all. They are absent from their work. For all that, Plato takes these poets to be pretenders and sets out to unmask them. And of course he succeeds in showing that they are not sages.

If you are looking for the wisdom of sages, you will not find it anywhere on the human stage, and it follows that you will not find it on the stage that art theater creates either. But there is another wisdom, as I have said, and it is what I have been calling "human wisdom." No one can pretend to human wisdom. How could you set out to show off something of which you know that it never shows? Simply to claim that you have wisdom would be enough to prove that you do not have it. Human wisdom always hides.

But not deliberately. The humanly wise do not try to keep us away from their wisdom, far from it. But they know that to flaunt what they have is to lose it. And even if they could unmask themselves for us, they know that what we would see and take away for ourselves would be false. No one can give to another the wisdom that is self-knowledge. You may only find it for yourself.

Good theater carries wisdom, but the wisdom it carries is human and in disguise, with the result that only artful watchers take it in. A wise audience is able to unmask a piece of theater and glimpse the wisdom that hides in the form of entertainment. Theater is the finest of the masks that wisdom can wear. Plato thought theater disguises its foolishness as wisdom, but he had it exactly backward. Theater does not wear the mask of wisdom, not ever. But wisdom always wears a mask, and sometimes the mask it wears is theater. At its best, theater just is the mask of wisdom.

12.3 "Many Wonders, Many Terrors"

The quarterback takes the snap, falls back, and looks for his receiver. Seeing that his man is blocked, he dodges sideways and begins to run. He is fast, graceful, unpredictable; and he makes fools of the defenders. As he crosses the goal line, eighty thousand people are on their feet. Half of them are elated by his team's victory, but all of them are elated by something else. They have all seen something wonderful. A great athlete is a wonder, and what he does reminds us how splendid a human being may be.

A famous ode in Greek tragedy begins, "Many wonders, many terrors, but nothing more wonderful than the human race—or more dangerous." The poet is Sophocles, the play is *Antigone*, and the lines seem to interrupt the conflict between a ruler and his niece over the burial of a young rebel, her brother. What the lines mean in this context is a puzzle, but in the greater context of theater this is no puzzle at all: "This is what we are," says the poet. "What you see on this stage is a species that is wonderful, but dangerous too, and for all that, vulnerable." He runs through the many things we human beings have conquered—the earth, the sea, the animal kingdom, the violence that would destroy society—but we have not conquered death. And we have not conquered injustice. Later, the play will show something else we have not conquered: ignorance. Even when knowledge is put before us, we may overlook it, owing to the pride we take in our own opinions. Death, injustice, ignorance, and the hubris to forget that we are subject to these weaknesses—somehow these must be remembered alongside the wonders.

In the great game, our quarterback was a wonder. But we saw more than wonders on the field that day. There was injury, foul play, and even a little foolishness. After all, one side was defeated in the end. And the players who were victorious—we know that some defeats lie in store for them as well. This is who we are. I have never scored a touchdown, and I never will, but still there is something about me that the brilliant quarterback has shown. I am a member of the same species as he, and he has just proved that we are capable of what he accomplished. He has proved this, but I do not believe that I have learned it.

Don't ask the thrilled, buzzing audience what they have learned as they swarm away from the theater of sport, where the great game has just now been played out. None of them are aware of having learned anything. They are thrilled because they have watched a close and beautifully fought contest. But if we could weigh their human wisdom before and after the game, we would find that many of them are carrying a heavier load now than when they entered. Not that they have learned anything new; every fan already knows the wonders and terrors of the game. But here has been a spectacular reminder of the wonders that human beings can be, an opportunity to deepen their appreciation of these wonders and terrors. And that has been part of the thrill, at least for some of them.

Human wisdom—knowing ourselves—is not like knowing the way home from the stadium or knowing how many yards our hero chalked up today. These things you may learn once and retain, if you have a healthy memory. Human wisdom, by contrast, must constantly face its enemies, which lie in wait for it in our minds. The main enemy is our need to think well of ourselves. We prefer the wonders to the terrors. Every success brings a new distortion of our self-images, a new strain on our self-knowledge. "I did that! Look how wonderful I am!" So, looking at that, I help myself forget the less-convenient parts of self-knowledge.

The wise, however, realize that self-knowledge requires ceaseless maintenance. Socrates says that his pursuit of self-knowledge is a full time job, leaving him no opportunity to follow other interests. Human wisdom is not an acquisition; it is a process sustained by frequent reminders of the wonders and terrors that we are. That is why we can make progress in human wisdom by seeing *Hamlet* more than once— not because we need to see it often to understand the play (although that is true), but because we need to understand the same thing many times over so as to provide for it the deep roots from which it may flourish over time. But many reminders are not enough; we need to take them to heart, and this calls for courage and attention over time. Those who watch wisely do not watch absentmindedly; they watch with care and keep what they have seen on their minds afterward.

We will find it easier to be good watchers in good theater. The football game was not very good; nothing in it called attention to the actions from which we might learn the most, and a great deal of it called attention to the twin distractions of victory and defeat, which by themselves teach us nothing. To make matters worse, the game draws us in as supporters, identifying so closely with the success or failure of our team that we are unable to step back and evaluate the larger drama.

Good mimesis makes good watchers because it selects certain elements of its original (or imagined original) and spins them to produce selected effects. In *Antigone*'s Creon-Haemon debate, for example, the artist helps us see how both father and son go too far, though each has some wisdom on his side. The debate was artfully constructed to have just this effect on us. In *King Lear*, our introduction to Edmund is artfully couched so that we feel the sting of Gloucester's contempt for his illegitimate son at the same time that we recognize the father's basic goodness. Both father-son scenes offer us seeds for wisdom that we would not easily find in real-life squabbles between fathers and sons. Mimesis is more selective than life. That is why, sometimes, it can teach us more.

If you were angry to see me place football side by side with *King Lear* in the basic theory of this book, now you should forgive me. The theory showed why *King Lear* is better theater than a football game. It has a better plot than a typical football game, as we saw many chapters ago, and now we see something more important: better than any football game could possibly do, *King Lear* presents us with opportunities for growing wisdom.

12.4 How to Watch Wisely

Only the brave have the courage to grow braver. Only the reverent can advance in reverence. This is a hard truth about all of the virtues—that you must have a virtue in order to grow more of that virtue. Wisdom is the easiest case to understand: because human wisdom always hides, you must be wise already in order to recognize wisdom in its hiding places. Only the wise see wisdom in the other people who have it, and only the wise find wisdom in theater. Luckily, we all have a little wisdom. So this hard truth is no reason for the rulers to reserve theater for an elite or the well educated. Rather, it is a reason for all of us to summon up what wisdom we have when we attend the theater.

Only the wise can unmask theater. If a piece of theater carries wisdom to its audience, it does so because both watchers and watched are practicing the art of theater well. Bad watchers won't gain anything from watching a good *Hamlet*, but good watchers may be better even after seeing a poor performance.

First, if you wish to watch wisely, *watch the whole thing*. Do not avert your eyes from the injured player or tune out during Hamlet's soliloquies. Do not leave before the end. You must take the good with the bad.

Second, in order to watch wisely, you must *know what you are watching*. "O brave new world!" exclaims Miranda when she sees for the first time a cluster of her species. "How beauteous mankind is!" As indeed they are, in their fine clothes. But these are mainly rascals who would kill for power, although they have arrayed themselves to look as if they deserve to be admired. Ordinary life presents many false appearances of this sort. Miranda does not know what she is seeing. How could she, after growing up on an island where the only other human being is her extraordinary father? The men Miranda sees are making a fine show— as so often occurs in theater—but the show is deceptive. We are never as good as we seem. Plato was right this far about mimesis: if we do not recognize mimesis when we see it, we will be sadly deceived.

That business with the quarterback was only a game. Tomorrow, the same young man may stumble into a venal contract and show another side of his nature. And tomorrow, we will be attending his wedding. The next day we will see a matinee of *Hamlet*, and that is mimetic theater. This very evening, when we return from the matinee of *Hamlet*, our children will perform for us. They know we have been in the theater, and so they have been preparing all afternoon, wishing us to see that they too are worth watching. With our children, we will be watching something else, for which we do not have a name, the theater of children trying to interest their parents. We need to know which is which, because they carry different opportunities for wisdom.

So you must watch the whole thing, and know what you are watching. There is a third, and most important, rule for watching wisely: *remember who you are, and who you are not*. And a fourth: *practice to become your own best audience*.

12.5 Remember Who You Are

Here we come to the center of human wisdom, to self-knowledge. A wise audience comes to know itself more deeply while watching a play; a foolish one may be untouched. "Your majesty, and we that have free souls, it toucheth us not," says Hamlet to his uncle, the king. As he suspects, however, the king does not have a free soul, and neither do most of us.

On stage, in a tragedy, you may watch a character understand for the first time who he is and what he has done. So we see Creon take upon himself the blame for his family's catastrophe and Oedipus realize that he has become a curse on his city. Hamlet, through his soliloquies, shows us a stream of self-recognitions, and Claudius is revealed to himself by a play within a play. Claudius's moment of truth is beyond the edge of what can happen to a wise audience. Faced with his own guilt, he drowns the stage in light, storms out of the theater, and tries to find solace in prayer. For him, self-recognition ends his experience of theater. For you, the wise watcher who is watching this scene in *Hamlet*, self-recognition should be a process that lasts the whole measured time of the play. Claudius sees only himself; you in the audience are mainly seeing Claudius, but, while watching him, you do not forget who you are. He is not so wicked that you do not know that he is of one species with yourself. But Claudius himself has not learned much from watching the play; he already knew full well that he was guilty. All the play has done is remind him of that fact.

Lear is a better example for us to follow when we watch human beings. He has been a foolish old man, blind to what he is doing, oblivious to the feelings of those around him, unaware of the dementia that is growing upon him. And now he is given the sight of Tom O' Bedlam, naked in the lashings of the storm. He watches this poor fork'd creature, unaccommodated, mad. We in the audience know that poor Tom is a fake; this is all an act. But the mimesis has its effect. As he watches Tom's act, Lear finally begins to see who he is, to appreciate the enormity of his loss, to take responsibility for it. He sees Tom as himself, bereft because of a bad decision to give all to his daughters. Now his journey toward wisdom finally begins, spurring us, who are watching him, along a similar path. Lear's growing wisdom is no less because it began in watching a man fake madness; his own madness is real, and that is what he now understands. Our wisdom is no less if we gain it by watching an actor pretend to be real; we are real, and we are the subject of our new understanding. Mimesis is mimesis because its effects are in the real world.

Oedipus has learned who he is and begins his long lament. You are not he, and he is not you, but you share his recognition of what it is to be human. At one level, this man is Oedipus, realizing that he is the one who killed his father the king; at another, this is a human being, recognizing that his gift for solving riddles did not amount to much. Yes, he saved the city from disaster once upon a time, but now he is the source of trouble. So it is with you: if you are wise, you recognize that your wisdom does not always save you and that your goodness is no more reliable than your wisdom. You too can be a bane.

And now, seeing these human possibilities heightened by art and deepened by the emotions they cultivate in us, we may even take responsibility for the web of choices that lead a human being in ways such as these of Oedipus. We like to forget who we are, and, in our forgetfulness, we congratulate ourselves too easily on our wisdom, on our goodness. But not forgetting, not giving in to the temptation to self-congratulation—that is tragic wisdom.

In comedy, of course, you won't see characters stumbling on self-knowledge. The Misanthrope, Alceste, never sees that he is to blame for his own misery. He is right to blame society for its hypocrisy, but he is blind to his own. Lost in a cloud of unhappy self-congratulation, he does not notice the affection that his friends truly have for him. But we, the audience, seeing Alceste storming offstage and out of society, are able to recognize what is going on in him, because he is so familiar. He is one of us, and his failure represents one of our human possibilities, writ large. We too might condemn a fault we fail to see in ourselves.

A foolish audience would recognize none of this. If, on leaving the theater, you congratulate yourself on not being Hamlet or Oedipus or Alceste, you have forgotten who you are, and you have escaped this opportunity for growing in wisdom. Such escapes are all too easy.

12.6 Your Own Best Audience

In watching other people, practice to become your own best audience. This is the fourth rule for watching wisely. Human wisdom is knowing yourself, and to attain this you must go beyond watching others. We often think of altruism as growing outward: I start caring about myself, then about my mother, then about other relatives, and so on toward the frontiers of caring. Distant people are harder to love, and that is why we start nearby. But distant people are easier to watch, and that is why watching starts at a distance and moves inward.

A good audience understands what it watches, through an emotional attunement that is governed by ethical virtue. After practicing the virtues of good watching on other people, now turn them back on yourself. Above all, honor yourself as someone worth paying attention to, but do not lose the ability to laugh at yourself when you are silly. And when you laugh, do so with respect. That's reverence. Pity yourself when you have suffered. That's compassion, and you deserve it too. Fear for yourself when in danger, but not so much that you'd let your fear deter you from doing what you should. That's courage. And be angry when someone treats you outrageously, and be satisfied when the wrongdoers have paid. That's justice.

To live wisely, you must pay attention to yourself. Practice paying attention to others. Then bring this ability back home, and be your own best audience. But keep in mind that self-watching carried to excess would drive you crazy. Do only what you need to know yourself. There is a time to watch others, and there is a time to perform for others. And those are times when you should forget yourself.

12.7 "Both Sides Spoke Well"

Father and son, man and boy are locked in a disagreement that will kill one and bring the other to his knees. Haemon and Creon have come to the end of their formal debate and are about to start bandying lines toward a violent breakup. But first the chorus of old men tells them to listen to each other. "Both sides spoke well," they say. "Listen to each other." You may want to dismiss these old men as weak, shilly-shallying, and ineffective, but please don't. And don't for a minute think that they are relativists.

They are wise, and their wisdom could have saved this family from disaster. They have the wisdom that allows them to appreciate both sides, a wisdom that flows from human self-knowledge. They know how to find the good in what people say on both sides, and they recognize that no human being, old or young, knows enough to have the last word. We must all listen to each other because we are human, because we see only what we can see from where we stand, because there is more to be seen than any one of us can appreciate alone.

This is both the tragic heart of wisdom and the mainspring of democratic wisdom. Both sides did speak well. But neither spoke well enough to go it alone. You may watch a contest simply to see who wins or to appreciate the skill of the contestants; but you can also watch a contest to see how people's different strengths may complement one another's.

Voters are often the despair of politicians. Like the old men, they seem to be so susceptible to persuasion that they slosh this way and that like water in a pail. But being open to persuasion is part of what I have elsewhere called citizen wisdom—the wisdom on which democracy depends. The old men are a good audience for the Creon-Haemon debate, and we should consider following their example.

The larger conflict of the play, between Creon and Antigone, strikes the Chorus in much the same way. The old men cherish Antigone: they see the strength of her position, but they are shocked by her intransigence. She is as stubborn as her father, they say, and they do not mean this as a compliment. And in cherishing Antigone, they are not disloyal to Creon, for whom they have great respect. I too, in watching this play unfold, am in love with Antigone. But I see that people I love can go wrong. I respect Creon also, for his experience and the depth of his arguments. But he too can go wrong.

The wisdom of dialogue grows from the wisdom of self-knowledge. A wise audience, like the old men of the Chorus, is reverent in its acceptance of human limitations. We love Antigone, but we recognize her limitations, and so we feel the need to pay close attention to those who oppose her. The limiting case is the love of self; Creon loves himself, but, if he is reverent, he will listen to those who oppose him—as, eventually, he does. Only he is too late. The catastrophe startles us, it comes so fast, and it reminds us how immediate is our need for dialogue.

The wisdom of dialogue is part of the wisdom of democracy. In the theater of politics, as in the theater of Antigone and Creon, we are invited to take sides. And this is fine, as long as partisanship does not block dialogue and lead to violence. In the early years of the Federal Republic, politicians found it hard to be partisan and respectful at the same time. So Adams signed laws against those who opposed him, and so Burr slew Hamilton. And so, in time, rebels fired on Fort Sumter. But there is no wisdom in using violence to suppress debate.

We need a compassionate sense of human limitations and of the value of competing claims on human love and loyalty. Compassion, reverence—these are the feelings that support democracy, in Athens as in the United States. They preserve the people as a people against destruction by its partisan divisions. They allow dialogue to go on, as an active embodiment of mutual respect. Good government, like good theater, plays on multiple sympathies and allows them to compete.

Of course, theater can be one-sided, and so can the ruling body of a democracy. But not for long. One-sided theater is boring; without a conflict that engages our sympathies, the thing will not be worth watching. The art of theater uses plot, and plot gives life to the conflict that defines it. A conflict that engages multiple sympathies is captivating. A pushover is a yawn. We don't have to love the villains of the piece, but we must see something in them to respect. There is no thrill in a game between a team we love and a team that is worthless. So it is in theater: we can respect Shylock, we can see in him the possibility of sympathy, and we may even be sorry for him at the end. That is why Shakespeare's *Merchant of Venice* is far stronger as theater than Marlowe's *Jew of Malta*, which has a paper-thin villain straight out of the silliest anti-Semitic myth. So much for one-sided theater.

As for one-sided democracy, it is on the way to being something else—it is turning into the tyranny of one faction over the others. Even the majority can be tyrannical.

12.8 Performer Wisdom

Playing villains

Let us now consider infamous men and women. Here is Claudius. He killed his brother so that he could be king and marry his brother's wife. There is Edmund. He tried to bring about the deaths of his father and his brother. And over there is Goneril, who cared little about her father, tried to have her husband killed, and succeeded in killing her sister.

You may play one of these parts and find it delicious to perform. You would find the joy of crossing a forbidden line, pretending, at least, to fulfill the darkest desires of your heart, making yourself the sole survivor of your family. But mimesis has real effects, as we have seen. What does it do to you to perform the part of such a villain?

Plato, and those who follow him, would warn you against doing this. Practice being like your wise teacher, they would say, and you will begin to become as wise as she; practice being like evil Goneril, and you will begin to become as wicked as she. Mimesis is bad for the performer, says Plato, unless the original that it brings to life is good. You must watch the Form of Justice then, and that of Beauty, and the Forms of all Virtues, beyond where the human eye can see. With your mind only. And in this watching, you will be drawn to emulate the good things that you watch, to give them a sort of life in your own action and in the ideas you bring to birth in your mind. So Plato. He is right about trying to watch justice in the mind's eye; we have no other hope of seeing it. But he is wrong about performance.

I have rarely known an actor take on in real life the villainy he performs. Crossing the forbidden line in mimesis is a temporary delight. I leave the explanation for this to psychology. My subject here is the wisdom that wise performers may gain from performance. This wisdom is not available to every performer, only to the wise ones. As is generally the case, only the wise may become wiser by these means. And you may become wiser by playing the part of Goneril or Claudius or Edmund.

If this is true, there is little more to say about it. If I could tell you what this wisdom is, then you would not have to play the part of Edmund to obtain it. But I can say this much. After playing Edmund you may find you have expanded your range of human sympathies. Shakespeare wrote your part well: insulted in public by your father, talented but thwarted, you learn to hate the legitimate brother who has been given what you are not allowed even to earn. And so you come to a deeper, emotional understanding of Edmund's villainy by walking in his shoes, through mimesis. But there is more: you would never have admitted the murderous feelings that are part of your human endowment. You too have the capacities of an Edmund. You too are human, and your potential to fail morally is no cleaner than his. *Et tu, Brute*. This is not far from who you are.

Performance-based learning

There are more parts to play than villains. In *Lear* you might play Kent or Edgar or the Fool. And then you would have an opportunity to learn how it is to embody someone whose beliefs are true and whose actions are noble.

In *Antigone*, you might play a member of the Chorus. In fact, if you were a young male citizen growing up in Athens, you would probably perform in at least one Chorus before you attained full manhood. If you performed in *Antigone*, you would learn what it is like to serve in a wise council during debate—to feel that, indeed, "both sides spoke well," and then offer clear advice for action. That is what the Chorus does after the debate between Creon and Haemon; they compliment both sides, urge them to listen to each other, and then advise the King, rightly, not to kill Ismene. Performing in such a Chorus would be part of your training for citizenship in democracy. It would have been a lot more fun than the courses in government that young Americans are forced to take—and probably a lot more effective.

Suppose you graduate from the Chorus to an individual role. You are Haemon, and you are learning what it is like to embody this young man who begins his scene with respect for his father and ends it in a shouting match. At the start of the scene, many endings seem possible, but, by the end, you are on a fixed course, and you have lost the ability to change direction. Your choices have led you into a defile from which there seems to be no escape. How did this happen to you? Did it have to come out this way? Was there a turning point after which you felt the power of choice slipping away from you? You will learn the answers. Perhaps you will find that you lost control of yourself when your father insulted you as a "woman's toy." In any event, you will come away from the performance with a deeper sense of how choice leads to choice, how passion clouds judgment, and how you could find yourself bent on self-destruction. A terrifying lesson, but a valuable one.

In modern theater, since Stanislavsky, preparation for performance may itself be educational. You will explore the larger context for your character, imagining, if necessary, a background story not supplied in the text. That is good practice for working out ways to understand other people in real life, a laboratory for empathy. Then as you perform your scene, you will learn to be sensitive to the emotions you are trying to elicit from others. Performers may develop multiple sympathies much more deeply than we others do when we merely watch.

12.9 The Furthest Wisdom: Inverting Theater

If theater is necessary, it is necessary both ways, both watching and being watched. Language is necessary, and for this the need for reversal is obvious. If you can manage a language, you know how to cease speaking and begin to listen, and you also know how to cease listening and begin to speak. If all you can do is speak, or if all you can do is listen, you have not mastered the use of a language. Learning when to speak and when to listen is the hardest lesson for a language learner. Many of us never get it right, and none of us gets it right all the time.

So it is with theater, but it is even harder there, and less obvious that we must master the reversal in order to be fully in possession of the art of theater: The performer must learn to watch, and the watcher must learn to perform. In the classroom, it is easy for teacher and students both to sink into permanent roles of watched and watchers. But not much learning happens in such a classroom.

In the political theater, we divide readily into watchers and watched, terrified of changing places. How may this man become an agent of change, when he has so long been only a disaffected spectator? Or how may this colleague step back from the turbulence of campus politics and watch, with, like most of her colleagues, a sense of powerlessness? The mere spectator is fooling himself: he can do more than he thinks he can to effect change. The mere performer on this stage is fooling herself too; we, who only watch, know that she is not doing as much as she thinks she is. Human institutions do not so easily change course.

In the art theater, mimesis is an obstacle to reversal. On the stage, mimetic performers are playing parts, while we in the audience are only ourselves. If for a moment the people on stage pretend to watch us, that is in the script, and it is make-believe. But there is no script for us to perform, and we are not here to pretend to be anything but ourselves, watching the action on stage.

Theater is most theater when it fulfills the goals of its two parts, watching and being watched. If so, then theater is most theater when it is not theater at all, when the arts of watching and being watched merge and give way to shared action, shared experience, a shared moment of transcendence, beyond theater.

Epilogue
The Defense of Theater

Plato had reasons to believe that theater would cause a healthy society to turn sick, and he has not been alone. Enemies of theater have been outspoken in many periods, even in the enlightenment, when Rousseau defended Geneva's ban on theater. Geneva was led at the time by Puritans, whom you—my theater-loving reader—may be tempted to dismiss as irrational. But Rousseau's attack on theater makes no appeal to religion as such. Like Plato, he has a cogent argument that brings principles of stagecraft into collision with ethics. If either Plato or Rousseau is right, then theater is far from being necessary; it would actually be destructive of a healthy society. Their arguments need to be appreciated and answered, and I will answer them. But not at length, for they are not the subject of this book.

When theater is well adjusted to its purpose in human society, it is good, and good for us. But it is not always good. We should resist the objections made by Plato and Rousseau, but we need to do so with great care. We'd go very wrong if we fell into giving an often-heard defense against them—what I call the "fine-arts defense." Fine art is supposed to be exempt from criticism that is not art-based; in judging a work of fine art as art we are not supposed to ask whether it is useful or instructive, whether it is morally sound, or whether it is good or bad for the community. We should, on this view, look only to a kind of evaluation that is unique to the arts.

If the fine-arts defense is right, Plato and Rousseau are missing the point about theater: we should not care what effect theater has on the fiber of a community—so runs the art-based defense—because theater may be judged only by the standards of art. If an artwork did turn out to serve a need, that would be a welcome accident, but not—on this theory—relevant to how good an artwork it is. Nothing outside art matters. But many things outside art do matter in our lives. And if we make this defense we deprive ourselves of any reason for thinking that theater is necessary. The fine arts would be an exotic luxury, alien to our needs. The fine-arts theory would defend art theater against the philosophers, but at too high a cost. Art theater would be saved, but it would have to be written off as useless, and other kinds of theater would fall under the philosopher's ax.

Answering Plato and Rousseau calls for better arguments, arguments showing that what is essential to theater is not at odds with ethics. I believe that I have done so throughout this book, especially in the chapters on characters, mimesis, empathy, and wisdom.

I do not mean this book to be an answer to Plato and Rousseau, however, because I think theater in our time is not powerful enough to have real enemies. Theater does have false friends, however, and they would confine it to a precious realm in the fine arts. We need to pull theater away from its false friends, but we have a greater task. We need to defend theater against the idea that it is irrelevant, that it is an elitist and a dying art, kept alive only by a few cranks in a culture attuned only to film and television. I want to support the entire boldness of my title: *The Necessity of Theater*.

Notes

INTRODUCTION

p. 12. "A democratic speaker spoke": Cleocritus, as reported in Xenophon, *Hellenica* 2.4.20–21 (author's translation).

p. 14. "But poetry is not so easily surrendered": The project by Robert Pinsky and Maggie Dietz (1999) assembles favorite poems of people from all walks of life, showing how deeply and widely art poetry continues to be valued in our culture.

p. 19. "I shall say that theater is mimetic when it depends make-believe": This is in accordance with Walton (1990); for more general count of mimesis in theater, see chapter 7.

p. 20. "W. H. Auden sees what Brueghel painted": "Museé des Beaux Arts" in Auden (1945), p. 3.

p. 27. "I cannot simply say that *The Laramie Project* serves a need": For the *Laramie Project*, see Kaufman and Members of Tectonic Theater Project (2001).

CHAPTER 1

p. 38. "What Theater Is": I do not attempt to solve all the boundary issues here; we have many art forms that live on the margins between theater and something else. I am inclined to treat live-voice performances as theater, as talking is a kind of action. But radio drama is something else. Puppet shows with live voices behind the screen are theater on my account. Opera simul-casts of theatrical productions have many of the features of theater, as do live broadcasts of sports events in sports bars. In these cases, however, the audience cannot affect the action on stage; I would classify them outside theater for this reason. But nothing hangs on how we classify these borderline cases. The important question to keep in mind in each case is whether, and in what way, the art of theater may be brought to bear.

p. 43. "Film": Recent practice in theater blurs the distinction between film and theater as actors work alongside video images of themselves, simulta-neous or recorded at an earlier date. Film is one of the arts that can be used in theater. But film in theater is an accidental feature—like formal scenery. We can have theater without either one.

p. 44. "'Cinema is a time machine'": Sontag (1969), p. 113. Sontag's essay is a searching study of the differences between film and theater; her view is that film is the more rigorous art form (also p. 113), but she predicts that both art forms will continue and will continue to influence each other.

p. 46. "The modern notion of the fine arts": Kristeller (1980 [1951]).

CHAPTER 2

p. 53. "Is Trobriand cricket a kind of cricket?" The Trobriand Islands, off the east coast of New Guinea, were visted by British missionaries who brought with them the game of cricket. Cricket aimed to bring the islanders into a larger British dominated community; Trobriand cricket (a ritual contest rather like a dance performance) brought the islanders together around their own cultural values. So Neumann (2006).

p. 54. "I have taken *Hamlet* and football together in this chapter because they have important features in common": My strategy is consistent with sug-gestions in Walton (1990) and Saltz (1991)

CHAPTER 3

p. 64. "A baseball game that remains tied for eleven innings has an excit-ing plot": I owe the example to Matthew Johnson.

p. 69. "Oedipus takes his seat on sacred ground": In Sophocles, *Oedipus at Colonus*, at the very start of the play. See the translation in Meineck and Woodruff (2003).

p. 70. "Such an exercise of imagination is anthropomorphic": We may stage action that follows from the choices of persons other than human beings such as gods or angels, if we believe that these are persons. I must allow for this in my scheme, but I would argue that this too would be anthropomorphic.

CHAPTER 4

Thanks to David Sosa for comments on an earlier draft of this chapter, and in particular for his asking whether a play is any better at representing choice than is a painting.

p. 80. "Compatibilism": I will not mount a full-scale defense of this family of positions here, but I will confess to being—like most playwrights—a compatibilist of some kind. I hold that we do not know enough about ourselves to declare that we are free of will and also that we do not know enough science to predict how much science will tell us about factors that limit our freedom. Whatever freedom we find we have, we should expect that sort of freedom to be compatible with our minds' being as explainable by science as is anything else in the universe. I can't see why we—or our minds, for that matter—should have a special exemption from science. I expect that little by little our minds and our behaviors will be better understood and more easily predicted. So far, the success of social science (for behavior) and neuroscience (for minds) has been promising, and we cannot know in advance how far the promise will carry us, or where it will be stopped. Arrogance blocks clear thinking. It is arrogant to suppose that we know now the limits of science in the future; it is arrogant to suppose that human beings are a special case and lie outside the realm of the explicable.

p. 83. "If we are to judge only by his work as a playwright, we cannot conclude that he is a determinist": See Woodruff (2007b). Sophocles' plays show human actions carrying out divine plans, but the actions are always human, and their agents are responsible. Sophocles generally does not use the *deus ex machina* as a plot device.

An account of responsibility common in Sophocles' time would have held Oedipus responsible even when his mind had been seized by a god. It was on the basis of such an understanding that Agamemnon holds himself responsible, while citing Zeus as cause, in the *Iliad* 19. But Oedipus himself would have objected to this, as he does in *Oedipus at Colonus* (he denies responsibility first at line 265 and then at length at 960 and following). Sophocles (unlike Euripides) avoids scenes of divine intervention in favor of those that show human action as entirely susceptible to human explanation.

p. 91. "Socrates cared deeply that the whole of it be coherent": That, on one view, is why he had promised a cock to the god of healing. The poet Carl Dennis makes this point beautifully in "Socrates and I":

> "Can't you see," I say, "that he feels blessed
> To be able to end his life as he lived it,
> Loyal to one luminous purpose?" (Dennis [2004], p. 7)

CHAPTER 5

p. 94. "No stage is big enough for both a romantic couple and a quarreling family": Opera is an exception, because it can stage competing scenes in counterpoint. Although we cannot attend equally to the words in both scenes, we can attend equally to the music, if we are trained to hear polyphony.

p. 96. "Stage characters may be mimetic whether they are fictional or historical": Bringing a historical character to life is a kind of mimesis. For my account of mimesis, see chapter 7.

p. 98. "The text-based account of character": See Gass (1970).

——. "A false way of reading Aristotle": G. de Ste. Croix has shown (rightly, I think) that Aristotle elsewhere must take historical characters also to be types in the relevant sense: "If we are to derive episteme from it [a particular action] we have to take the further step of recognizing the general (the universal or the necessary) in the particular." Quoted in Rorty (1992), p. 28.

p. 99. "That is, if what it is to be Rosalind is to have a mixture of courage and loyalty and sensitivity, then she must show that mix of qualities consistently": Rosalind may be prone to change character traits in certain ways, but being prone to change is a universal human characteristic and so could not define her character.

p. 101. "What is consistency of *êthos?*": Aristotle uses the word *êthos*, translated "character," for the mainly ethical qualities of agents: "It is in view of their characters that the agents are of a certain sort" (*Poetics* 50a18, author's translation). These qualities are reflected from the agents onto their choices, when these have no clear ethical qualities in themselves (50b8). He thinks that a good playwright brings out the characters of his agents through their speeches and actions but that a tragedy can go forward without character altogether (50a24). Certainly it cannot go forward without actions, however, and there is no action without an agent. For Aristotle on character, see Woodruff (2004) and (2007b).

——. "We should expect people to do unexpected things": Aristotle quotes Agathon with approval as saying that it is *eikos* (i.e., expectable) for many things to happen against *eikos* (56a24). This explains his rule for character, which allows agents to be "consistently inconsistent" (*homalos anomalon*; 54a27): they may violate *eikos*, but only in accordance with *eikos*.

p. 102. "Harold Bloom asks": Bloom (1998), p. 6.

——. "The first great artist of character in the European tradition is Sophocles": Woodruff 2007b.

p. 104. "Now in my dial of glass appears": Douglas (1998), p. 119. Douglas was killed during the Normandy landings, and his collected poetry was published posthumously.

p. 105. "Gorgias made a case against truth in theater": Gorgias wrote: "Tragedy produces a deception in which the one who deceives is more just than the one who does not, and the one who is deceived is wiser than the one who is not." Fragment 23 (Gagarin and Woodruff [2005], p. 204.10; cf. p. 302).

CHAPTER 6

I am grateful to T. K. Seung for starting me on the theme of this chapter, which I had neglected in my book on reverence.

p. 113. "A very old man shambles onto the stage": The opening of *Oedipus at Colonus*. All references to the Oedipus plays are to the Meineck/Woodruff (2003 and 2007) translations.

p. 114. "Oedipus has come under a curse, his own curse": Sophocles, *Oedipus Tyrannus*, lines 244–51. The curse entails that he must not be in the public eye; although he does not believe he is untouchable, his people shrink from him, and he says himself: "By all the gods, you must hide me away" (line 1410).

p. 115. "Classical languages have the same word for 'sacred' and 'cursed' ": For example, Latin *sacer*.

p. 116. *The Nine Worthies* in *Love's Labor's Lost* is performed in act 5, scene 2. "This is not generous, not gentle, not humble.": line 629.

—. "The best in this kind are but shadows": Shakespeare, *A Midsummer Night's Dream*, act 5, scene 1, lines 212–14.

p. 117. *The Knight of the Burning Pestle* by Francis Beaumont was published in 1613.

p. 118. *Dionysus in 69*: Performance Group (1970).

p. 120. "Alienation effects": Devices for making the familiar feel foreign to the audience. See Bertolt Brecht, "Short Organon for the Theatre," sections 42–44, in Willett (1964), p. 191–92, and section 12, p. 276: "When our theatres perform plays of other periods they like to annihilate distance, fill in the gaps, gloss over the differences. But what comes then of our delight in comparisons, in distance, in dissimilarity—which is at the same time a delight in what is close and proper to ourselves?"

p. 122. *The Laramie Project*: Kaufman and Members of Tectonic Theater Project (2001).

CHAPTER 7

p. 123. "Let's suppose": The scene described is the opening of Sophocles' *Oedipus at Colonus*.

p. 124. "Modeling": Modeling leads from mimesis to authenticity. Consider the stage example, in which an actor models grief and then actually begins to feel it, and real tears start to fall. In *Hamlet*, the First Player shows his ability by working himself into what appears to be overwhelming grief. Over nothing, or, at least, nothing we can see. He is playing the part of Aeneas, a refugee from Troy who tells Dido about the death of Priam during the sack of Troy. Priam's wife Hecuba sees it all:

> When she saw Pyrrhus make malicious sport
> In mincing with his sword her husband's limbs,
> The instant burst of clamor that she made,
> Unless things mortal move them not at all,
> Would have made milch the burning eyes of heaven,
> And passion in the gods. (Shakespeare, *Hamlet* 2.2, lines 513–18)

The player has brought tears to his eyes, but he has not heard "the instant clamor." Far from it. Hecuba is not even represented on stage. We've known all along that the Player is doing this to show Hamlet what a fine actor he is, so we know he is not really grieving over Hecuba. Yet his tears are real, and he seems truly to be in pain.

His method is familiar. If you smile, you simulate happiness, but then you often begin actually to feel happier. If you frown... and so on. The Player, wailing and grimacing, easily works himself into a state. He does not even need to be a good actor. The First Player began by simulating emotion for a cause that does not touch him, and now he is wallowing in strong feelings. Hamlet, watching him, is ashamed. Hamlet has good reason to feel grief and anger, but the feelings do not come as they should. Real life often suffers by comparison with mimesis, and mimesis is often a way to make things become real.

p. 125. "Septimus": A character in Virginia Woolf's *Mrs. Dalloway* (1925). The scene is at p. 14 of the 1981 Harcourt publication.

—. "Defining Mimesis": See Woodruff (1992), pp. 73–95. Walton's (1990) account of mimesis is revolutionary and powerful in a general theory of the arts. I will neglect it in these pages, however, so as to fill out the classical conception and show its application to the art of theater. For the ancient concept of mimesis, see the essays in Halliwell (2002), Nehamas (1982), and Keuls (1978).

p. 126. "But the painting cannot actually perform mimesis": Plato stretches ancient usage to treat painting as mimetic. See Nehamas (1982), p. 56: "These terms were originally connected with speech and poetry rather than painting, with hearing rather than with seeing."

—. "Essential to the idea of mimesis is a theory of natural causation": Where mimesis involves imaginary worlds, as in myth or fiction, the imagination must be sufficiently robust to sustain a concept of natural causation native to that world. For the vampire game, teacher and children need to imagine the same rules about how vampires behave. Most children know such rules very well and will not allow you to change these rules in midgame, as parents know. The plea, "but there are no vampires" cuts no ice with a child who knows very well how vampires behave.

p. 126. "The Ancient Greeks said that art is mimetic of nature": Aristotle says that art is goal-directed in imitation of nature (*Physics* 2.2, 194a21 ff.). "On the whole," he says a few pages later, "art completes some of the things that nature is unable to bring off, while imitating others" (*Physics* 2.8, 199a15–16). Medicine is an example of the sort of completion he has in mind, since health is a natural goal that we may foster by art.

—. "Mimesis does not have to be unnatural, but it does have to be secondary to a natural process": The theory of mimesis requires a robust commitment to natural processes that allows for this distinction between natural products and by-products.

p. 127. "Learning is a pleasure for human beings, as Aristotle tells us": In *Poetics* 4, 1448b13–14.

p. 128. "Plato was afraid that acting would change people for the worse, and that was one of his objections to theater": *Republic* 3, 395c–398b.

—. "Complicity occurs when those who are affected by mimesis help it along through an effort of imagination, through make-believe": A brilliant book about mimesis by the philosopher Kendall Walton (1990) develops a theory of make-believe through elegant distinctions to account for a great deal of what occurs in all of the arts.

p. 129. "The Chorus in the *Bacchae*": The opening choral ode, lines 73–166 in the Woodruff translation (1998), could come at least in part from an actual hymn to Dionysus, as Dodds (1960, p. 71) points out, following earlier scholars. Also, the performance is part of a festival to Dionysus, who has a prominent (though relatively new) part at the center of the state religion. The ode is presented, however, from the perspective of the Asian women whom the young men impersonate, as lines 64–72 show. On the whole, however, the ode appears to be a devotional exercise that involves mimesis. I would compare it with the Christmas carol, "We Three Kings." When we sing it, we are playing the parts of the kings, but the devotion may be real. Through such examples we are familiar with the overlap between mimesis and reality.

—. "Mimesis of terrible actions may lead to real emotions, and real emotions normally lead to real actions": Mimetic theater usually moderates its effect on action through emotion; I discuss this in chapter 8.

p. 130. "First, he complains that poets play the part of wise men and so enjoy the respect that belongs to the wise." He makes this argument in the opening of Book 10 of the *Republic*.

—. "As Plato points out, Homer never won any wars or founded any cities": *Republic* 10, 599d.

—. "Plato holds that we can achieve knowledge only by focusing our minds on what is most real": The theme runs through many of his works, surfacing most famously in the image of the Cave, *Republic* 7, 514–18.

p. 132. "Fearlessness can be stupid": Plato, *Protagoras* 350b.

p. 133. "Poetry presents material that is twice removed from reality": Plato's claim is in *Republic* 10, 597e. The passage is often mistranslated to imply three removes. Poetry is third from the top, separated from the top by two intervals.

—. "Then justice requires you to keep the weapon": Plato, *Republic* 1, 331c.

—. "Plato holds that the original of Justice is out of this world": Plato's "two-worlds" theory appears to be laid out at the end of *Republic*, Book 5.

—. "His pupil Aristotle was probably the first": Aristotle's *Poetics* is often read as a reply to Plato, although Aristotle nowhere in the *Poetics* explicitly takes on Plato's arguments against the poets. For the *Poetics*, see the excellent translations by Halliwell (1995) and Janko (1987).

p. 134. "Mimesis is enjoyable in itself": So Aristotle, *Poetics* 4.

—. "Our knowledge serves, Plato tells us, as an inoculation against being led astray by mimesis": *Republic* 10, 595b.

—. "This strategy is attributed to Aristotle": In the *Poetics*.

p. 135. "There is nothing in the music that can possibly refer to either of the lovebirds": W.H. Auden wrote: "If I were a composer, I believe I could produce a piece of music which would express to a listener what I mean when I think the word *love,* but it would be impossible for me to compose it in such a way that he would know that this love was felt for *You* (not for God, or my mother, or the decimal system). The language of music is, as it were, intransitive, and it is just this intransitivity which makes it meaningless for a listener to ask: 'Does the composer really mean what he says, or is he only pretending?'" (Auden [1960], p. 36)

—. "Moods and emotions are not the same things." For the distinction between mood and emotion, and for an explanation of the importance of subject and object to emotion, see chapter 8.

—. "Much of this is a purely physical response": The physical feeling caused by the music fails all four tests for emotion. It has no intentionality and so cannot move us to action. More surprisingly, it has no subjectivity. We do not even recognize the feeling as ours. Nietzsche noticed this in the *Birth of Tragedy* (1967 [1872], p. 37) when he identified music as the art of Dionysus that breaks down individuality and brings a crowd into an irrational sense of unity. Music is nevertheless often expressive of emotion. See Harré (1997).

p. 136. "Aristotle says he knows that music contains likenesses of virtue and vice": *Politics* 1340a22, a41, with the discussion that runs through *Politics* Book 8, chapters 5–8.

—. "In a little-read text": The *Problemata* 919b–920a.

p. 137. "Mimesis calls up emotions and other feelings in an audience": Whether the feelings engendered by theatrical mimesis are real emotions or are merely mimetic of emotions is controversial.

p. 138. The Rodney King beating: In 1991, a bystander caught on videotape a scene in which a suspect was beaten by the police who were arresting him.

p. 139. "In mimesis, the agent produces certain effects of the original but not others": For example, harmless insects that mimic poisonous ones may do so with markings of exaggerated clarity, but they do not reproduce all of the features of the poisonous species—just the ones they need to do the job.

CHAPTER 8

The forerunner of this chapter is my unpublished essay "Trying to Care about Hamlet and Hecuba: From Mimesis to Emotion in Theater," written during a stay at the Humanities Center at the University of Michigan, for which I am very grateful.

My work on emotions follows a recent trend toward a moderate cognitivism in emotional theories, started by my late colleague Robert Solomon (1976, 2007). Martha Nussbaum (2001) has developed a modern version of the thorough cognitivism of the ancient Stoics, who understood emotions as judgments. The theory I propose here, however, calls for only enough cognitive content to pick out objects in the world, a kind of theory that John Deigh (1994) calls "traditional cognitivism."

Important recent philosophical work on the emotions includes de Sousa (1987) and Wollheim (1999). For a survey of work on emotion in response to art, see Levinson (1997), and for an important cross-cultural study, see Higgins (2007).

p. 145. "Oh what a rogue and peasant slave am I!" *Hamlet*, act 2, scene 2, line 550.

p. 146. "How weary, stale, flat, and unprofitable / Seem to me all the uses of this world!" and "Man delights not me, no nor woman neither.": Shakespeare, *Hamlet*, 1.2.133–34 and 2.2.322–23

p. 148. "I care about Iago": Iago is the villain from Shakespeare's *Othello* who deceives and betrays his former friend.

p. 149. "To experience a full human life, you must take the risk of caring about other people": Nussbaum (1986), chapter 12.

p. 151. "Stung by the opening of *The Murder of Gonzago*, King Claudius rises, calls for lights, douses the performance, and goes off to pray": Shakespeare, *Hamlet*, 3.2.145–280.

p. 154. "When Clytemnestra hears of her son's death and reacts with a mixture of pain, relief, and joy, then we are engaged on her behalf as well": Sophocles, *Electra*, lines 766–68 (Meineck and Woodruff [2007]).

p. 160. "Noël Carroll has put it this way": Carroll (1990), p. 62. His elegant solution to the problem is to replace beliefs in the third premise with thoughts that are entertained in imagination, so that our emotion depends on a thought (Hecuba is real) that is not consistent with what we know (Hecuba is not real). (See also Carroll [1997], p.210).

p. 160. "Indeed, Macbeth is genuinely frightened by his vision of Banquo's ghost, and the ghost could be a creature of his imagination": Shakespeare, *Macbeth*, 3.4.93–107

p. 161. "This solution is due to Kendall Walton": (1990), pp. 241–55. In such circumstances, Walton contends, "we do actually experience something" (p. 247), but this something is fictionally (that is, by make-believe) an experience of fear.

CHAPTER 9

This chapter is based on Woodruff (1988), "Engaging Emotion in Theater: A Brechtian Model in Theater History." See also valuable pieces by Moran (1994) on the role of imagination, Gordon (1995) on simulation theories of empathy, and Deigh (1995) on failures of empathy in psychopaths, as well as Solomon's recent chapter on sympathy and compassion (2007, pp. 63–71).

For a recent study of empathy, see Hoffman (2000). Psychologists distinguish between cognitive and affective models of empathy (Hoffman, p, 29). In this chapter, I develop a theory that considers a number of models of empathy, culminating in one that I would argue is both affective and cognitive, in keeping with my cognitivist theory of the emotions.

p. 166. "In its original use": See Gauss (1973) and Lee (1913, 59–69). Lee guards against two misinterpretations of this use: as projection of the ego (the ego is not felt in empathy on Lee's view) and as felt mimicry or sympathy (which on Lee's view presupposes an earlier act of empathy). Lee is using the term primarily for a certain kind of response to the visual arts.

p. 167. "Bertolt Brecht…[and] theater without empathy": See Willett (1964), especially pp. 15, 23, 70–71, 182–83, and 270–71.

—. "When Plato criticized theater": *Republic* 10, 605a–607a. For an impressive defense of emotion in the arts against Plato, see Carroll (1997).

—. "This complaint was revived by Rousseau": Rousseau's complaint against comedy is translated in Bloom (1960), p. 34: "The very pleasure of the comic is founded on a vice of the human heart."

p. 168. The quotations from Brecht: Willett (1964), p. 71.

p. 174. *Painting Churches* is in Howe (1984).

—. "Brecht's ideal audience": Of his theater for instruction he writes: "The theater became an affair for philosophers, but only for such philosophers as wished not just to explain the world but also to change it" (Willett [1964], p. 72).

p. 178. "If *Love's Labor's Lost* were simply a romance, the ending it has would ruin the play": Shakespeare ends the play by bringing in the news that the father of the princess has died, and the couples must separate for a year. Berowne says:

> Our wooing doth not end like an old play;
> Jack hath not Jill: these ladies' courtesy
> Might well have made our sport a comedy. (act 5, scene 2, lines 874–876)

p. 179. "The sonnet scene in *Romeo and Juliet*": act 1, scene 5. The young couple exchanges love talk in the form of a sonnet.

p. 186. "Aristotle gnawed at it in the *Poetics*": "Since the poet is supposed to provide pleasure through mimesis from pity and fear" (*Poetics* 14, 1453b11–13).

—. "*The Laramie Project*": The play performs interviews with townspeople concerning the violent death of Matthew Shepard (Kaufman [2001]).

p. 187. "Aristotle is right about this: we take great pleasure in coming to understand things": *Poetics* 4.

CHAPTER 10

I have treated this subject more thoroughly in Woodruff (1977) and (1997).

p. 188. "She [Juliet] can't very well feel any emotion for Alice while she is laughing at her": Bergson famously defended the complementary position that emotion negatives laughter: "Indifference is its natural environment; laughter has no greater enemy than emotion" (1911), p. 4; also in Morreal (1987), p. 118. For a similar contemporary view, see Morreal (1983), pp. 101–13), and Morreal (1987), pp. 212–24.

p. 189. "Moss Hart knew he finally had a success when an audience laughed through the last act of his first play": Hart (1959), pp. 385–402.

—. "The Duke and the Dauphin in *Huckleberry Finn* knew they had a flop when the audience roared with the wrong kind of laughter": Samuel Clemens [Mark Twain] (1884), chapter 23.

p. 190. "Agave cradles the...head of her son": Euripides, *Bacchae*, line 1484

—. "Holofernes runs offstage": Shakespeare, *Love's Labor's Lost*, act 5, scene 2.

p. 191. "All laughter, Rousseau believes, bubbles up from wicked recesses of the human heart": See his *Letter to M. D'Alembert*: "And since the very pleasure of the comic is founded on a vice of the human heart, it is a consequence of this principle that the more the comedy is amusing and perfect, the more its effect is disastrous for morals" (Bloom [1960], p. 34). See also de Sousa (1987), p. 277, 289, and Frye (1957), pp. 167–68.

—. "Plato proposed to ban the use of comedy": *Republic* 10, 606c; *Laws* 7, 816e ff., and 11, 935d ff.

p. 193. "In the *Clouds* of Aristophanes": This work contains a debate that is ridiculous on both sides (lines 889–1104 in Meineck's translation [1998]).

p. 194. "We have comic characters and moments in ancient tragedy": These include:

The Watchman: Sophocles, *Antigone*, lines 223 ff.

Dionysus's cleverness: Euripides, *Bacchae*, especially scene 4, 923–72.

The porter's drunken monologue: Shakespeare, *Macbeth*, act 2, scene 3, 1–25.

Hamlet's mockery of Polonius: Shakespeare, *Hamlet*, 2.2, 398–439.

CHAPTER 11

The forerunner to this chapter is Woodruff (1991), "Understanding Theater." I owe a huge debt to F. M. Berenson's paper, "Understanding Music" (which I believe is unpublished) and to her book of 1981. Her work started me on the reflections that led to this chapter. I owe debts also to Arthur Danto (1981, 1984, 1986) and to work on the emotions by Robert Solomon (1976, 2007), and Ronald de Sousa (1987). I am also grateful for advice to friends who work in theater, especially Michael Holden and James Loehlin.

p. 200. Danto (1984) p. 16; cf his (1986), pp 154–55.

p. 201. "*The Murder of Gonzago*": *Hamlet*, act 3, scene 2.

—. "Claudius understands Hamlet's production of *The Murder of Gonzago*": act 3, scene 3, line 36.

p. 202. "Agave's mad scene": Euripides *Bacchae*, lines1168–1264 in Woodruff (1998).

p. 205. "Aristotle left us with a famous question": *Poetics* 14, 1453b11–13. On this, see Woodruff (2007a).

—. "Those who put out Gloucester's eyes": Shakespeare, *King Lear*, act 3, scene 7 ("out vile jelly!," line 82).

—. "There must, there must, there has to be a way": Brecht (1965 [1940]). The lines end an epilogue that Brecht added to prevent misunderstandings of the play. Bentley translates the title as "Woman," although the German is gender neutral *Mensch* (person"); the title character changes gender as circumstances require.

p. 207. "The death of Ophelia": Shakespeare, *Hamlet*, act 4, scene 7.

p. 208. "The wooing of Katherine": act 5, scene 2.

CHAPTER 12

I am grateful to James Collins for insights into performer wisdom.

p. 211. "The curtain falls on Fortinbras": act 5, scene 2, lines 373–414.

p. 212. "The principles of textual criticism as practiced by A. E. Housman": Stoppard (1997), p. 37–39.

—. "Polonius...mingles wisdom and platitudes": *Hamlet*, act 1, scene 3, lines 59–80.

—. "Great lecturers may embody the truth of what they say, even in a classroom setting, if they show their students what it is like to live as those who believe the things they teach": I owe the point to James Collins.

p. 213. "Before democracy,...the rulers of Athens introduced Homer and other poets of performance in the hope of improving the common people": Reported in Plato's *Menexenus*, not accepted by many scholars.

—. "During democracy, theater evolved as a treasure of the people": See Woodruff (2005), pp. 199–200.

—. "In other words, if there is wisdom in a poem, it could not have come from the poet": See especially the argument of Plato's *Ion*, with his *Apology* 22ab.

—. "So when anyone claims wisdom for a poet, he is taken in by mimesis": see above, pp. 130–32.

p. 214. "Human actions...have features that make them seem right in one context and wrong in another": Plato makes the point in many contexts, but sums it up in *Republic* 5, 479a. My particularist account of Plato's theory of virtues grows out of my interest in the work of Jonathan Dancy, who does not share my view of Plato.

—. "Plato says that philosophers must try to die to this world, to practice philosophy as if practicing for death itself": *Phaedo*, 61b ff., especially 65a–6t7b.

p. 216. "A sage could even cloud our minds to protect us from truths that would torment us or lead us astray, like a parent who knows best what truths a child should face": Plato's philosopher kings would tell us things that are not true, but that we are better for believing (*Republic* 3, 414).

p. 218. "Many Wonders, Many Terrors": Sophocles, *Antigone* line 332. The speech that explains this line is at 332–75 (Woodruff [2001b).

p. 219. "Socrates says that his pursuit of self-knowledge is a full-time job": *Phaedrus* 229e–230a, a passage that I did not fully appreciate until A. P. D. Mourelatos helped me see the point.

p. 220. "You must have a virtue in order to grow more of that virtue": See Woodruff (2001a), p. 73, where I follow Aristotle's *Nicomachean Ethics* Book 2, chapter 1; a similar theme runs through the tradition in Confucian thought that begins with Mencius.

p. 221. "'O brave new world!' exclaims Miranda when she sees for the first time a cluster of her species. 'How beauteous mankind is!'": Shakespeare, *The Tempest*, act 5, scene 1, lines 183–84.

p. 222. "Your majesty, and we that have free souls, it toucheth us not": *Hamlet*, act 3, scene 2, lines 241–42.

—. Creon in Sophocles, *Antigone*, lines 1261–69; Oedipus in *Oedipus Tyrannus*, lines 1436–37. See p. 000.

—. "Hamlet...shows us a stream of self-recognitions": For example, "Oh what a rogue and peasant slave am I!" (act 2, scene 2, line 550).

—. "And now he is given the sight of Tom O' Bedlam, naked in the lashings of the storm": Shakespeare, *King Lear*, act 3, scene 4, lines 44–189.

p. 224. "Both Sides Spoke Well": Sophocles, *Antigone*, line 725.

p. 226. "Tyranny of one faction over the others": See Woodruff (2005), p. 65.

—. "Plato…would warn you against doing this": See above, p. 128. Goneril is one of the villainous sisters in Shakespeare's *King Lear*.

p. 228. "After the debate between Creon and Haemon": Sophocles, *Antigone*, lines 683–725. Father and son ignore this advice from the Chorus and dive into a contest of insults—not what works best in democracy.

—. "Woman's toy": Line 756 in my translation of the *Antigone* (Woodruff [2001b]).

EPILOGUE

Much has been written about Plato's work on poetry and theater. Recent valuable studies include Halliwell (2002), Janaway (1995, and Winn (1998).

p. 230. "Rousseau defended Geneva's ban on theater": In Bloom (1960).

Bibliography

Auden, W. H. (1945). *The Collected Poetry of W. H. Auden.* New York: Random House.
——— (1960). *Homage to Clio.* New York: Random House.
Berenson, F. M. (1981). *Understanding Persons: Personal and Impersonal Relationships.* New York: St. Martin's.
Bergson, Henri (1911). *Laughter: An Essay on the Meaning of the Comic.* Trans. Cloudesley Brereton and Fred Rothwell. New York: Macmillan.
Bloom, Allan (ed.) (1960). *Politics and the Arts: Rousseau's Letter to M. D'Alembert on the Theater.* Ithaca, N.Y.: Cornell University Press.
Bloom, Harold (1998). *Shakespeare: The Invention of the Human.* New York: Riverhead.
Brecht, Bertolt (1965 [1940]). *The Good Woman of Setzuan.* Trans. Eric Bentley. New York: Grove Press.
Carlson, Marvin A. (1993). *Theories of the Theatre: A Historical and Critical Survey, from the Greeks to the Present* (exp. ed.) Ithaca, N.Y.: Cornell University Press.
Carroll, Noël (1990). *The Philosophy of Horror, or Paradoxes of the Heart.* New York: Routledge.
——— (1997). "Art, Narrative, and Emotion." In M. Hjort and S. Laver (eds.), *Emotion and the Arts.* New York: Oxford University Press, 190–211.
Clemens, Samuel [Mark Twain] (1884). *The Adventures of Huckleberry Finn.* Many editions.
Danto, Arthur (1981). *The Transfiguration of the Commonplace: A Philosophy of Art.* Cambridge, Mass.: Harvard University Press.
——— (1984) "Philosophy as/and/of Literature." *Proceedings and Addresses of the American Philosophical Association* 58, pp. 5–20.

———— (1986). *The Philosophical Disenfranchisement of Art*. New York: Columbia University Press.

Deigh, John (1994). "Cognitivism in the Theory of Emotion: A Survey." *Ethics* 104: 824–54.

———— (1995). "Empathy and Universalizability." *Ethics* 105: 743–63.

Dennis, Carl (2004). *New and Selected Poems*. New York: Penguin.

de Sousa, Ronald (1987). *The Rationality of Emotion*. Cambridge, Mass.: MIT Press.

de Ste. Croix, G. E. M. (1975). Ed. B. Lewick. *The Ancient Historian and His Materials*. Gregg Publishing. Cited in Rorty (1992), pp. 23–32.

Dodds, E. R. (ed.) (1960). *Euripides: Bacchae. Edited with Introduction and Commentary*. 2d ed. Oxford: Oxford University Press.

Douglas, Keith (1998 [1978]). *The Complete Poems*. Intro. Ted Hughes. 3d ed. London: Faber and Faber.

Fischer-Lichte, E. (1992 [1983]). *The Semiotics of Theater*. Abr. and trans. J. Gaines and D. Jones. Bloomington: Indiana University Press.

Frye, Northrop (1957). *Anatomy of Criticism: Four Essays*. Princeton, N.J.: Princeton University Press.

Gagarin, Michael, and Paul Woodruff (eds.) (1995). *Early Greek Political Thought from Homer to the Sophists*. Cambridge: Cambridge University Press.

Gass, William (1970). "The Concept of Character in Fiction." In his *Fiction and the Figures of Life*. New York: Knopf, pp. 34–54.

Gauss, Charles Edward (1973). "Empathy." In Philip P. Weiner, ed., *Dictionary of the History of Ideas*. New York: Scribner. Vol. 2, pp. 85–89.

Gombrich, E. H. (1960). *Art and Illusion: A Study in the Psychology of Pictorial Representation*. Princeton, N.J.: Princeton University Press.

Gordon, Robert (1995). "Sympathy, Simulation, and the Impartial Spectator." *Ethics* 105: 727–42.

Griffiths, Trevor (1976). *Comedians*. New York: Grove.

Grotowski, Jerzy (1968). *Towards a Poor Theatre*. New York: Simon and Schuster.

Halliwell, Stephen (1995). *Aristotle: Poetics*. Cambridge, Mass.: Harvard University Press.

———— (2002). *The Aesthetics of Mimesis: Ancient Texts and Modern Problems*. Princeton: Princeton University Press.

Hart, Moss (1959). *Act One: An Autobiography*. New York: Random House.

Harré, Rom. "Emotion in Music." In M. Hjort and S. Laver (eds.), *Emotion and the Arts*. New York: Oxford University Press, 110–18.

Higgins, Kathleen Marie (2007). "An Alchemy of Emotion: *Rasa* and Aesthetic Breakthroughs." *Journal of Aesthetics and Art Criticism* 65, 43–54.

Hjort, Mette, and Sue Laver (eds.) (1997). *Emotion and the Arts*. New York: Oxford University Press.

Hoffman, Martin (2000). *Empathy and Moral Development*. Cambridge: Cambridge University Press.

Howe, Tina (1984). *Three Plays by Tina Howe*. New York: Avon Books.

Janaway, C. (1995). *Images of Excellence: Plato's Critique of the Arts*. Oxford: Clarendon.

Janko, R. (1987). *Aristotle: Poetics*. Indianapolis: Hackett.

Kaufman, Moises, and Members of Tectonic Theater Project (2001). *The Laramie Project*. New York: Vintage.

Kaufmann, Walter (1969). *Tragedy and Philosophy*. New York: Doubleday.

Keuls. Eva (1978). *Plato and Greek Painting*. Leiden: E. J. Brill.

Kivy, Peter (1988). *Osmin's Rage: Philosophical Reflections on Opera, Drama, and Text*. Princeton, N.J.: Princeton University Press.

Konstan, David (2001). *Pity Transformed*. London: Duckworth.

Kristeller, Paul (1980 [1951]). "The Modern System of the Arts." In his *Renaissance Thought and the Arts: Collected Essays*. 2d ed. Princeton, N.J.: Princeton University Press, pp. 163–227.

Lee, Vernon (1913). *The Beautiful: An Introduction to Psychological Aesthetics*. Cambridge: Cambridge University Press.

Levinson, J. (1997). "Emotion in Response to Art: A Survey of the Terrain." In M. Hjortand and S. Laver (eds.), *Emotion and the Arts*. New York: Oxford University Press, 20–34.

Mamet, David (2000). *Three Uses of the Knife: On the Nature and Purpose of Drama*. New York: Vantage.

Meineck, Peter (1998). *Aristophanes I: Clouds, Wasps, Birds*. Indianapolis: Hackett.

Meineck, Peter, and Paul Woodruff (2003). *Sophocles: Theban Plays*. Indianapolis: Hackett.

——— (2007). *Sophocles: Four Tragedies*. Indianapolis: Hackett.

Moran, R. (1994). "The Expression of Feeling in Imagination." *Philosophical Review* 103: 75–106.

Morreall, John (1983). *Taking Laughter Seriously*. Albany: State University of New York Press.

——— (ed.) (1987). *The Philosophy of Laughter and Humor*. Albany: State University of New York Press.

Nehamas, Alexander (1982). "Plato on Imitation and Poetry in *Republic* 10." In Julkius Moravcsik and Philip Temko (eds.), *Plato on Beauty, Wisdom, and the Arts*. Totowa, N.J.: Rowman and Littlefield, pp. 47–78.

Neumann, Birgit (2006). "Re-Membering Cricket: Sport as an Instrument of Decolonisation in *Trobriand Cricket* (1976) and *Lagaan. Once Upon a Time in India. Contemoorary Theatre Review* 16, pp. 468–82.

Nietzsche, Friedrich (1967 [1872]). *The Birth of Tragedy and the Case of Wagner*. Trans. Walter Kaufmann. New York: Vintage.

Nussbaum, Martha (1986). *The Fragility of Goodness: Luck and Ethics in Greek Tragedy and Philosophy*. Cambridge: Cambridge University Press.

——— (2001). *Upheavals of Thought: The Intelligence of Emotions*. Cambridge: Cambridge University Press.

Performance Group (1970). Ed. Richard Schechner. *Dionysus in 69*. New York: Farrar, Strauss Giroux.

Pinsky, Robert, and Maggie Dietz (1999). *America's Favorite Poetry*. New York: Norton.

Rorty, Amélie. (ed.) (1992). *Essays on Aristotle's Poetics*. Princeton, N.J.: Princeton University Press.

Saltz, David Z. (1991). "How to Do Things on Stage." *Journal of Art and Art Criticism* 49: 31–45.

———— (1998). "Theater." In Michael Kelly (ed.), *The Encyclopedia of Aesthetics*. Oxford: Oxford University Press. Volume 4, pp. 375–80.

Schechner, R. (1977). *Essays on Performance Theory, 1970–76*. New York: Drama Book Specialists.

Seaford, R. (1994). *Reciprocity and Ritual*. Oxford: Oxford University Press.

Segal, C. (1996). *Dionysiac Poetics and Euripides' Bacchae* (2d ed.). Princeton, N.J.: Princeton University Press.

Solomon, Robert C. (1976). *The Passions: The Myth and Nature of Human Emotion*. New York: Anchor.

———— (2007). *True to Our Feelings: What Our Emotions Are Really Telling Us*. New York: Oxford.

Sontag, Susan (1969). *Styles of Radical Will*. New York: Farrar Strauss Giroux, pp. 99–122.

Stoppard, Tom (1997). *The Invention of Love*. London: Faber.

Thom, Paul (1993). *For an Audience: A Philosophy of the Performing Arts*. Philadelphia: Temple University Press.

Walton, Kendall (1990). *Mimesis as Make-Believe: On the Foundations of the Representational Arts*. Cambridge, Mass.: Harvard University Press.

Willett, J. (1964). *Brecht on Theatre*. New York: Hill and Wang.

Winn, James Anderson (1998). *The Pale of Words: Reflections on the Humanities and Performance*. New Haven, Conn.: Yale University Press.

Wollheim, Richard (1999). *On the Emotions*. New Haven, Conn.: Yale University Press.

Woodruff, Paul (1977). "Rousseau, Moliere, and the Ethics of Laughter," *Philosophy and Literature*, 1, 325–336.

———— (1988). "Engaging Emotion in Theater: A Brechtian Model in Theater History." *Monist* 71: 235–57.

———— (1991). "Understanding Theater." In D. Dahlstrom (ed.), *Philosophy and Art*. Washington D.C.: Catholic University of America Press, 11–30.

———— (1992). "Aristotle on Mimesis," in A. Rorty, 73–90.

———— (1997). "The Paradox of Comedy." *Philosophical Topics* 25: 319–35.

———— (1998). *Euripides: Bacchae*. Indianapolis: Hackett Publishing Company.

———— (2001a). *Reverence: Renewing a Forgotten Virtue*. New York: Oxford University Press.

Woodruff, Paul (2001b). *Sophocles: Antigone*. Indianapolis: Hackett Publishing Company.

——— (2003). "Aesthetics of Theatre," in J. Levinson (ed.), *The Oxford Companion to Aesthetics*. Oxford: Oxford University Press, pp. 594–605.

——— (2004). "Who Is Creon? Aristotle on Character." Unpublished essay.

——— (2005). *First Democracy: The Challenge of an Ancient Idea*. New York: Oxford University Press.

——— (forthcoming a). "The Aim of Art and the Nature of Tragedy." In Georgios Anagnastopoulos, ed., *Blackwell Companion to Aristotle*. Oxford: Blackwell.

——— (forthcoming b). "Sophocles' Humanism." In William Wians (ed.), *Logos and Mythos: Philosophical Essays on Greek Literature*. Albany: SUNY Press.

PLAYS DISCUSSED IN THESE PAGES

Jean Anouilh
  Antigone

Samuel Beckett
  Endgame
  Waiting for Godot

Bertolt Brecht
  A Man's a Man
  Mother Courage and Her Children

Euripides
  Bacchae

Tina Howe
  Painting Churches

Trevor Griffiths
  The Comedians

Moises Kaufman
  The Laramie Project

Living Theater
  Dionysus in 69

Arthur Miller
  Death of a Salesman

Molière
  Le Misanthrope

Eugene O'Neill
  Long Day's Journey into Night

Shakespeare
  As You Like It
  Hamlet
  Henry IV, Parts 1 and 2
  King Lear
  Love's Labor's Lost
  Macbeth
  Merry Wives of Windsor
  A Midsummer Night's Dream
  Much Ado about Nothing
  Tempest

Sophocles
  Ajax
  Antigone
  Electra
  Oedipus at Colonus
  Oedipus Tyrannus

Tom Stoppard
  The Invention of Love
  Rosencrantz and Guildenstern Are Dead

Thornton Wilder
  Our Town

Index

Note: Plays are listed under their author's name in the index. A list of plays discussed is provided on p. 250.

subjectivity: of emotion, 155, 157
sympathy: caring about contrasted,
    148; empathy contrasted, 166–67;
    tonal, 157–59, 175–76, 180, 194

text: character and, 98; theater and,
    36, 52–53
theater: defined, 38–42; kinds of, 33;
    necessity of, 22–24; product of,
    49–62; understanding of, 196–210
theater of presence: definition, 34;
    transformative, 180, 183; weddings
    as, 172–73
tonal sympathy. *See* sympathy
tragedy: characters in, 107; comedy
    and, 194–95; contests and, 23;
    fate and, 76–78; pleasure in,
    186–87
truth: in theater, 57–58, 105, 211–12

value judgments: implied by
    definition, 65–68
video documentary, 138
villains, 226–27
virtues: cardinal virtues applied to
    watching, 204–5, 220; humaneness,
    20–21; choice and, 86; represented
    in poetry, 132–35

Walton, Kendall, 161–62
watching: definition, 18, 141–43;
    virtues in, 204–5, 220
weddings: choice and, 78–80;
    empathy and, 165, 171–84;
    need witnesses, 8, 23; theater of
    presence, 172–73
wisdom: human wisdom, 215–18;
    performer wisdom, 226–28; sage
    wisdom, 216–17